William Fenton

The Iroquoians and Their World

EDITORS
José António Brandão
William A. Starna

William Fenton
Selected Writings

William N. Fenton / Edited and with
an introduction by William A. Starna
and Jack Campisi

University of Nebraska Press / Lincoln & London

Acknowledgments for the use of previously
published material appear on pp. xiii–xxi,
which constitute an extension of the
copyright page.

Library of Congress Cataloging-in-
Publication Data

Fenton, William N. (William Nelson), 1908–2005.
[Selections. 2009]
William Fenton : selected writings / William N.
Fenton ; edited and with an introduction by Wil-
liam A. Starna and Jack Campisi.
p.   cm.—(The Iroquoians and their world)
Includes bibliographical references and index.
ISBN 978-0-8032-1607-5 (pbk. : alk. paper)
1. Iroquois Indians—Folklore. 2. Iroquois
Indians—Rites and ceremonies. 3. Iroquois
Indians—Social life and customs. 4. Iroquois
Indians—Historiography. I. Starna, William A.
II. Campisi, Jack. III. Title.
E99.I7F463   2009
398.2089′9755—dc22
2009016371

Set in Minion by Bob Reitz.

Contents

Illustrations

Introduction

The origins of William Nelson Fenton's (1908–2005) distinguished career in anthropology are traceable to Dartmouth College and then Yale University's Graduate School. Of his mentors at Yale—Edward Sapir, George Peter Murdock, Leslie Spier, Clark Wissler, and Sir Peter Buck (Te Rangi Hiroa)—Sapir's influence was of particular significance, coming as it did from his broad knowledge of the Iroquois, especially the Six Nations at Brantford, Ontario, gained from his years as the director of the Anthropological Survey of Canada. It was at Sapir's urging that Fenton first undertook fieldwork among the Allegany Senecas in the early 1930s, a task made easier by his close ties to this Indian community fostered by summers spent on his family's nearby farm and the generous assistance he received from the Seneca people who sponsored him.

So it was that for most of his seven decades as an active and productive scholar, Fenton focused his considerable research and writing talents on the Iroquois. Ever the consummate field-worker, he relished the opportunities he was afforded to spend time with Iroquois colleagues, exploring with them the many and varied facets of their rich culture and societies. He was their student and friend who sought to understand the complexities of the past as told and shared with him by those who had been deeply schooled in the texts, songs, dances, networks of kin, and symbols of Iroquois ritual life.

Fenton looked back from what he was taught and had on many occasions observed at the longhouses at Allegany, Cattaraugus, Tonawanda, and Six Nations and in the homes of many of the renowned Iroquois ritualists—Simeon Gibson, Johnson Jimerson, Howard Sky, Chauncey Johnny John, Henry Redeye, and others—to uncover the sources and meanings surrounding the great ceremonies and medicine societies he was privileged to attend. He also sought to reconstruct the historical context from which Iroquois societies had emerged, functioned, and flourished. To accomplish the latter task, he immersed himself in the full range of surviving colonial administrative, treaty, mission, and travel records housed in scores of libraries and archives in the United States, Canada, Great Britain, and Europe. In addition, on his journeys through two continents, Fenton searched out and studied items of Iroquois material culture held by some of the world's great museums—masks, canoes, rattles, war clubs, condolence canes, and wampum—to both broaden and augment his research program.

Fenton's archival and material culture investigations remained focused on problem solving: how better to understand the information he was given by Iroquois culture bearers and ceremonial practitioners, and how it shed light on Iroquois culture history. His approach was both pragmatic and conservative: pragmatic in the sense that, through it all, he sought answers to a series of questions he first posed in a 1940 article, "Problems Arising from the Historic Northeastern Position of the Iroquois," and then added to in "Iroquois Studies at the Mid-Century," published in 1951; conservative because in his efforts to first apprehend and then describe the belief system of the Iroquois, he concentrated his research on the stability of those beliefs and not on the far-reaching changes that had occurred over the centuries since the Dutch, French, and English first intruded on North America. The result has been an impressive and lengthy list of published works on precisely these questions.[1]

It is worth noting that Fenton always claimed to be a Boasian, yet his theoretical interests were, in their application, far more eclectic. Anthony F. C. Wallace, an eminent scholar and one of Fenton's oldest and most valued friends, perhaps best put his finger on the intellectual character of this anthropologist:

Fenton's career also can serve as the epitome of a certain kind of professional life in anthropology. He is and has always been an Iroquoianist, allowing himself only so much time with other subjects (Taos, Klamath, Blackfoot, Maori) as to give some added perspective to his view of Iroquois. This single-minded devotion to one group, and the emphasis on ethnographic and historical description and classification (although always illumined by, and illuminating, theory) makes Fenton's role unique among American anthropologists of my acquaintance.[2]

In 1985 and 1986, scholar Elisabeth Tooker compiled and edited three sourcebooks with the stated goal "to make more accessible a number of the most significant articles on Iroquois culture and society that have appeared since the publication of Lewis H. Morgan's classic *League of the Ho-de-no-sau-ne or Iroquois* (1851)." Organizing this material under three themes—political and social organization, calendric rituals, and medicine society rituals—Tooker singled out fifty-nine works published between 1858 and 1971. No fewer than eighteen had been produced by Fenton, who shared authorship on three of these, two with J. N. B. Hewitt.[3] Fenton, however, would continue to write for more than three decades, until a few months before his death.

Although the articles reprinted here are rightly regarded as being among Fenton's best, they represent but a small part of his total scholarly output. There remain a number of other works, perhaps not as well known, that add significantly to both our understanding of Iroquois conservatism and Fenton's contributions to the fields of anthropology and, in particular, ethnohistory, of which he is considered a founder.

In selecting the articles for this collection from Fenton's extensive and wide-ranging bibliography we were guided by several objectives: to illustrate the manner in which Fenton approached his chosen profession; to provide insights into his thinking; to demonstrate the value he placed on his friendship with his Iroquois colleagues; to make explicit his views on fieldwork, research methods, and anthropological theory; and finally, to bring to public attention the emphasis he placed on literary skill and style.

Notes

1. William N. Fenton, "Problems Arising from the Historic Northeastern Position of the Iroquois," in *Essays in Historical Anthropology of North America*, Smithsonian Miscellaneous Collections 100: 159–252; Fenton, "Iroquois Studies at Mid-Century," *Proceedings of the American Philosophical Society* 95, no. 3 (1951): 296–310.

2. Anthony F. C. Wallace, "The Career of William N. Fenton and the Development of Iroquoian Studies," in *Extending the Rafters: Interdisciplinary Approaches to Iroquoian Studies*, ed. Michael K. Foster, Jack Campisi, and Marianne Mithun (Albany: State University of New York Press, 1984), 2. Wallace provides the best summary of Fenton's career, paying special attention to Fenton's contributions in ethnology and ethnohistory.

3. Elisabeth Tooker, ed., *An Iroquois Sourcebook*, vol. 1, *Political and Social Organization* (New York: Garland, 1985), vol. 2, *Calendric Rituals* (New York: Garland, 1985), vol. 3, *Medicine Society Rituals* (New York: Garland, 1986).

Further Reading

Campisi, Jack, and William A. Starna. "William Nelson Fenton (1908–2005)." *American Anthropologist* 108, no. 2 (2006): 456–58.

Fenton, William N. *Iroquois Journey: An Anthropologist Remembers*. Ed. and intro. Jack Campisi and William A. Starna. The Iroquoians and Their World. Lincoln: University of Nebraska Press, 2007.

Fenton Papers—Précis

General Works

"Iroquois Indian Folklore." *Journal of American Folklore* 60, no. 238 (1947): 383–97. Reproduced by permission of the American Folklore Society.

As a student of the Boasian tradition, Fenton early on recognized the utility of examining folklore as one of the keys to understanding culture. In this article he proposes a classification for folkloristic topics or genres that he considered valuable adjuncts to his research on the Iroquois. He would later create and apply another kind of classification to Iroquois False Faces, the masks worn by members of the False Face Medicine Society, in an effort to better interpret the social context in which they appeared. See William N. Fenton, *The False Faces of the Iroquois* (Norman: University of Oklahoma Press, 1987). Collecting and organizing ethnographic information—a search for the patterns and systems in a society—was a hallmark of Fenton's theoretical approach.

— — —

"Letters to an Ethnologist's Children: From Simeon Gibson to the Children of William N. Fenton Who Took Them Down." *New York Folklore Quarterly* 4, no. 2 (1948): 109–20. Reproduced by permission of the New York Folklore Society.

Here, in the form of letters written from the field, are folktales told to Fenton by a close colleague from the Six Nations Research, Simeon ("Simmy") Gibson. Other collections of Iroquois stories have been published, but these, whether they are tales not previously reported or variations on older themes, are in Gibson's unique and accomplished voice.

— — —

"The Training of Historical Ethnologists in America." *American Anthropologist* 54, no. 3 (1952): 328–39. Originally published by the American Anthropological Association (http://www.anthrosource.net).

This is one of the earliest and most influential statements on the disciplinary hybrid called *ethnohistory*, and in particular, on the role of its practitioners whom Fenton named "historical ethnologists." Here Fenton discusses how the gap between the distinctive approaches and objectives of history and ethnology could be bridged. In addition, he identifies source materials ethnohistorians might use in a method he styles "upstreaming," a term now firmly rooted in the literature of ethnohistory. An oft-forgotten suggestion Fenton offers, innovative for its day although now commonplace in universities, is to teach courses on American Indians "in a truly historical fashion." He also addresses the subject of ethnologist as expert witness, an acknowledgment of ethnohistory's origins in the Indian Claims Commission created by Congress in 1946 and the requirement to research the historical bases for land claims that American Indians were bringing before that body. For important assessments of ethnohistory see Robert M. Carmack, "Ethnohistory: A Review of Its Development, Definitions, Methods, and Aims," *Annual Review of Anthropology* 1 (1972): 227–246; James Axtell, "Ethnohistory: An Historian's Viewpoint," *Ethnohistory* 26, no. 1 (1979): 1–13.

— — —

"Cultural Stability and Change in American Indian Societies." *Journal of the Royal Anthropological Institute of Great Britain and Ireland* 83, no. 2 (1953): 169–74. Reproduced by permission of Blackwell Publishing.

In 1952 Fenton published a paper on factionalism that he had presented at the Fourth International Congress of Anthropological and Ethnological Sciences, held that year in Vienna. It was a straightforward description of political processes operating among the Klamath, the Blackfeet, the Iroquois, and at Taos Pueblo. Fenton had undertaken fieldwork while he was temporarily reassigned to the Bureau of Indian Affairs from the Bureau of American Ethnology. The essay presented here expands on that earlier research chiefly by providing additional theoretical background. But it also shifts focus from the question of factionalism to that of stability and change in American Indian communities. This demonstrates Fenton's use of "upstreaming," but it also illustrates his attraction to the "old culture," the conservative elements present and functioning within present-day Indian communities, a perspective that is evident in much of his written work. It remains, however, that no work better addresses the persistence and purpose of traditional culture than Annemarie Anrod Shimony's *Conservatism among the Iroquois at the Six Nations Reserve* (New Haven: Department of Anthropology, Yale University, 1961; reprinted with a new introduction by Annemarie Anrod Shimony, Syracuse NY, 1994), Fenton's review of which is included in this collection.

— — —

"The Hyde de Neuville Portraits of New York Savages in 1807–1808." *The New-York Historical Society Quarterly* 38, no. 2 (1954): 118–37. Reproduced by permission of the New-York Historical Society.

In this essay Fenton describes and puts into historical context a few of the early-nineteenth-century portraits of the Indian residents of Iroquoia painted by Baroness Hyde de Neuville (d. 1849). The drawings and accompanying text are demonstrative of Fenton's abiding interest in the arts and material culture as sources of ethnographic insight.

— — —

"This Island, the World on the Turtle's Back." *Journal of American Folklore* 75, no. 298 (1962): 283–300. Reproduced by permission of the American Folklore Society.

The cosmological myth of the Iroquois—the Earth-grasper or the Woman Who Fell from the Sky—is of crucial importance to Iroquois people as well as to any understanding of their culture. Its three epochs furnish the philosophical, symbolic, and psychosocial bases for Iroquois society. In short, the myth explains what it is to be Iroquois.

A revised version of this essay appears in Fenton's *The Great Law and the Longhouse: A Political History of the Iroquois Confederacy* (Norman: University of Oklahoma Press, 1998), 34–50.

— — —

"'Anthropology and the University': An Inaugural Lecture." State University of New York at Albany. 24 pp. 1969. Reproduced by permission of the Department of Anthropology, SUNY–Albany.

In 1968 Fenton left his position as director of the New York State Museum and the State Museum and Science Service to join the faculty of the State University of New York at Albany as research professor of anthropology. There he was instrumental in the development of the graduate program in anthropology, chairing the committee of its first PhD. In his inaugural lecture Fenton touches upon the major themes of anthropology and its place in the university and society, all within the framework of Iroquois ceremony and ritual language.

— — —

"Return to the Longhouse," in *Crossing Cultural Boundaries: The Anthropological Experience*, ed. Solon T. Kimball and James B. Watson, 102–18 (San Francisco: Chandler, 1972).

Fenton did his first ethnological fieldwork among the Senecas in 1933 on the Allegany Reservation. In this essay he recalls those early times but also reflects on his bittersweet return to the community in 1968.

— — —

"The Advancement of Material Culture Studies in Modern Anthropological Research," in *The Human Mirror: Material and Spatial Images of Man*, ed. Miles Richardson, 15–36 (Baton Rouge: Louisiana State University Press, 1974). Reproduced by permission of Louisiana State University Press. Copyright © 1974 by Louisiana State University Press.

At several junctures in his career Fenton published papers advocating a particular approach to research or pointing scholars involved in studies of the Iroquois and other Indian communities to areas in need of investigation. Examples are "The Training of Historical

Ethnologists," included in this collection; "Iroquois Studies at Mid-Century," *Proceedings of the American Philosophical Society* 95, no. 3 (1951): 296–310; and *American Indian and White Relations to 1830: Needs and Opportunities for Study* (Chapel Hill: University of North Carolina Press, 1957). In this essay, Fenton urges colleagues in ethnology, museology, and archaeology to work cooperatively in advancing material culture studies.

— — —

"The Iroquois in the Grand Tradition of American Letters: The Works of Walter D. Edmonds, Carl Carmer, and Edmund Wilson." *American Indian Culture and Research Journal* 5, no. 4 (1981): 21–39. Reproduced by permission of the American Indian Studies Center, UCLA. Copyright © Regents of the University of California.

Fenton read a wide range of literature, and in particular, early works on the philosophy of science and ethnology, as anyone who took his graduate seminar, "The History of Anthropological Thought," will attest. His curiosity in this regard extended to "men of letters" whose subjects were the Iroquois, one of whom, the eminent writer and literary critic Edmund Wilson, became a colleague and friend. It was Fenton who in the late 1950s introduced Wilson to the Iroquois as a historical and modern people, and then sponsored him among the Senecas. The result of this collaboration was Wilson's highly regarded *Apologies to the Iroquois*. For Fenton's reminiscences on Wilson see his introduction to the reprint of *Apologies* (Syracuse NY: Syracuse University Press, 1992).

— — —

"Return of Eleven Wampum Belts to the Six Nations Iroquois Confederacy on Grand River, Canada." *Ethnohistory* 36, no. 4 (1989): 392–410. Copyright 1989, the American Society for Ethnohistory. All rights reserved. Reproduced by permission of the publisher, Duke University Press.

As a state official, museum director and trustee, and scholar, Fenton found himself a party to the controversy that surrounded demands for and resistance to the repatriation of cultural objects to American

Indians, an issue that surfaced in the late 1960s. His first published statement on the proposed return of wampum belts held by the New York State Museum lays out his position on the matter. See "The New York State Wampum Collection: The Case for the Integrity of Cultural Treasures," *Proceedings of the American Philosophical Society* 115, no. 6 (1971): 437–61. In the article presented here, Fenton provides a "case study" in repatriation, which contains a discussion of the historical research requirements in addition to ethical and legal considerations of the process, along with a description of the Native ceremony that attended the return.

– – –

"He-Lost-a-Bet (Howanʔneyao) of the Seneca Hawk Clan," in *Strangers to Relatives: The Adoption and Naming of Anthropologists in Native North America*, ed. Sergei Kan, 81–98 (Lincoln: University of Nebraska Press, 2001). Copyright © 2001 by the University of Nebraska Press. Reproduced by permission.

In this very personal account, Fenton recalls how he came to know and was accepted by the Snow family of Allegany Senecas, and in 1933, adopted into the Hawk clan.

Book Reviews

Of Fenton's numerous book reviews, we have selected five he wrote on what are landmark studies of Iroquoians.

Review of *The Wars of the Iroquois: A Study in Intertribal Trade Relations* by George T. Hunt (Madison: University of Wisconsin Press, 1940; 209 pp., 1 map). *American Anthropologist* 42, no. 4 (1940): 662–64. Originally published by the American Anthropological Association (http://www.anthrosource.net).

Review of *Indian Affairs in Colonial New York: The Seventeenth Century* by Allen W. Trelease (Ithaca: Cornell University Press, 1960; xvi, 379 pp.). *American Anthropologist* 63, no. 2 (1961): 416–18. Originally published by the American Anthropological Association (http://www.anthrosource.net).

Review of *Conservatism among the Iroquois at the Six Nations Reserve* by Annemarie Anrod Shimony (Yale University Publications in Anthropology, No. 65; New

Haven: Department of Anthropology, Yale University, 1961; 302 pp., 19 figures, 2 tables). *American Anthropologist* 65, no. 2 (1963): 444–47. Originally published by the American Anthropological Association (http://www.anthrosource.net).

"Huronia: An Essay in Proper Ethnohistory." Review of *The Children of Aataentsic: A History of the Huron People to 1660* by Bruce G. Trigger (Montreal: McGill-Queen's University Press, 1976; xxiii, 913 pp. in two vols.). *Ethnohistory* 80, no. 4 (1978): 923–35. Copyright 1978, by the American Society for Ethnohistory. All rights reserved. Reproduced by permission of the publisher, Duke University Press.

Review of *The Ordeal of the Longhouse: The Peoples of the Iroquois League in the Era of European Colonization* by Daniel K. Richter (Chapel Hill: University of North Carolina Press, 1992; xvi, 436 pp., illustrations, maps). *Ethnohistory* 41, no. 2 (1994): 343–46. Copyright 1994, by the American Society for Ethnohistory. All rights reserved. Reproduced by permission of the publisher, Duke University Press.

Obituaries

Fenton's old friend Anthony F. C. Wallace probably said it best: "For Fenton, field work has always been an intensely personal experience, a type of bond that fellow workers share in a valued common undertaking, and he gave his Indian collaborators the traditional Western scholar's farewell to a departed colleague" ("Overview," in Michael K. Foster, Jack Campisi, and Marianne Mithun, eds., *Extending the Rafters: Interdisciplinary Approaches to Iroquois Studies* [Albany NY: State University of New York Press, 1984], 5).

We have added to these Fenton's obituary for John R. Swanton, one of America's most distinguished ethnologists, for whom Fenton held great admiration.

"Simeon Gibson: Iroquois Informant, 1889–1943." *American Anthropologist* 46, no. 2 (1944): 231–34. Originally published by the American Anthropological Association (http://www.anthrosource.net).

"Twí-yendagon' (Woodeater) Takes the Heavenly Path: On the Death of Henry

Redeye (1864?–1946), Speaker of the Coldspring Seneca Longhouse." *The American Indian* 3, no. 3 (1946): 11–15. Reproduced by permission of the Association of American Indian Affairs.

"John Reed Swanton, 1873–1958." *American Anthropologist* 61, no. 4 (1959): 663–68. Originally published by the American Anthropological Association (http://www.anthrosource.net).

"Howard Sky, 1900–1971: Cayuga Faith-Keeper, Gentleman, and Interpreter of Iroquois Culture." *American Anthropologist* 74, no. 3 (1972): 758–62. Copyright © 1972 by *American Anthropologist* and reproduced by permission of Blackwell Publishing Ltd.

Conference on Iroquois Research

The annual Conference on Iroquois Research, which Fenton founded with Merle Deardorff and Charles Congdon at Red House on the Allegany Reservation in 1945, may turn out to be Fenton's greatest legacy. True to its informal organization, there are just a handful of reports on meeting activities, several of which we include here. Still, here and there in the file cabinets of longtime participants may be found a folder containing a collection of the typed one-page conference programs, although one would have to ask.

"Conference on Iroquois Research." *American Antiquity* 12, no. 3 (1947): 207. [This is a report on the Second Iroquois Conference, which also describes the first.] Reproduced by permission of the Society for American Archaeology.

"Fourth Conference on Iroquois Research." *American Antiquity* 14, no. 2 (1948): 159–60. Reproduced by permission of the Society for American Archaeology.

"Seventh Conference on Iroquois Research." *American Antiquity* 17, no. 3 (1952): 292–94. Reproduced by permission of the Society for American Archaeology.

"Iroquois Research." *Science* 123, no. 3185 (1956): 69. Reproduced by permission of the American Association for the Advancement of Science (AAAS).

"History and Purposes of the Conference on Iroquois Research." In *Iroquois Culture, History and Prehistory: Proceedings of the 1965 Conference on Iroquois*

Research, ed. Elisabeth Tooker, 3–4 (Albany: University of the State of New York, 1967). Reproduced by permission of the New York State Museum, Albany NY 12230.

"Iroquois Research Conference after 25 Years." *Newsletter of the American Anthropological Association* 10, no. 10 (1969): 9. Reproduced by permission of Wiley-Blackwell.

General Works

-

Iroquois Indian Folklore

Methodology and Techniques

When checking the Index to the *Journal of American Folklore* (1930), for titles of articles, reviews, and notes contributed by authors working in eastern North America, and for the names of tribes, and regions, one is at first overwhelmed with the enormous amount of material that has been collected and published in the name of the discipline. Not only do many titles relate to the Plains and Eastern Woodlands Indians, but the topics exhibit a wide range. All of it is folklore of a sort, as the topics reflect some aspect of the traditional life of people. No other discipline concerns itself mainly with the subject matter of myths and tales, their classification, analysis, comparison, and distribution. Otherwise, Indian folklore, judging by the *Journal*, comprises much ethnology, which may be defined as the science of folkways.

I have attempted to classify the topics of folklore in my field of research, as they appear in the *Journal* and other media. Those topics that are principally folkloristic appear first, followed by others that move progressively into the field of ethnology.

1. *Myths, tales, and historical legends.* Aware of pitfalls in distinguishing these three, we depend (later) on how the folk classify tales. These comprise the bulk of literature in folklore, filling our Memoir series. Cosmogony and cosmology belong here.

2. *Beliefs: signs governing activities.* Signs controlling weather, and

such activities as love, gambling, and the chase; disease concepts and curing; omens regarding death; and dreams greatly concern the folklorist. These topics are on his agenda and he collects them, often without regard to the cultural matrix in which he finds them.

3. *Folk Knowledge: Science.* Here I list star lore (astronomy), plant lore and herbalism (ethnobotany), animal, bird, and reptile lore (ethnobiology), and place names and related activities (ethnogeography). Depending upon the interests and capabilities of the investigator and the wealth of such materials among the folk with whom he works, any of these topics may become the subject of monographic studies that relate them to other aspects of culture. Of themselves, items in these categories are interesting for comparative purposes, but they are liable to misinterpretation unless evaluated critically.

4. *Crafts.* Unlike Scandinavia, where so much attention has been lavished on native arts, the folklore of material culture remains an undeveloped field in America, judging by the publications of the American Folklore Society. In Indian studies, crafts as part of material culture have received the serious attention of American anthropologists, but principally in museum collections. Of late years this subject has attracted few students. Here lies a great opportunity in relating collections to folk knowledge of crafts, their use, meaning, and the perpetuation of the folk arts. Recently the U.S. Indian Service has entered the field of the crafts in relation to education. A series of Indian Handcraft Pamphlets have appeared; they are well illustrated, and some are comprehensive, possibly too comprehensive for technical uses. In Canada, Barbeau has pursued with some success the historic ties between French and Indian folk arts and crafts. The Rochester Museum of Arts and Sciences, under the able directorship of Dr. Arthur C. Parker, recovered some Indian arts and revived others among the Tonawanda and Cattaraugus Senecas of western New York. The resulting collections have not been described although the materials have been widely exhibited.

5. *Amusements: tale-telling, riddles, and games.* Folklorists and

ethnologists have devoted too little space to describing the circumstances of tale-telling, how the art is learned, and its significance in the life of a people. To what extent is tale-telling ritualized? Archer Taylor has recently shown that American Indian riddles are a neglected subject of inquiry (*JAF*, 57 [1944], 1–15). The Huron-Iroquois Dream Feast offers background material for a historical study of the practice.

Folklorists have collected games from diverse cultures, and Indian games occupy much space in the literature, having been monographed by Culin (1907). Many are continental in their distribution. Here again these activities take place in social and ceremonial contexts of which they are an integral part. Play activities of children offer an interesting lead to studies of child development and personality structure. Few changing cultural activities are as well documented as the *Pawnee Ghost Dance Hand Game* (Lesser, 1933).

6. *Ceremonialism: rituals, dances.* Indian ceremonialism of the Plains and Eastern Woodlands of North America has given rise to an enormous literature in ethnology, comprising extensive descriptive accounts of ceremonies and dance associations, theoretical considerations of the relation of myth to ritual, studies of diffusion of ceremonials, analyses of ceremonial patterns, and discussion of other historical problems (Lowie, 1915). Ceremonies distributed over wide areas like the Calumet ritual, the Sun Dance, and Peyotism lend themselves to varying interpretation. Descriptions of social dances, dissociated from their social setting, recur in earlier issues of the *Journal.* Unless a historical or psychological problem underlies our approach to the study of widely distributed social dances, we see no point in expanding the literature with duplicate data.

7. *Music.* Songs and musical notation of Plains and Woodland Indians claim fewer titles in the *Journal of American Folklore* than ballads and regional folk songs of the United States. Alice Fletcher and later Frances Densmore collected on the central and northern Plains and around the Western Great Lakes; and published mainly

in the series of the Bureau of American Ethnology. In the Eastern Woodlands Iroquois music is distinctive, but demonstrations of its relations to northeastern Algonquian, Plains, and southeastern Woodland music await transcription of large existing record collections. Such collections did not abound when Roberts (1936), citing Goldenweiser's records (1910) which have since vanished, isolated a distinctive melodic pattern for Iroquois songs which reminded her some of Plains songs and at other points with Yuchi (southeastern) songs, as we might expect. The only work on recent collections, based on a short series of "Tutelo" songs collected by Speck (Herzog *in* Speck, 1942) among the Six Nations Iroquois, calls attention in the material to a general similarity with melodies of other southeastern tribes, occasionally with Pueblo, and quite specific agreements with Iroquois melodies. Throughout the areas under discussion nonsense or burden syllables predominate in song recitative. To their phrasing and structure might be applied a method of analysis that Herzog (1935) devised for demonstrating affinities of Plains Ghost Dance and Great Basin music. Perhaps the technique of the ballad collectors might contribute to problems of historical reconstruction. Analysis of verses, of ritual poetry, and of stomp dance cries offer promising lines of inquiry.

8. *Religion.* While more nearly of an ethnological character, the religious ideas of the Indians represent the systematics reflected in myths which we have said are the peculiar property of the folklorist's discipline. Moreover, ideas about sacred power, the sacred bundles containing tribal fetishes, and conceptions of the supernaturals are transmitted orally. They belong to the folk literature. Likewise the means of controlling these classes of phenomena are acquired along with other folk knowledge to the end that folk science, witchcraft, revelation, and divination come by education that does not isolate clearly the categories or levels of application. The relationship of myths to rituals has provoked recent theoretical discussion (Kluckhohn, 1942). The Ghost Dance on the Plains, Peyotism, and other Messianic

cults provide contemporary materials for the study of religious beginnings, of the relation of the individual to culture (prophets), and of cultural change.

9. *Social Usages.* Social usages attendant upon life crises afford topics of article length to the folklorist and anthropologist. Personal names and naming practices constitute another aspect of social organization which might yield considerable material of unique character that folklore well might claim e.g., Dorsey's materials on Siouan names and Goldenweiser's collection of over a thousand Iroquois personal names, belonging to members of certain clans and tribes, that, apart from their place in social organization, have formal and distributional aspects which might be treated comparatively. What is the distribution of various types of names in the Eastern Woodlands and on the Plains? How are choice of names and totemism related? Are new names being invented? What is the process? English equivalents of Indians names, such as Hotbread, Steeprock, Rolling Thunder, etc., now belong to the stock of English patrilineal family names among these Indians. Other Indian families have taken names of captives: Crouse, Jemison, Tarbell, etc. Colonial officials and army officers sired others. What is the process and what changes are at work in it? How do the folk regard family history? How do Chauncey Johnny John's grandsons come to call themselves the "J. John's"?

10. *Acculturation.* We have touched the topic of acculturation several times in the discussion. European tales, loan words in English, and foreign elements in Indian tales have been noted for many years. These have been derived, in the Eastern Woodlands, from French, English, possibly Dutch and Swedish, and Negro sources. Barbeau has published Wyandot tales including foreign elements (*JAF*, 28 [1915], 83–95), Skinner collected European tales from the Plains Ojibwa (*JAF*, 29 [1916], 330–340), and Menomini (*JAF*, 26 [1913], 64–80); Speck found them among the Penobscot of Maine (*JAF*, 26 [1913], 81–84; also *JAF*, 48 [1935], 1–107); in 1939 Hallowell recorded European tales from non-English-speaking Berens River Saulteaux (*JAF*, 52 [1939],

155–179), and Teit reported them from the Upper Thompson River Indians of interior British Columbia (*JAF*, 29 [1916], 301–329). Judging by the wealth of French folklore extant, which is found among Indians from Nova Scotia to the Rockies, those Indians whom the French furtraders reached assimilated considerable French lore. Stith Thompson (1919) has surveyed this material. In the southeast, Negro influence is strong in animal tales, but Swanton who collected them among Indians of the Muskhogean stock (*JAF*, 26 [1913], 193–218) believed that whatever the origin of the separate Rabbit tales, that this animal was one of the Tricksters of the Southern Indians in pre-Columbian times.

We should like to know how European tales were disseminated. For example, in collecting tales among the modern Iroquois contemporary informants are as likely to give me something from Grimm as a tale from the *Skanawundi* Trickster cycle. They have learned the former along with the latter, and both are told in the Iroquoian dialects. Possibly a study of missionary primers printed in Indian dialects would discover that Indian children carried home European tales which they learned from such sources as Asher Wright's elementary reading book in the Seneca language.

Contacts between Indian herbalism and colonial medicine (Fenton, 1941) have hardly been explored. We may infer, again, from the presence of Indian herbs in our pharmacopoeia and the number of introduced or escaped European species which Indian herbalists now employ the extent of contact and the directions of borrowing. In the case of certain species we can document the interchange. My data from the Iroquois indicate that names of new plants differ markedly more than names of indigenous species which the Iroquois peoples had used for many generations until each dialect carried a name for the species that frequently obtained consistently from group to group. Down to our own time Indian herbalists have plied their trade among neighboring whites. A generation ago the Indian Medicine Show was an institution in many parts of the country, and I have met within my limited field experience old Indians like Rolling Thunder who were professional showmen. Yet no one has made a study of Indian Shows, either the Wild West Show of the Plains, or the Medicine Barker of the woodland and prairie states. What are the common elements and basic patterns in the organization and conduct of such enterprises? To what extent have they influenced the popular American conception of the Indian? How far has this stereotype become part of the Indian's thinking to the end that show costumes and behavior are reintroduced to "native" ceremonies. Show costumes in the "Plains" mode have practically supplanted the nineteenth-century dress of Iroquois Indians in New York, and only a few of the more conservative longhouse lovers in Canada affect the old tribal dress. And they distinguish between sacred and "show" songs.

Among the Iroquois at least, new songs both in the traditional modes and for "show" purposes are continually being composed. I have witnessed the introduction of a new song to a neighboring tribal group and sat with hosts as they learned the new Women's Dance song. Every year in the several longhouse communities the leaders of singing societies compose new sets of these songs in anticipation of entertaining guests from other longhouse communities. The guests come and learn them and carry them home to become part of the tribal repertoire. If the song takes hold, if "it's a good song," it continues to be sung. Years later in Ohsweken, a certain song is ascribed to "Twenty Canoes" of Allegheny. In another generation, the composer being dead, no one remembers the composer and the next generation forgets where the song originated. Other field workers unquestionably can duplicate this instance many times. But here is dissemination that we can study in movement, not infer later from internal evidence, and working out the process now should help us to understand how folk songs spread in ancient times.

We may also learn something about the growth of mythology by paying more heed to the myths that contemporary Indian communities hold regarding tribal history. Nor is such investigation entirely lacking in practical significance. Indian treaties with the United States summoned as delegates some of the ablest minds of the time. The Indian tribes sent their best men and required oral reports supported by wampum belts and other mnemonic devices. The lore attending such treaties, anecdotes relating to great Indian leaders, and reinterpretations of the lore weigh heavily on the minds of contemporary Indian leaders who revere their national past. A central tenet in the lore of the Iroquois longhouse maintains independent nationhood for the Six Nations of Canada and individually for their remnants in New York. The myth of independent nationhood coming down from the "treaties" (Haldimand Treaty in Canada, and Pickering Treaty at Canandaigua, New York, 1794) crops up in any issue that may be interpreted as threatening the national existence. How does the "Indian agitator" get that way? Folklorists might gain some controlled data and earn the respect of men of affairs by pursuing such problems.

Let us look at some marginal groups of mixed racial composition who are neither Indians nor whites, but who live as outcasted groups between the dominant white caste and the nether Negro caste in our society. Dr. W. H. Gilbert, in a preliminary research paper on the Wesorts of southern Maryland (1945), demonstrates the importance of studying Indian survival groups that are distributed from New England to Louisiana: the Jackson Whites of the New Jersey–New York border, the Moors and Nanticokes of Delaware (treated by Weslager in a popular book, 1943), the Croatans of Carolina, and the Melungeons of Tennessee. In the main, relegated to poor lands in isolated areas, these folk live an acculturated existence, unassimilated by the surrounding population, and they betoken a kind of society toward which other Indian groups may be drifting. They should be studied not so much for the survivals of their Indian past as for what their folklore may lead us to expect of other deculturated groups.

In the main, however, all scientific collectors aim at securing verified data. They are not satisfied in securing a tale from one informant alone, and they exercise some rule of thumb in judging informants. Sometimes anyone is the best available, as Speck, for example, found among the Catawba Indians of Carolina. Ideally, the collector works where practicable in the native language and records the exact language of the narrator. Thus the collector of English ballads encounters little difficulty, but the folklorist among American Indians rarely commands an Indian language, and that only after long years of work with a single tribal dialect, or stock of languages. Two Indian ethnologists achieved this facility: La Flesche of the Omaha and Osage, and Hewitt of the Iroquois; both were natives, but the latter had to learn several dialects. We think of Lowie's work among the Crow, but he has denied that he commands the language. Others, perforce, operate through interpreters, but even so they put down the exact language of the narrator.

Thus on the basis of how they were collected, Boas, a generation ago, distinguished two types of collections. In his day the greater body of data included tales taken down in English or in other European tongues directly from informants, usually through interpreters. The second type of collection, then the smaller group but greatly augmented by the prodigious labors of Boas and his students, comprised tales taken down from dictation by natives, or recorded in the native language by natives, and later revised and edited. Boas would relate tales to the corpus of folklore. He demonstrated that texts in the native language are necessary to the study of literary form; and the best translation does not admit an adequate grasp of literary form and style because the best interpreters cannot convey in English the totality of the tale in the original language.

The collector must be trained in phonetics, and he must cope with the language. Michelson could meet these standards among the Fox and other Central Algonquian tribes. Geary has carried on his work. Hewitt's aimed at completeness, an objective which deterred him from publication. His Onondaga text, the epic of the founding of the League (289 pp. MS), never went to the printer. Goldenweiser had the same from the identical informant, some 525 pp., but never essayed to translate it.

Yet there is a middle ground between strict scientific accuracy and mere story collecting. Beckwith makes a pretty good case for taking materials in Indian English, allowing for lapses of Indian memory and not retouching the material to enhance its attractiveness. Unless we listen to reason the folk materials and the story tellers will vanish before students are trained. The story tellers available in Iroquois about equal the number of collectors who can take texts. A greater number know tales that they can tell in English. Therefore, besides the group that Voegelin is training in methods of scientific linguistics to take Iroquois tests, we need some folklorists who will concern themselves with the literature now available and work incidentally in the field. Possibly we can look to the Folklore Institute for some of them.

Speck, for example, has published collected tests, but he employs an alternate method in Delaware and Cayuga field work when rapid dictation permits only sketchy notes (see Fenton, *American Anthropologist*, 48, 424).

Recording machines have been greatly improved since the day when Alice C. Fletcher sallied forth to the Omaha with a "Perfected Graphophone" and Frances Densmore first went to the Chippewa with a precursor of the Dictaphone. But even the most modern machine cannot supplant the folklorist. They enable the informant to proceed at normal speech rates, capturing stylistic and literary devices of the tale-teller that might be lost from other dictation. They are to be recommended for recording prayers, preaching, and oratory which have distinctive styles of speaking among the Iroquois and presumably among other tribes. The collector may make the necessary comments on the record to identify singers, place, group, and the matter taken; but it is still incumbent on the folklorist to keep a notebook of texts, particularly for music. The wire recorder makes possible records of whole interviews, and now entire rituals may be had for preservation. The ethnologist may now spare a little time and space to acculturative materials: hymns sung in Indian, for which published hymnals go back a century, and gospel preaching in Indian and "Reservation English," which offers interesting leads to dialect geography.

The *Journal of American Folklore* seems adequate for papers of a general nature, for short research papers, and for bringing to the attention of folklorists important collections of modest proportion. In its Memoir series the Society faces the same problems as other publishers in bringing out large systematic collections. Possibly some bulky collections might be microfilmed and copies deposited in centers of folkloristic research. For example, the Library of the U.S. Department of Agriculture has taken over the work of the American Documentation Institute (1719 N Street, N.W., Washington DC) which was created by Science Service to meet such problems. Reproduction costs are minimal. Limitations of the use of movable type, excess charges for foreign language material, and conservatism of printers have influenced a number of publishers to refuse texts. Perhaps use of multilith offers an answer. Records are another means.

Classification and Interpretation

Such attempts at analysis and comparison of folk data as have been made in Eastern America have been predicated on the geographical-historical method (Beckwith, 1931, pp. 50–51). Collectors have sometimes analyzed their own materials, but with the notable exceptions of Barbeau (Huron), Swanton (Southeast), Dixon (Central and Eastern Algonkins), Lowie and Beckwith (Northern Plains), the method has not been applied rigorously and followed through.

Classification may be approached from the viewpoint of geography and convenience, or from the viewpoint of the folk. The first defines a limited workable field, the Central Lakes area, the Southeast—which implies cultural homogeneity, and asks the question what is the folklore of the area? But in all such areal studies cultural and linguistic affinities weigh heavily, as in Dixon's comparison, a generation ago, of Central and Eastern Algonkin Mythology (1908).[1]

The Oglala Dakota of the Plains distinguish two classes of tales: "true" and "lying" on the basis of lead lines—"A tribe was settled …," and "Spider was traveling …." Of the Iroquoians, Huron, Seneca, Onondaga, and Cherokee make similar distinctions. Huron (Barbeau, 1915) and Seneca-Iroquois (Curtin and Hewitt, Parker, 1923; Fenton) distinguish between things and events "which truly happened," i.e., myths; "they went to hunt for meat tales," experiences with supernaturals which gave rise to medicine societies; and tribal history. Barbeau segregates these into myths, tales and traditions. Actually, there are two types of myths, as distinct from tales, and traditions. Likewise, the Delaware (Brinton) distinguish *tomoacan*, tales for leisure hours vs. *machtanha*, "those who are bewitched." Cherokee myths have been classified roughly into sacred myths (genesis, astronomical, life, death, monsters, hero gods), animal stories, local legends, and historical traditions (Mooney, 1900, p. 229). Mooney assumed that the stock of myths was probably not original with the Cherokee (p. 234), and earlier pointed out a number of Iroquois parallels (*JAF*, 11 [1898], 67), which ought now to be followed out in greater detail.

Analysis of myths from the Eastern Woodlands has not proceeded beyond the impetus given by Boas to the work of Radin and Barbeau 1912–1915 at the Geological Survey of Canada.[2] Evidently Radin was never able to carry out his intention, expressed in the preface to one collection (Radin, 1914), to publish a systematic study of Ojibwa mythology. But his "Literary Aspects of North American Mythology" (1915), written between Ojibwa field trips, drew heavily on Eastern Woodland materials. Radin exploded Ehrenreich's theory of a primary version, and showed that the mere insistence of an informant that his version is true indicated individual literary diversity. He laid the grounds for myth analysis as to plot, elaboration, actors, episodes, and motifs; he found that elaboration of a tale may be the function of the episodes, actors, and that "in every case that the motivation of the episode is extremely variable and that the constant element is always the plot" (p. 30). With regard to myth-complexes as unit cycles, differences were found in the way that various elements of the myth-complex were welded together; these are attributed to individual selection of episodes and motifs and to historic causes. In selecting Trickster cycles for comparison he followed Boas' insistence (Boas, 1940, p. 431) that all comparisons be based on material collected from contiguous areas. Establishment of myth centers and demonstrating their relation to transmission of tales rests on Dixon's study, already cited, which defined a Western and an Eastern group of Algonkins, the former much influenced by the Huron-Iroquois version of the myth of the twin brothers, particularly the Ottawa and Pottawatomi.

The Introduction to Barbeau's *Huron and Wyandot Mythology* (1915) approaches a satisfactory analysis of the material collected. The methods of Boas and Radin are carried out with considerable vigor, and comparisons are made with collections from adjacent tribes, both Iroquois and Algonquian. It is evident that Huron and Iroquois comprise one mythological center with distinctive creation myths and a body of tales relating to supernatural tutelaries of medicine fraternities. He attributed the Wyandot Trickster and Raccoon cycles, shared by the Seneca, to borrowing from neighboring Algonkins (p. 13). During analysis he refers (p. 19, n. 1) to a list of leading Huron-Wyandot themes with indications of their distribution which he then was preparing for publication. What happened to it?

F. W. Waugh was preparing a similar analysis of his Cayuga materials from the Six Nations Reserve (MS), for he annotated each of the tales as it was typed for publication, but he had not made a synthesis. The above two studies taken together with Parker's published collections (Converse and Parker, 1908; and Parker, 1923), of which the latter carries nice discussions of "fundamental factors in Seneca folklore," themes and materials, and the relationship of legends to Seneca culture, might be compared with the Curtin and Hewitt collections and Beachamp's Onondaga folklore publications (*JAF* index, and Syracuse, 1922). Without benefit of these collections Mooney (1900, p. 234) attempted to place Cherokee myths in relation to surrounding tribes. In synoptic fashion, Swanton (1929, pp. 267–275) related myths of the southeastern tribes which he collected to Mooney's Cherokee data, Speck's Yuchi materials, and to a wide range of folk tales over the continent. These relations might be made clearer by further study.

Of five possible means of interpreting Plains and Eastern Woodland folklore—historical-cultural, psychological, literary, educational, and functional—only the first and fourth have received attention. Sapir's classic *Time Perspective in Aboriginal American Culture* (1916) defined the method of using direct and indirect evidence in historical interpretations. While critical of legendary history referring to the distant past, Sapir suggested criteria for admitting native testimony on the spread of cultural features in recent time. Clearly Sapir influenced Barbeau (1915, p. 24 ff.) who in discussing antiquity of Huron-Wyandot mythology, as to form, style, ending formulae, and subject matter, segregated direct and indirect evidence. He compares his own collections with those of Connelly, somewhat earlier, and for these he finds exact antecedents in the writings of Sagard (1623) and of Brébeuf and his Jesuit colleagues ca. 1634–1648. Cosmogonic myths, journeys to the land of the dead, and origin legends relating to sources of supernatural power (The Little Water Medicine Society, and the False-faces) exist in fragmentary form but of sufficient diagnostic value to establish their aboriginality. This enables us to infer that similar legends among the Iroquois go back to the same period. The absence of written documents relating to the Trickster cycle throws the investigation back upon inferential methods of distribution, dissemination, which rest on the theory of age and area, for determining their antiquity. Moreover, acculturated myths are plainly recognizable in their derived American versions, which have not been integrated with other cycles.

Unlike the Muskhogeans of the Southeast, the northern Iroquoians, and the Cherokee for that matter, have no extensive migration legends such as the "Walam Olum" of the Delaware, which we might expect, considering the other evidence that they were intrusive in their historic seats. Their traditional history did not enable Swanton and Dixon (1914) to assign them a former home.

Eastern American mythology has not been treated from the viewpoint of how it reflects the psychology of the peoples. How do the Iroquois personify their gods and what does this tell of their own personality? For example, a preoccupation with dreams that the Jesuit Fathers first noted in Huronia finds its expression in the ritual pageants of the medical associations or confraternities which dramatize the behavior of supernaturals in tales. Considering Iroquois ceremonialism we should not be surprised to find a folk literature peopled by ghosts, ghouls, and witches. Moreover, Iroquois genius for political organization finds its expression in long detailed sagas of the beginnings of the Confederacy—the Deganawi:dah epic—and in the Cosmogony emerges a philosophy which bears certain kindred to the Delaware world view of superimposed heavens and high gods. How reconcile fear of demons with political sagacity and breadth of comprehension?

A qualitative analysis, however, of the folklore of various groups in the Eastern Woodland area should indicate the terms of their artistic expression. Only secondary students have collected them for human interest. The star lore of the Plains tribes and the Iroquois tales of otherworld journeys have definite appeal.

Functional interpretations of folklore offer new problems. A few collectors have indicated how the literature functions in the daily life of the people, e.g., Parker's Introduction to his *Seneca Myths and Folk Tales* (1923). Of course, functional problems may not always be practicable for field study in broken cultures. However, the obverse problem—reflection of culture in mythology—may be sought in the older collections, such as those for Fox and Seneca, which afford rich material for cultural analysis.

The theories relating to the study of Indian mythology have been stated by Beckwith and Boas. Apart from Radin's stricture with Ehrenreich, only Swanton of the Eastern collectors has contributed to the body of principles (*JAF*, 23 [1910], 1–7). Others attempted to derive myths from phenomena in nature, or spent themselves in the futile search for the original and ideal myth. Just such an aberration plagued Hewitt's study of the League. To Boas' principles of dissemination Goldenweiser, who may hardly be considered a folklorist, contributed the idea of convergence and the principle of limited possibilities in the development of culture. Of late ethnologists have come to appreciate the unique character of each culture, which, although it may be comprised of many diffused elements and complexes, manifests intense localism in its patterning. In this sense the myths of two peoples never exhibit true identity. Although as Boas pointed out (p. 429), the composite character of myths may reflect borrowing, and usually does, secondary interpretations and grafting of new elements onto old myths have proceeded until their explanations of the tales bear no relation to their history.

An interesting lead to the study of Iroquois myth making and ceremonialism lies in a general theory of myths and rituals which Kluckhohn (1942) has based on a broad study of the literature in the perspective of his Navaho field work. Two fields of inquiry beckon. Medicine fraternities have origin legends which in two cases go back to aboriginal times. Handsome Lake, the Seneca prophet, stood to preach a new religion in 1799, and his preachments have since come down in codified form that now amounts to a myth. From Morgan, Parker, Hewitt, and from modern preachers come materials for checking its growth; in the study of Seneca ceremonialism in various longhouse communities the student enters the theater to witness the fulfillment of one in the other. A study of Iroquois dreams would reveal the type sources of ritualism. But it will be demonstrated that much of modern Iroquois ceremonialism antedates the Code of Handsome Lake and that some is shared with Delaware.

Iroquois mythology is little affected by European contact; what has been adapted constitutes an added literature. The old Iroquois literature has been reduced rather than hybridized. The tales which Curtin collected are no longer to be had among the Seneca; possibly the same is true of Cherokee. Yet what does remain manifests the remarkable stability of the Iroquois cultural pattern generally in its resistance to French, British, and Yankee culture during 400 years.

Nevertheless, whole folklores have vanished in many sectors. Hallowell has recently told me of visiting with children among the Minnesota Chippewa who did not recognize characters in tribal fiction such as Nanabush and Wisakehä. Few Seneca children can tell one much about Skanawandi or Raccoon, and my informants were convulsed by Hatcinondon, a former traditional hero.

Aims and Accomplishments

So far coverage has consisted mainly of collecting the lore of the Woodland and Plains tribes before the last informant expired. Completeness has been the cardinal principle of the Iroquois collectors, especially Hewitt. Mooney succeeded for the Cherokee, and Dorsey for the eastern and southern Plains. Topical studies have been made by Densmore (music); Speck (ethnobiology); his students; Mooney, Huron Smith, LaBarre, and the writer (ethnobotany).

A number of analytical studies, continental in scope, cover Eastern and Plains materials: Lowie, Test Theme (*JAF*, 21 [1908], 97–148); Waterman, Explanatory element (*JAF*, 27 [1914], 1–54); Reichard, Literary types and dissemination of myths (*JAF*, 34 [1921], 269–307); Gayton, Orpheus motif (*JAF*, 48, 263–293); and Benedict's monograph on Guardian spirit. While Lowie's and Benedict's materials were oriented in the Plains or Central Woodlands, no such study has originated within the Northeastern or Southeastern areas. Swanton was interested in Lodge Boy and Thrown Away and the writer with the Roc Legend as the origin of the Seneca Eagle Society.

Stith Thompson has pointed out that "no other tribes show such thorough independence in their tales and detachment from other sections as do the Iroquois." Although as Dixon indicated, their creation myth has elements shared by the Central Algonkians (*JAF*, 22 [1909], 1–9), "the rest of their tales show little outside influence." Thompson was impressed by "a great monotony of motivation and treatment. Accounts of cruel uncles, wicked brothers, cannibalistic mothers, flying heads, and ravaging monsters are given but slight relief through an occasional trickster tale or a beautiful myth of other-world journeying" (Thompson, 1929, p. xxii).

As Swanton had demonstrated "animal tales and migration legends mark the collections from the Southeast." Mooney, and to some extent Swanton, thought the Rabbit Trickster cycle was aboriginal, although Thompson suspects it of being as much Negro as Indian.

Save Swanton's brief comparisons of his Southeastern tales no study has been made of the areal affiliations of Iroquois tales to determine whether they really are unique and whether a study of them does solve the obscurities in Cherokee mythology as Mooney hoped. Again eastern studies have not attained the level of far western studies by the California group.

Following Speck's leads in his studies of Mahican and Delaware ceremonialism the writer has collected Iroquois folklore and employed it in treatment of the medical fraternities and in a study of the League as an adjunct to the study of Iroquois culture. Tales have not been taken for their own sake. However, Ehrlich (1937), following the lead of Boas on the Northwest Coast, made a study of "Tribal Culture in Crow Mythology," finding striking congruence with published ethnography. Flannery made use of folklore collections in "An Analysis of Coastal Algonquian Culture" (1939), but the method used by Ehrlich commends itself to the examination of Huron, Iroquois, and Cherokee collections.

The extent to which folklore collecting aims to increase our knowledge of cultural history, psychology, and cultural contacts has not been realized, if at all appreciated, by Eastern students.

In attempt to assess coverage by areas, the writer mapped the recorded folk tales east of the Rocky Mountains. The data show up tribes that have received most attention, some that vanished before collecting began, and certain lacunae. Flannery, in her report, has suggested the Albany River as a place for gathering borderline Ojibwa and Cree folklore.

The Plains, particularly to the north, seem well covered. Possible gaps are Plains Cree (Mandelbaum?), Assiniboin, Yankton Dakota, Santee Dakota (?). The Crow (Lowie), Blackfoot (Wissler, Uhlenbeck), Teton Dakota, Hidatsa and Mandan (Beckwith) Cheyenne (Grinnell) are represented by substantial collections. The southern Plains appears enigmatic. Substantial early collections by the Dorseys, Fletcher, and LaFlesche leave something to be desired, but is further field work possible? Collier and Mishkin are supposed to have Kiowa materials; Linton, Comanche. What of the Missouri and Quapaw?

Turning north, Shawnee materials of Trowbridge have been expanded by Erminie Voegelin. The Central Lakes area is in good shape with substantial collections from the Central Algonquians in both text and translation, excepting possibly Pottawatomi.

We have fine Huron and Seneca collections. Beauchamp's Onondaga materials are the best extant. Cayuga is in Waugh's ms. Oneida of Green Bay, Wisconsin are covered by Basehart and Lounsbury's study. Modern Mohawk of Caughnawaga, St. Regis, Bay of Quinte, and Six Nations Reserve are worth investigating.

Delaware presents an enigma. Brinton's "Walam Olum" has been overrated. Speck is supposed to have ms tales.

Of the Northeastern tribes, all have vanished save Abnaki, Penobscot, Micmac, and Malecite, south of the St. Lawrence. Speck assures me that much could be done with Passamaquoddy. For the others we have to depend on earlier collectors: Rand, Leland, etc. Flannery has discussed the Laurentian area.

The following appear as specific needs:

(a) A systematic analysis of Iroquois mythology, based on existing collections.
(b) Publication of the Waugh collection.
(c) Systematic comparison of Northeastern Algonquian and Central Algonquian folklore with Iroquois, coupled with a comparison of Delaware and Shawnee elements in Iroquois.
(d) An inquiry into how Iroquois folklore complements Cherokee.
(e) Collection of the folklore of marginal Indian groups, with a study of the growth of tribal myths concerning tribal history and relations with the whites, in answer to the question of how has folklore developed (Boas, 437).
(f) A study of hymns in Indian languages, with records and texts, noting song alteration and language alteration.

There remain these general needs.

(a) Characterizations of the folklore of major areas (Boas, 478), showing how it is adjusted to tribal life.
(b) A series of studies of cultures based on folklore materials, as contrasted with ethnographic materials.

Immediate needs are the following.

(a) A bibliography of American Folklore, 1929–1945.
(b) A list of manuscripts in archives and in possession of scholars.
(c) The training of more folklorists, as scholars.
(d) New media for publication such as multilith or photo-offset which are ideally suited to reproducing texts.

Altogether too much random collecting has gone on in the past. Let us have less irresponsible collecting and more synthetic studies erected around problems. Next, at expense of repetition, we commend to ethnologists the use of myths as source materials on culture and urge them to collect them in text, if possible, or in faithful translation whenever possible. In general ethnologists have shied away from using abundant existing collections of folklore as tools or counters for working out problems. We leave comparisons to linguists and archaeologists, confining ourselves to "culture traits," ignoring folklore elements. Finally, here is a body of information for the students of both psychology and culture.

Notes

1. Since this report was written Margaret W. Fisher's "The Mythology of Northern and Northeastern Algonkians in Reference to Algonkian Mythology as a Whole" has been published (Papers of the Robert S. Peabody Foundation for Archaeology, Vol. 3, 1947, pp. 226–262).

2. Fisher, *loc. cit.*

Literature Cited

Barbeau, C. Marius
1915   *Huron and Wyandot Mythology* (Canada Geological Survey, Memoir 80. Ottawa).

Beauchamp, William M.
1922   *Iroquois Folk Lore Gathered from the Six Nations of New York* (Onondaga Historical Association, Syracuse, New York). (Contains much other material.) See other entries in Index of JAF, p. 15.

Beckwith, Martha Warren
1931   *Folklore in America: Its Scope and Method* (Publications of the Folklore Foundation, No. 11, Vassar College, Poughkeepsie NY).

Benedict, Ruth Fulton
1923   *The Concept of the Guardian Spirit in North America* (Memoir 29, American Anthropological Association).

Boas, F. "Mythology and Folk-Tales of the North American Indians." Reprinted in:
1940   *Race, Language and Culture* (New York), pp. 451–490.

Brinton, Daniel G.
1890   "Folklore of the Modern Lenape." In *Essays of an Americanist*, by Daniel G. Brinton (Philadelphia), pp. 181–192.

Converse, Harriet Maxwell, and Arthur Caswell Parker (eds.)
1908 *Myths and Legends of the New York State Iroquois* (New York State Museum, Bulletin 125, Albany).

Culin, Stewart
1907 *Games of the North American Indians* (24th Ann. Rep., BAE, pp. 3–809).

Curtin, Jeremiah (J. N. B. Hewitt, Ed.)
1918 *Seneca Fiction, Legends, and Myths* (32nd Ann. Rep., BAE).

Curtis, Natalie
1923 *The Indians' Book* (2nd ed.; New York) (Plains music.).

Ehrlich, Clara
1937 "Tribal Culture in Crow Mythology," *JAF*, 50 (1937), 307–408.

Fenton, William N.
1941 "Contacts between Iroquois Herbalism and Colonial Medicine." (Ann. Rep. for 1941, Smithsonian Institution, pp. 503–526).

Flannery, Regina
1939 *An Analysis of Coastal Algonquian Culture* (Catholic University of America, Anthropological Series, No. 7).

Gilbert, William Harlan, Jr.
1945 "The Wesorts of Southern Maryland: An Outcasted Group," *Jour. of the Washington Academy of Sciences*, 35 (1945), 237–246.

Herzog, George
1935 "Plains Ghost Dance and Great Basin Music," *AA*, 37 (1935), 403–419.
1942 "Transcriptions and Analysis of Tutelo Music." In *The Tutelo Spirit Adoption Ceremony*, by Frank G. Speck, Pennsylvania Historical Commission, pp. 83–120.
Journal of American Folklore: Index to Volumes 1–40 (MAFS, Vol. 14).

Kluckhohn, Clyde
1942 "Myths and Rituals: A General Theory," *Harvard Theological Review*, 35 (1942), 45–79.

Lesser, Alexander
1933 *The Pawnee Ghost Dance Hand Game* (Columbia Univ. Cont. to Anthro., Vol. 16).

Lowie, Robert H.
1915 "Ceremonialism in North America" (*Anthropology in North America*, NY, pp. 229–258).

Mooney, James
1900 *Myths of the Cherokee* (19th Ann. Rep., BAE, pp. 3–548).

Parker, Arthur C.
1923 *Seneca Myths and Folk Tales* (Buffalo Historical Society Pubs., Vol. 27).

Radin, Paul
1914 *Some Myths and Tales of the Ojibwa of Southeastern Ontario* (Canada Geological Survey, Memoir 48, Anthro. Series, No. 2, Ottawa, pp. 1–83).
1915 *Literary Aspects of North American Mythology* (Canada Geological Survey, Bulletin 16, Anthro. Series. No. 6, Ottawa, pp. 1–51).

Roberts, Helen H.
1936 *Musical Areas in Aboriginal North America* (Yale Univ. Publ. in Anthro., No. 12).

Sapir, Edward
1916 *Time Perspective in Aboriginal American Culture, A Study in Method* (Canada Geological Survey, Memoir 90, Anthro. Series, No. 13, Ottawa).

Swanton, John R., and Roland B. Dixon
1914 "Primitive American History," AA, 16 (1914), 376–412.
1929 *Myths and Tales of the Southeastern Indians* (Bul. 88, BAE).

Thompson, Stith
1919 *European Tales among the North American Indians* (Colorado College Publs., Language Series, Vol. 2, No. 34, pp. 319–471).
1929 *Tales of the North American Indians* (Cambridge MA)

Voegelin, Erminie Wheeler
1944 *Mortuary Customs of the Shawnee and Other Eastern Tribes* (Indiana Historical Soc., Vol. 2, No. 4, pp. 227–444).

Weslager, C. A.
1943 *Delaware's Forgotten Folk: The Story of the Moors and Nanticokes* (Philadelphia).

Wright, Asher
1836 Diuhsáwahgwah gayádoshah .... Wastok (Boston) (Elementary reading book in the Seneca language).

Letters to an Ethnologist's Children

From Simeon Gibson to the Children of William N. Fenton Who Took Them Down

[The following folk tales are substantially as told by the late Simeon Gibson at Brantford, Ontario. They were written on the typewriter in the form of letters home at the end of long days of interpreting and translating the Deganawi:dah legend of the founding of the League of the Iroquois in the month before Pearl Harbor. My children have enjoyed the letters, and they contain several tales not represented in the Iroquois literature. For these reasons they seem worth publishing.—W. N. F.]

THE MAGIC POT
An Old Iroquois Children's Story of How Mush Was Made of Chestnuts

There was at one time an old lady and her grandson who lived in the woods in a house by themselves. Just the old grandmother and her little boy, her grandson. So the boy used to watch his grandmother to learn the way she cooked chestnut meal and made mush of it in a pot. The boy used to watch her when she left her chestnuts in a basket high out of his reach. She would take the basket down and take a few chestnuts out and scrape the chestnuts into powder. At the same time she would have the pot half full of water hanging over the fire. She did this every day.

So when he grew bigger, about a year older, his grandmother was away all day for one day. He made up his mind that he would cook the chestnut meal for himself, so that he would have a meal ready when she returned to the house. He worked for a long time to get the basket down from its high place near the rafters. Finally he succeeded, and he found there was only one chestnut left in the basket. So he took this one chestnut and scraped it and made powder, using it all up. At the same time he put the pot over the fire and put water in it and got the wooden ladle which she usually hung on the wall above the fireplace. When the water was boiling he started to put the powder into the pot, and he commenced stirring as his grandmother did when she made chestnut mush.

The pot soon boiled over, and he struck the side of the pot as he had seen his grandmother do to make it stop boiling over. But, to his surprise, the kettle grew larger; but he kept on stirring it, and every little while it would start to boil over again, and he would strike the kettle with his ladle. Again, every time he struck the pot it would grow larger. He was laughing and saying, "Oh, we will have enough mush to last us for several days now!"

So after a while he had struck that pot so many times, and it had grown so large that the room was filled with it, and there was no room for him inside the house. He went out the door and around the bark house and climbed up on the roof to the smoke hole so he could stir his kettle which filled the whole house. He was sitting on the roof stirring the kettle down through the smoke hole.

Just at that time, his grandmother came back. She saw him sitting on top of the roof. So she saw it was the pot that he was stirring. She hollered to him and at the same time weeping, cried, "You have cooked all the chestnuts that we had."

And the boy answered, saying, "Don't cry, Aksot [grandmother], don't worry. I'll get some more chestnuts."

She said, "You can't do it, they are hard to get."

And he asked her, "Where do you get those chestnuts?"

She told him, she said, "There is a house on the other side of the bush [woods]. There a family lives in the house with five young girls. That is where the chestnut tree stands by the house. One girl is always guarding the tree throughout the day. They won't let anyone have any of their chestnuts."

So next morning he told his grandmother, "I'm going to the house where the chestnut tree grows and where there is always one of the five girls guarding it." So she did not want to let him go. She wept again. She said, "They might kill you." But he said, "Grandmother, don't worry, they can't kill me."

So he left. He walked through the woods. Then when he saw the house quite a ways away, he just talked to himself, saying, "Mice, I want you to help me. I want to turn into a mice myself. And I want to go to that house standing over there to get chestnuts." So he did that. He changed himself and became a mice.

Then it went that way toward the house under the leaves, under the weeds. When he got to the tree by the house, he came out from the weeds, and he saw a lot of chestnuts lying on the ground. He picked up all he could carry. The guards did not even seen him. And he went back again to the place in the forest. When he got back where he had changed into a mice, he changed into a young boy again, and he was carrying these chestnuts with him when he returned to his grandmother's house.

When he returned, he said, "Here, grandmother, whenever we eat that up I can get some more." She shouted out, saying, "Nyawenh [thanks] that you got back safely."

"Onenh netho nigagais [now this is the end of the story]." (Simmy thought this extremely funny.)

Letter of November 21, 1941

It is hard to remember stories over the summer because the old people told us not to relate stories during the summer. They said snakes would come to the house if one told stories in summer time.

HOW THE BEAR LOST HIS TAIL

An Onondaga Tale via Europe

There was once a fox and he was in his hollow stump where he lived—

Wait, now this is not the beginning.

On the start there was a fox who went out to look for fish. He was running on the road, and as he looked back he saw the fish man driving on the road with his horse and rig. And this fox thought he would get the fish out of the fish man's buggy. So he made up his mind that he would lay down across the road and pretend that he was dead. So he did. He laid down across the road and pretended to be dead fox.

The fish man came along, and he saw this fox lying in the road. So he stopped his horse and walked up to where the fox was lying, and he shook him up. But the fox was dead, he thought, so he just grabbed him by the leg and carried him back to his rig and tossed him into the box where the fish were. So he drove on and thought no more about it.

So the fox thought now it must be time to start. So he got up to where the fish were piled and grabbed one at a time and tossed the fish out to the side of the road as they were going along. So he thought surely now that is enough fish. So he jumped down off the wagon box and away he ran back along the road to pick up the fish that he had tossed out of the wagon.

So he carried home as many of the fish as he could put into his mouth. So when he got back to his hollow stump where he lived, he went into the hole and started to eat his raw fish.

Just then the bear came walking around there. He saw this fox in the hollow stump eating the fish. The bear went close to the stump and said to the fox, "Where did you get your fish?" The fox replied, saying, "I got the fish out of that ice hole down by the river. You just put your tail in the ice hole and the fish will bite your tail, and when you think you have enough just pull your tail out and the fish will all be hanging on your tail." So the bear believed that story.

So in the evening the bear went to that river. He was walking along the river, and presently he spied an ice hole. So then, he thought, "I am going to fish now." He sat down by the ice hole and put his tail in the ice hole in the water. My, it was a cold night! He was sitting there quite a while, and he felt that his tail was getting heavy. So he stirred a little and said to himself, "I guess I will stay a little longer. I will catch more fish then."

So he was sitting there towards morning; but when he tried to pull his tail out he couldn't do it. His tail was frozen in the ice. So he was struggling there until daybreak.

People lived in houses atop the hill, and one came down with a pail in the morning for water. She saw this bear sitting on the ice hole with his tail frozen into the ice. He was struggling hard to break loose. So this woman ran back to the house. She told her folks what she saw there. The people all ran out of the house and down to the river to see the bear. They had one shotgun.

When the poor bear saw the crowd coming, he struggled hard and twisted to get loose, for he thought surely they would kill him. All of a sudden it broke off—his tail. He could not break the ice. So he ran in the opposite direction without his tail.

So that's how he lost *his* tail—that bear.

That's the end.

(Simmy says that the old people told him this as being an old Onondaga story. However, the incident of the fox and the fish man sounds like Grimm's fairy tales.)

Letter of November 24, 1941

NÉ HADÓWETS: THE HUNTER (AND HIS DOGS)
Magic Flight from a Bodyless Head

A hunter started out from his house in the settlement and took five dogs with him—all different breeds of Indian dogs. They went straight north for two overnights. They made camp twice over a night and then went on when the day came.

The third day when he reached the place where he was going to hunt the hunter made a shanty of bark from the great elm tree and made a roof of the same material. And he made a fireplace—a ring of stones and a hole in the roof for the smoke to pass out—for the Indians had no chimneys, only a hole in the roof.

Then he went out to hunt. He killed a deer every day, and bears, and he would bring the carcass back and skin the animal by the house. He would save the meat, hanging it around the wall inside the house where it would dry for use during the winter. He was hunting three days. The third night in the evening when he was inside his house sitting at the side of a good fire, he heard his dogs barking outside. They were barking and barking—oh, until pretty near midnight.

The smallest one of the five dogs they call *gayei nadehagóedá*— four eyes. It has its natural eyes and a yellow spot over each eye which makes him appear to have four eyes. His body is black, and he is the smallest dog in the pack.

This four-eyed dog came into the house and spoke to his master, saying, "We all are going to die. But we will try to save you. We will do our best to save you." And then the dog started to tell him what he must do in order to escape from this thing that was making the dogs bark outside.

There is a *hononhwaígon* [only a head, no body], which is sitting way up in the tree—high in the branches. That is a witch. It has hair all over it. Its eyes are fire, and it has a great mouth with long teeth. That is the one that is going to kill us.

I am going to tell you that the only way you can save your life is to start out at once to go back home. Go east when you go out of this house. Go straight to the east.[1] When you have gone for a ways, then turn directly south. Run as fast as you can go. Don't stop to take anything with you. Leave everything—all your meat and hides here. Just take your rifle.

The way that witch is going to do is that it will come down into the house and eat up the meat that you have got. After that it is going to follow your tracks. We will be after that Witch. It is going to kill one dog at a time only until it has eaten us all. So we want you to run as fast as you can. Go right straight back to the reserve.

So this little four-eyed dog ran out and went back to the place where the other dogs were barking around the tree and looking up at the witch there. This man got ready and took his rifle down, and he went out the door and went straight eastward into the dark. He went for a way, and then he turned to the south on the run as fast as he could go.

It was not daylight yet when he got back to the reserve. People on the reserve were having sadahgiiwe, the all-night Feast for the Dead. Therefore young men were outside the long house walking around and talking. And they heard this man, shouting the war cry of distress: Guuuuuu weh Guuuuuu weh! *This is the cry of distress*, an Indian sos. It meant to them that some one of their people needed help. So they ran back to the long house and reported to the old people what they had heard. So the old folks hurried and got down the torches of dry hickory bark wound on ends of poles which they always kept overhead against such emergencies. So they lighted up those torches. They selected the warriors who were swiftest and told them, "Run as fast as you can in the direction where that man is shouting and meet him." Then they lighted those torches and started out on the run as fast as they could go through the woods. They carried spare torches to light when the first had burned out.[2]

They could hear that man yelling, and his shouting was getting closer. They met him at last, and he told them what had happened. In a few minutes that witch came flying that way, but it would not come down because they had the woods all lighted. It sat up in a high tree, and they all got a good look at it—these warriors. It was just a head with no body to it—hair all over its head, fire pits for eyes, big mouth, and long teeth. Then they took this man back to the long house where the old people were waiting.

When the rescuing warriors met the hunter they escorted him to the long house with the torches. When they arrived back at long house, they walked inside where the people were having the Dance for the Dead. The warriors led this hunter to the men's side of the long house, and he sat down there.

Then he stood up and spoke, telling the chiefs and the people what had happened to him in the forest. He repeated the same story from the time the little four-eyed dog came into his shanty and warned him until he arrived safely back at the long house. (The old-time Indians always repeat here the whole episode telling the story of the hunter.)

And the hunter lost all of his dogs. The little dog with four eyes was the last one to be killed. He was the one who used to carry messages to the hunter warning him how close the monster had approached. He would tell him how many dogs are now left. Towards the last he said: "I am the last one now. I will never come back again. So do your best. Don't stop any place. You will never see me again." At that the little four-eyed dog who had a black body and a yellow spot over each eye to make him look as if he had four eyes ran out into the night to meet this Monster.

So next day when the hunter got over being frightened a party of warriors went back with him over the trail of his flight. They found the bones of the smallest dog. Only the bones remained, for the flesh had been eaten by this Monster. Then they went on. And presently they found the second dog. It was just the same way. They found only bones without flesh. And then they went on again following the trail until they found the third one, and then they went on again until they found the fourth. The fifth and last one was near the tree where the dogs had first been barking; and then they arrived at the shack where he had camped. They entered the house, but the meat from his hunting was entirely gone, and the hides were missing— only bones were left from the hunter's quarry.

So the warriors and hunter went back at once on the trail to the settlement. The hunter picked up the bones of the first dog, and he put them in a bag, making up his mind to take them home, and as he came to another pile of bones he picked that up too, and they walked on to the next pile of bones, and he did the same way— picked them up, put them in the bag, and so on—they did that with all the bones of his five dogs. When they got back to the village, he dug a grave by his house and buried the bones of his five dogs in a common grave.

And then he went in his shack.

That's the sum of my words.

(Comment: The old people used to tell me this about *hai hai*, the Eulogy chant on the road when they have Condolence (council) for dead chiefs. Some chiefs possibly died afield away from the villages. When they installed the new chief his maternal people would go after his bones and bring them from his temporary grave, and they would keep them in a bag ready for the Condolence ceremony. At the starting place, where the condoling party sings on the road, the party of followers (procession) would include one carrying these bones in a sack following the singer who recites the roll call of the first chiefs (founders) of the League. They follow this parade until they get to the long house. When the singer enters the long house of the bereaved nation, the bone-carrier and his people go right straight on to the graveyard where a grave would be already prepared for the bones, and there they bury the bones. After the funeral they go back to the long house and join the ceremony of installing the new chief. That's what they used to tell me how they did in the old times.—SIMEON GIBSON.)[3]

Letter of November 26, 1941

THE BOY AND THE CROW
A European Folk Tale

There was an old farmer, and he had one son, a boy, and their cow took sick and died. When it died the father said to the boy: "I will give you that dead cow if you will skin it. Perhaps you can sell the hide." So the boy said, "All right, I'll skin it." So he sharpened his jackknife and went over to that dead cow and started to skin it. When he finished skinning that dead cow, he cut up the hide, making holes all through the hide, punching it here and there with his jackknife. He made long slits in it. Then he took the hide with him and went away. He told his folks that he was going uptown to sell it.

He went out toward the edge of the bush [woods] and lay down on the ground himself and covered himself up with this cowhide. In just a little while a great bunch of crows came along and sitting up in the trees. They saw what looked to them like a dead cow lying there. All these crows flew down to where the boy was lying covered with the cowhide. One of the crows hopped up on top of the hide. The boy could feel the crow hopping on top of the hide. It stuck its foot through a slit in the hide, and the boy grabbed the foot of that crow. He grabbed the crow's leg. Then the boy stood up, for he had caught the crow.[4]

Then the boy made up his mind that he would go to the neighbor's house and sell that crow to the neighbor. He just left the hide there and went to the house. When he got to the house he went by a window in the house, and he saw the boss of the house crawl under the bed to hide.

The boy went around to the door and rapped. The lady looked out. She told him to come in, and so he did. And she gave him a chair to sit down, and the boy spoke, he said, "Where is your husband gone?" She replied, "He has gone away."[5]

So this boy knew where the house owner was. He was under the bed hiding. Then the boy squeezed the crow which he had under his arm and the crow said, "Gah." And the boy said, "Shut up!" Then the lady was surprised, and she asked the boy, "Do you know what he said?" And the boy said, "Yes, I know what he said." The boy said, "My crow says the owner of the house is hiding under the bed!"

So the owner of the house came out crawling from under the bed. He was surprised at what the boy had said. He asked this boy, "Will you sell that crow? How much money will you take? I will buy it if you will sell it." "Oh," the boy said, "I don't think I will sell it."

The owner of the house went to the next room, and when he came out he was carrying a great box full of money. He set this down on the table—this man did. He put coins in a hat until it covered up the bottom. He said, "I will give you that much for your crow." "Oh, no," the boy said, "I don't want to sell my crow." Then the man added some more money to the hat until the hat was pretty nearly half filled. "I will give you that," he said. So the boy made up his mind to take it. He thought, "That might be enough money for this crow which I caught at the wood's edge." "All right," he said, "I'll take it."

So the owner of the house took this crow. He said, "Take your money." So the boy stood up and went to the table and grabbed a handful of money and put it in one pocket, and another handful and stuffed it in his other pocket. Then the third pocket. Finally he took all the money that was in the hat. Then he said, "I'll go home now."

The owner of the house was glad. He said, "I am glad I bought this crow, for he talks." He had the crow under his arm as he was bidding the boy good-by. (You see he was surprised that the crow told that he was hiding under the bed. He thought it was great. It was so wise.)

The boy went out and went home. When he got back he showed his father all the money he had got for the hide of the dead cow. Three pockets full of money. His father said, "Where did you get all of that money?" He said, "I sold that cowhide." His father and mother were surprised at the pile of money he had got for that cowhide. He did not tell them what he had done with the hide, or how he sold the crow. That's the end of the story.[6]

(*Comment*: My father used to tell this story to us Indian children. He would tell it in Onondaga. Never told us where he learned it.— SIMEON GIBSON.)

Notes

1. East is good in Iroquois folklore—"Never go to the west," the boy is warned.

2. Hickory rind torches are hitherto unreported in the Iroquois literature.

3. While this precious bit of ethnology was suggested by the tale just told, it applies directly to the problem of how the Condolence Council, the ceremony for condoling the bereaved nations of deceased Founders of the League and installing their successors, is related to the present Feast for the Dead, and how both are descended from the decennial Death Feast which Brébeuf and other Jesuits described among the seventeenth-century Hurons of Georgian Bay. For a description of the former, which yet survives, see "An Iroquois Condolence Council of Installing Cayuga Chiefs in 1945" (*Journal of the Washington Academy of Sciences*, 36 (April 15, 1946), 110–127).

4. This is similar to the widespread Indian method of trapping eagles.

5. A typical situation at Six Nations, when a visitor calls.

6. The plot seems to be European, but the method of catching the crow sounds like the old Indian method of pit-trapping eagles for their feathers.

The Training of Historical
Ethnologists in America

I

The thesis of this paper is that cultural anthropology in America has not yet realized its potentialities as a strictly historical science[1] and that the maturity of our discipline depends in part on training ethnologists who will carry the perspective of field work to the library. We must enlist the help of historians to train some ethnologists in historical methods so that our students will be equally at home in the field and in the library and so that they may use the materials and methods of one research activity to enrich the other. While my perspective derives from the study of the North American Indian, what follows may apply similarly to the training of students in Britain, France, and elsewhere who will work perhaps in Africa, Asia, or the rest of the world. My own acquaintance with the general ethnological literature from the rest of the world leads me to believe that the following remarks have general validity.

American ethnology, at least, finds itself in the anomalous position of facing declining opportunities to do field work among primitives while books on the American Indian pour into the libraries yearly. Who are we training to read this literature intelligently? The abundant archival resources awaiting the ethnological student have scarcely been touched. The students and mature scholars whom I have encountered in libraries and archives are mainly biographers, colonial historians, historians of the West, and lawyers. Almost without exception none of these persons was trained in ethnology, and few had gained the perspective that comes from working with the living people. Library scholars have made me appreciate the value of knowing the main culture patterns of a period, and by rubbing elbows with them in the manuscript room and at the card catalog I have caught some of the theory and practice of historical study. In turn, I have furnished them information on ethnic entities—who were the Tutelo, where did they live, what happened to them? But to the question of where can a historian learn how to find out such information, I have no ready answer.

The main reason, I believe, why ethnology has matured slowly as an historical science is the long-standing preoccupation with diffusional studies and the neglect of direct history. Since studies of diffusion have passed out of fashion, direct history has been forgotten. In going back to Sapir's famous paper, I note that the problem of the use of direct evidence of history—documentary, native testimony, archeological—is allotted but five pages of comment, of which only one page is devoted to the importance of documentary evidence.[2] The greater part of the study is given over to discussing inferential evidence, methods of utilizing it, and critiques of each method mentioned. In one attempt to apply Sapir's suggested criteria, however, I discovered that it required some 90 pages to consider one aspect of the direct evidence alone.[3]

When diffusional studies were undertaken, it was assumed that the direct evidence of history was not forthcoming; that simpler peoples were without benefit of history. Elaborate methods were therefore devised for inferring history, with occasionally quite brilliant results, in which criteria of seriation, association, geographical distribution, age and area were highly developed. The students who were trained to use these criteria, employed them to the exclusion of all else, in areas and in problems on which the historians have since brought considerable direct evidence to light. Thus Spier ended his rigorous analysis of the Sun Dance on a note of frustration with a plea for better knowledge of the role of the innovating individual, and himself turned to the direct evidence of history in describing the movement known in the Northwest as the Prophet Dance.[4] In the former study, Spier proceeded analytically and comparatively to solve an historical problem with scientific methods. But I suspect that documentary materials are available for an historical study of the Sun Dance, and that Spier's results can ultimately be checked with diaries and records of the kind Ewers has been finding and Schaeffer has recently uncovered at the Blackfoot Agency.

This is not the place to review the controversy between history and science in anthropology, over which Kroeber and Boas disagreed fifteen years ago.[5] I concede that Boas' study of the dissemination of folktales in the Northwest had an historical objective which it achieved,[6] while I accept Kroeber's profession that the distinctive features of historical activity, as opposed to historical technique, are always an attempt at descriptive integration of societal phenomena in time and space; that all historical procedure is in the nature of a reconstruction; and that "sound history, and sound anthropology, concern themselves with finding patterns and putting them into their actual relations on the phenomenal level."[7] Later, in evaluating the work of Swanton, Kroeber recognizes a distinction between history and non-history of another sort when he points out that in America we have relied almost exclusively on diffusion and independent local developments to explain how cultures have come to be as they are,[8] and that ethnographers have shied away from problems in the study of tribal movements which demand long hours in the library and archive. I do not agree with Lowie that the historical ethnologist must largely dispense with documents, because they do exist;[9] and I do not think that the so-called "Historical Schools" of England and the Continent are historical at all, in any other than a purposeful sense. I insist that the historical ethnologist must confine his attention to manageable problems in which he can use his own descriptive integrations of a society as the frame of reference for organizing an abundant historical and ethnographical literature to obtain time depth and spatial relations for the major cultural patterns which he reconstructs. Such a literature exists for the history of many societies in Europe, Africa, and the New World. In selecting problems for historical treatment I recommend a method for employing internal evidence from the culture to formulate problems, which Radin first suggested in a provocative book nearly twenty years ago.[10]

If anthropologists have lacked a true understanding of history and have perforce pursued it beyond the frontiers of direct evidence into the limbo of inference, often employing indirect evidence when direct evidence was forthcoming, it is even harder to find historians who grasp the concept of a culture. Historians without culture are as common as anthropologists without history. Such an historian as Curti is all too rare; most members of that profession have only the vaguest ideas of what the anthropologists are doing, partly because we study cultures and write monographs, while they read and write books. And there is an inevitable time lag between fields.

I shall now attempt to bridge the gap between anthropology and history, as the two disciplines may contribute to the training of historical ethnologists, grouping the discussion under four heads: the history of American ethnology, the source materials for ethnohistory, the methods and practice of historical ethnology, and recommendations.

II

Scientific anthropology is now a century old. It is no longer possible for students to know its founders, and very few of the first generation of Boas-trained anthropologists are still teaching. But a knowledge of the history of American ethnology should be part of the liberal education of anthropologists. Wissler used to consider that it was important for ethnologists as it was for Indians to know their tribal lore, and he gave his students some formal indoctrination in addition to those anecdotal aspects of anthropology, at which he was master. Wissler distinguished four major periods in the history of American anthropology,[11] which I shall now project, by condensing his last two and adding one other:

1. The exploratory or survey period, 1492–1800
2. The discovery of research leads, 1800–1860
3. A century of ethnography, 1851–1950
   a. The museum period, 1860–1900
   b. The academic period, 1900–1950
4. The applied period, 1951–

When Wissler wrote, the academic period, his third, was at its height; it ended roughly with World War II, when anthropologists flocked to government in various capacities, some of which were on social science research. After the war old loyalties reasserted themselves, and the anthropologists and their colleagues went back to their teaching, so that for a time the academic period enjoyed an epi-climax. But it would appear that applied anthropology is here to stay, and while teaching goes on, just as the research of anthropologists in museums has continued, we witness daily the conversion of research and teaching organizations to training institutes, or to teams of specialists exploring some administrative problem. I believe that the theory which Kroeber developed in *Configurations of Culture Growth*[12] can be applied to the intellectual history of anthropology and to the history of the institutions with which anthropology has been associated, with quite practical results for the student.

Knowing the history of anthropology has a certain cash value for assessing the types of positions now open to the profession, and such knowledge may help in predicting the kinds of jobs which will open up. Traditionally history has been the avocation of gentlemen, and since the museum period there have always been a few posts of long tenure in state and federal establishments for historical ethnologists.

But we cannot expect to attract students to train in historical ethnology unless we can indicate that the positions at such institutions
show some likelihood of permanence and are supported by programs
of research which are geared to the present condition of world ethnological realities, or which offer some promise of new careers in
library, archival, or museum research. There is certainly room for
such scholarship if a way can be found to support it. But it would
appear that anthropology is dying at the core while it is expanding
at the periphery. A certain strength in historical ethnology may be
detected in the current flurry of demand by lawyers for the services
of anthropologists who were trained in ethnohistorical research,
and the challenge to adapt ethnological techniques to the materials of history for advancing or defending Indian claims against the
Government may develop a trend with a predictable future.

III

Ethnohistory is blessed with an abundance of source materials. Since
all ethnology starts with a problem that is taken to the field, I mention
first informants, the living sources of the culture, who to the best of
their ability, and according to their interest and that of the culture,
provide the ethnologist with his first leads of how things came to be
as they are. The work of Swanton and Dixon[13] shows that various
Indian groups vary enormously in their abilities to narrate traditional
history, yet Iroquois informants frequently have described to me a
functioning activity and then compared it with changed conditions
in the past. Often such traditional history can be corroborated with
direct historical evidence.

Collections of photographs illustrate physical types, costumes,
implements, activities and places at an earlier time, enabling the
student to measure change and note stability. To pick but one example
from the picture file at the Bureau of American Ethnology, we may
take Taos Pueblo, for which there is a continuous series of photographs

taken at ten-year intervals going back from my own photographs on the Plaza in 1950 to those attributed to Jackson in 1870.

The Library of Congress has perhaps the finest collection of recorded Indian music, from the time of Fletcher's Pawnee field work and the extensive collections which Frances Densmore made for the Bureau of American Ethnology. These are gradually being made available on LP discs in the Library's distinguished series, "Folk Music of the United States."

Our greatest and most neglected treasures, however, are the huge collections of ethnological specimens, which are frequently dated and documented with accession records. Yet where are we training students to use such collections intelligently? Ignoring for the moment the mass of Indian records at the National Archives which span the century and a half of Federal relations with the Indians, and considering only the archive of the Bureau of American Ethnology, which has some 4,000 manuscripts by such pioneer ethnologists as Gibbs, Gatschet, Powell, Dorsey, Mooney, Hewitt, and Michelson, and noting the expanding holdings of the American Philosophical Society Library, which already has the Boas and Speck papers, it appears that there are abundant literary materials for the ethnologist to carry his perspective backward and to broaden his comparative knowledge. Biographers have already begun to take up the early ethnologists, but why not direct a gifted student of anthropology into this field? Why should we not give the doctorate to students in the history of ethnology?

Elsewhere I have recently indicated the kind and character of manuscript materials bearing on the political history of the Six Nations.[14] That such materials are available for other ethnic groups seems altogether possible; the Clements Library at the University of Michigan, for example, has in a famous collection known to historians as the Gage Papers the detailed reports of John Stuart (1717–1779), who was His Majesty's Superintendent of the Indians in the Southern Department on the eve of the Revolution. No ethnologist to my knowledge has examined the Stuart correspondence. Nor have the 80,000 volumes and several thousand manuscripts in the Ayer Collection at Newberry Library, Chicago, commanded the attention from ethnologists which this noteworthy resource deserves.

Printed materials on the American Indian alone are reaching staggering proportions. The Library of the Bureau of American Ethnology counts over 40,000 volumes, which in part are comprised of general ethnology, foreign periodicals, and local history. It would be remiss not to mention the Library of the Peabody Museum at Harvard and its famous catalog. Murdock seems to be the first scholar since Pilling to tackle ethnographic bibliography for the continent as a whole.[15] And recently Rouse and Goggin have produced a regional bibliography for the Eastern Seaboard.[16] The usefulness of manuscript check lists, library catalogs, and bibliographies already in print recommends the publication of a catalog of the Bureau of American Ethnology manuscripts which has been prepared, and suggests the possibility of microfilming the catalogs of specialized ethnographic libraries.

Technical aids to documentation have improved immensely under the stimulus of the American Documentation Institute, to which the Association names a delegate; it holds an annual meeting at the Library of Congress at which manufacturers display the most recent aids to the library scholar such as microfilm readers, sorting and coding systems, a simple device known as *Contura*, a light source which enables the student to do his own photocopying in the library; while papers read at the annual meeting are published in a quarterly journal.[17] Yet I know of no University department of anthropology which is now training students in the methods of both history and ethnology with a view to using the vast store of materials and the new techniques just mentioned.

IV

In approaching the methods and practice of historical ethnology, I shall dwell briefly on the direct historic approach, I have several suggestions on time perspective, and I will point to some applications.

The direct historic approach, first associated with the work of Nelson on the Galisteo Ruins in New Mexico,[18] with the name of Swanton in the Southeast,[19] and with the work of Strong and Wedel on the Plains,[20] has the scientific virtue of working back from the known to the unknown. My own version of this method I have previously termed "upstreaming."[21] The method has been variously applied, but an understanding of the approach is fundamental to appreciating the work of such diverse personalities as Swanton, Speck, and Cooper. Speck, like Radin, applied the approach intuitively in broken cultures, working back from the present functioning society through the minds of individual informants to release cultural memories of which the informants themselves were but dimly aware. I have watched Speck apply his great fund of knowledge of eastern ethnography, his intense familiarity with patterns of Algonquian culture, so as to arouse the dim memories of boyhood experience in the minds of old Indian men. His method was deep-level ethnology at its best. The example of Speck bears out my own field experience that the ethnologist finds out what he knows.

No one expressed greater admiration for Speck's facility to get on with Indians than Swanton, who was the first academically trained ethnologist to join the Bureau of American Ethnology staff, and though now retired, was a field worker of prodigious accomplishment. But Swanton, despite his forays into linguistics at the insistence of Boas, loved history deeply, and when freed to follow his own inclinations, brought the Bureau tradition of historical ethnology to its greatest height. For a half century ethnologists at the Bureau have mainly concerned themselves with ethnic entities, by which Kroeber means the identities, locations, contacts, and movements of the various Indian tribes,[22] and the Bureau has been the place of final appeal on such matters, its staff answering the queries of school children, writers, librarians, historians, and citizens at large.

Next to its famous *Handbook of American Indians*, Swanton's fundamental monographs stand as models of the direct historic approach, combining a knowledge of Indian society with a feeling for the land, an uncanny familiarity with maps, and a mastery of printed and manuscript sources, all of which was filtered through a first-rate critical mind. Before he retired, a decade ago, several of us wrote *Essays in Historical Anthropology* . . . (1940) to honor his fortieth year at the Bureau; and I learned his method by visiting with him in his office frequently while assessing the historic problems of the Iroquois cultural position. By reading such essays and attempting to apply the method to a problem the student can appreciate what may be accomplished by this approach. In the Northeastern field one problem after another in archeology, ethnology, and linguistics has been taken up and solved by members of the Iroquois Conference.

The clearest exposition of the direct-historical approach to archeology is Wedel's paper on Pawnee, and his essay in the Swanton volume. Archeology is perhaps the most difficult proving ground for the method and requires the most exacting critical techniques, for if the site is not where the historian says it is, the method has failed. I understand that the Plains Conference has already considered some of the limitations of the method, but it should be spelled out for the historian and ethnologist.

The method of "upstreaming," which I am applying to collecting materials for a political history of the Six Nations,[23] rests on three premises: (1) major patterns of culture tend to be stable over long periods of time, so that one should watch out lest he commit the fallacy of assumed acculturation; (2) "upstreaming" proceeds from the known to the unknown, concentrating on recent sources first because they contain familiar things, and thence going to earlier sources; (3) a preference for those sources in which the descriptions of the society ring true at both ends of the time scale. I have confidence in Samuel Kirkland, Guy Johnson, and Conrad Weiser, though they lived in the eighteenth century, that they knew their Iroquois, just as I have confidence in Lewis H. Morgan, because the Indians they describe agree with what I know of the Iroquois today. It is only by prolonged concentration of an area and a people that students can acquire such perspective.

A suggestion of applying the direct historic approach to field work comes from John C. Ewers, who has worked out a technique of employing dated ethnological specimens as a means of eliciting historical information from informants and then checking tradition against accession records. The men on Wissler's team who did the fundamental ethnography of the Plains proceeded as if historical sources were not available to them, and treated Plains culture in flat perspective. Their data indicate that tribal composition varied considerably from period to period so that the student coming afterward is left wondering what tribe, or what band of that tribe, and just when. It is now late to complain that informants then living could have tied their information to the Maximillian, Catlin, and Lewis and Clark period—the first quarter of the nineteenth century. Collections were taken and described, often without reference to similar specimens collected in an earlier period. We have Plains collections spanning a century, and it still may be possible to get additional historical data on key specimens from a few old people and particularly what other events can be associated with their introduction and disappearance. I am inclined to favor this approach since in my own field work at Tonawanda I was able to reach Morgan's sources, a century earlier.

Of time perspective, I allude once more to Radin's method of determining cultural change from internal evidence in myths and ceremonials.[24] Native historians sometimes conceive their cultural past in periods marked off by great events—by the appearance of a culture hero, or by some disaster. Traditions of a more recent type can often be tied to dated documents. That stability and cultural change are facets of the same process has been stated by Herskovits,[25] but the factors that make for stability have received little attention in research. Most so-called studies of acculturation ignore the old culture, and students have neither acquired the interest, nor bothered to learn the probing techniques of Speck, or to gain the patient mastery of sources of Swanton. Realizing that complaining of students marks advancing age, I will summarize by saying that cultural history offers the best opportunity for testing theories of pattern growth and decline, for demonstrating cultural change, and for explaining stability.

American ethnology does not all lie in the past, however, and its program need no longer be aimed at recovery. Ethnology used to be justified on a plea of getting into the field to catch the last dying gasps of Beothuk, a now extinct Algonquian language of Newfoundland; but happily American Indian languages and cultures have refused extinction, for some 120 languages are still spoken and survive for study, while certain cultures show amazing resistance to assimilation. The American field can still be used as a training ground for field ethnologists.

In studies of diffusion, which I disparaged at the outset of this paper even where documents attest the dissemination of a cultural complex, direct history still requires support of the method of cultural analysis and comparison, which is best exemplified, in the work of Cooper, and his student Flannery.[26] Otherwise one cannot be sure that he is treating with the same complex phenomena as they are seen, in the historical literature, to move about in time and space. In tracing the roots of the Iroquois Eagle Dance, for example, direct history and tradition take the complex back to the Calumet ritual, which has its climax in the Pawnee Hako. The documents say that the Pawnee gave the ceremony to the Illinois, the Iowa, the Fox, and the Miami, from whence it can be traced to the Iroquois. Another line of diffusion carried the ceremony down the Mississippi to the Southeast, whence it reached the Iroquois about 1750. In making this study, I wanted to be certain that I was everywhere dealing with the same phenomenon, so each case was analyzed and compared with the next with which history connects it. Moreover, the problem and the data were submitted to a second person who repeated the analysis with special attention to the materials of the music and the dance and came up with similar conclusions. As it turned out, at least two complexes were involved.[27]

Two applications of the practice of historical ethnology will suffice. First, I would like to suggest teaching the American Indian course in a truly historical fashion. For the moment, let us forget the origin myth of American anthropology that man entered the new world via Bering Strait and that his culture reached a climax in Middle America whence all great developments radiated to the marginal peoples of the continents, and let us consider a more humble approach. It may come as a shock to anthropologists to discover that ethnography is secondary source material, and that all our direct knowledge of Indians comes from the literature of contact. Contact began on the East Coast, where our New England forebears exterminated the Algonquians for the glory of God; after that our knowledge follows the frontier. Ethnographic monographs commence after the middle of the nineteenth century and only to the extent that they describe cultures then in being are they primary sources; Mooney's justly famous "The Ghost-dance religion and the Sioux outbreak of 1890" in the main contains primary material, but Morgan's classic "League of the Ho-de-no-sau-nee, or Iroquois" documents survival two hundred years after white contact. In view of the time lag between culture areas, I have experimented with reordering Kroeber's culture areas to agree with Turner's concept of the frontier in American history, commencing the course with the marginal peoples on the Atlantic coast. The course then proceeds to the Appalachian Iroquoians who resisted conquest and whose history leads into the Southeast, from whence history takes us up the Mississippi to the Plains, and follows the trail of Lewis and Clark up the Missouri, and over the Rockies to the Basin-Plateau and Northwest Coast cultures. It is then possible to return and pick up the thread of history in the Southwest. The plan has the virtue of arriving on the Plains in the nineteenth century, which is better than inferring history from the flat perspective of the culture-area approach. I believe that the plan makes sense out of Kroeber's large Eastern area.

The second application is now in process as ethnologists are having their metal tested in the crucible of the courts. While the purposes of the law and anthropology are not the same, they have much in common at the research level, and there are possible gains for ethnology in acquiring some of the legal criteria for evidence. To the evaluation which ethnologists place on this experience may be added the opinion of historically minded lawyers who are employing ethnologists, and who are interested in gaining acceptance in court for more ethnological theory and fact. Every ethnologist who has appeared before the Indian Claims Commission will read his own experience into this situation, but I owe the following observations to Dr. J. A. Jones, who is the first trained ethnologist to be employed full time by the Department of Justice. The ethnologist soon learns the distinction between historical facts and legal facts. What the court has decided or what transpired at some legally endowed ceremonial such as a treaty has a certain prestige value in court although such interpretation may differ from the facts of history and ethnology. It becomes necessary to marshal the latter in terms of the former. Lawyers have an annoyingly critical attitude toward accepted authorities, regarding ethnography at best as secondary source material, which must be checked and documented with the printed record, so that the ethnologist finds himself bolstering his theory with historical fact. Beyond the record of the time it is important to know the cultural biases of a period such as the age of Jackson and its relation to the forces for Indian Removal, which policy represented an abrupt shift towards the rights of the States and contrasted markedly with Indian policy during the Federal Period, somewhat earlier; and such knowledge is basic to understanding sources like *The American State Papers—Indian Affairs*. Through research is not always practicable, however, and as in other government research positions the ethnologist learns to do an adequate job of spot research, using only the principal references. Finally, conveying the ethnological point of view to lawyers requires no little tact and considerable teaching ability.

A growing group of lawyers is learning about ethnology and the avant-garde of the profession understands ethnological theory and seeks to gain acceptance for it in court. But we ethnologists are not in the habit of proving our cases in court. We get by with untidy research sometimes, and in our willingness to consider all sides of a problem, make poor witnesses. Two types of persons are needed: the research worker and the confident teacher.

V

I have but four recommendations.

1. See to it that anthropologists learn historiography from professional historians.
2. As an educational experience for professional historians and professional anthropologists, a summer seminar in the methods of cultural history, composed of two archeologists, two ethnologists, and two historians might explore the common ground of the disciplines.
3. Push anthropologists, particularly historical ethnologists, for research and administrative posts in libraries and archives.
4. Survey the experience of anthropology in Indian claims.

Notes

This paper was prepared and read while the author was a member of the Bureau of American Ethnology staff; he joined the permanent staff of the National Research Council as Executive Secretary of the Division of Anthropology and Psychology on January 1, 1952.

1. Sapir, 1916, p. 1.
2. Lewis, 1942, p. 2.
3. Fenton, 1940, 1951.
4. Spier, 1921 and 1935.
5. Kroeber, 1935; Boas, 1936.
6. Boas, 1940, p. 307.
7. Kroeber, 1935, pp. 545–546, 547, 567.
8. Kroeber, 1940, pp. 5–6.

9. Lowie, 1937, p. 156.

10. Radin, 1933, pp. 33–37.

11. Wissler, 1942.

12. Kroeber, 1944.

13. Swanton & Dixon, 1914.

14. Fenton, 1951, pp. 298–303.

15. Murdock, 1941; Pilling, 1887–1894.

16. Rouse and Goggin, 1947.

17. American Documentation.

18. Nelson, 1914, p. 9.

19. Swanton and Dixon, 1914.

20. Strong, 1940; Wedel, 1938, 1940.

21. Fenton, 1949, p. 236.

22. Kroeber, 1940, p. 4.

23. Fenton, 1949, p. 236.

24. Radin, 1933, pp. 35–36.

25. Herskovits, 1948, pp. 18, 20, 26, and Chapter 28.

26. Flannery, 1939; Cooper, 1946.

27. Fenton, 1952; Kurath, 1952.

Bibliography

Boas, F., 1936, History and Science in Anthropology: A reply. *American Anthropologist*, Vol. 38, pp. 137–141.

———, 1940, Race, language and culture.

Cooper, J. M., 1946, The Culture of the Northeastern Indian Hunters: a Reconstructive Interpretation, in *Man in Northeastern North America*. Papers of the R. S. Peabody Foundation for Archaeology, Vol. 3, pp. 272–305.

Fenton, W. N., 1940, Problems Arising from the Historic Northeastern Position of the Iroquois. *Essays in Historical Anthropology of North America*. Smithsonian Miscellaneous Collections, Vol. 100, pp. 159–251.

———, 1949, Collecting Materials for a Political History of the Six Nations. *Proceedings of the American Philosophical Society*, Vol. 93, pp. 233–238.

———, 1951, Iroquois Studies at the Mid-century. *Ibid.*, Vol. 95, pp. 296–310.

———, 1952, The Iroquois Eagle Dance, a Variant of the Calumet Ritual, *Bulletin 156*, Bureau of American Ethnology (In press).

Flannery, R., 1939, An Analysis of Coastal Algonquian Culture. *Catholic University of America Anthropological Series*, No. 7.

Herskovits, M. J., 1948, *Man and His Works*.

Kroeber, A. L., 1935, History and Science in Anthropology. *American Anthropologist*, Vol. 37, pp. 539–569.

————, 1940, The Work of John R. Swanton. *Smithsonian Miscellaneous Coll.*, Vol. 100, pp. 1–9.

————, 1944, *Configurations of Culture Growth*.

Kurath, G. P., 1952, The Iroquois Eagle Dance: An Analysis of the Music and Choreography *Bulletin 156*, Bureau of American Ethnology (In press.).

Lewis, Oscar, 1942, The Effects of White Contact upon Blackfoot Culture . . . *Monographs of the American Ethnological Society*, No. 6.

Lowie, R. H., 1937, *The History of Ethnological Theory*.

Murdock, G. P., 1941, Ethnographic Bibliography of North America. *Yale Anthropological Studies*, No. 1.

Nelson, N. C., 1914, Pueblo Ruins of the Galisteo Basin, New Mexico. *Anthropological Papers of the American Museum of Natural History*, Vol. 15, Pt. 1.

Radin, P., 1933, *The Method and Theory of Ethnology*.

Rouse, I., and J. M. Goggin, 1947, An Anthropological Bibliography of the Eastern Seaboard. *Eastern States Archaeological Federation*, Research Pub., No. 1. New Haven.

Sapir, E., 1916, Time Perspective in Aboriginal American Culture, a Study in Method. Canada, Department of Mines, *Geological Survey*, Mem. 90, Anthropological Ser., No. 13. Ottawa.

Spier, L., 1921, The Sun Dance of the Plains Indians . . . *Anthropological Papers of the American Museum of Natural History*, Vol. 16, Pt. 7, pp. 451–527.

————, 1935, The Prophet Dance of the Northwest and Its Derivatives: the Source of the Ghost Dance. *Gen. Ser. in Anthropology*, No. 1.

Strong, W. D., 1940, From History to Prehistory in the Northern Great Plains, *Smithsonian Msc. Coll.*, Vol. 100, pp. 353–394.

Swanton, J. R., and R. B. Dixon, 1914. Primitive American History. *American Anthropologist*, reprinted in *Anthropology in North America* (1915), pp. 1–41.

Wedel, W. R., 1938, The Direct-historical Approach in Pawnee Archaeology. *Smithsonian Msc. Coll.*, Vol. 97, No. 7.

————, 1940, Culture Sequences in the Central Great Plains. *Smithsonian Msc. Col.*, Vol. 100, pp. 291–352.

Wissler, C., 1942, The American Indian and the American Philosophical Society, *Proceedings*, American Philosophical Society, Vol. 86, No. 1, pp. 189–204.

Cultural Stability and Change
in American Indian Societies

This paper will explore the problem of conservatism in the political structure and religious life of four American Indian tribes. The approach arises from the conviction that ethnologists are preoccupied with the process of culture change and are not paying enough attention to stability. Certainly one of the most remarkable facts of ethnology in America is that there are Indian societies and cultures yet available for study. No one has explained their tarriance satisfactorily. The prophecies of their doom have not been fulfilled, happily, by their rapid extinction, either as people or as societies or as cultures. Why?

I shall examine this question by references to the cultures of four societies—Klamath of Oregon, Blackfoot of Montana, Iroquois of New York and Ontario, and Taos Pueblo of New Mexico—which I know more or less at first-hand. The four cultures have been described systematically (Spier 1930; Wissler 1910, 1911; Morgan 1851; Parsons 1936) and studies of acculturation have been made of all four societies (Nash 1937; Lewis 1942; Fenton ed. 1951; Fenton N.D.)

Stability: Theoretical Aspects

Theoretical treatment of the stability of culture remains inadequate. I note, however, one useful lead in a recent work on cultural theory by Herskovits (1948, pp. 18, 20, 26) in which he states three paradoxes:

the first contrasts cultural universals with local diversity (cf. Fenton ed. 1951); a second paradox relates the individual to the culture of his society; and a third, which concerns us now, reads: "*Culture is stable, yet culture is also dynamic, and manifests continuous and constant change.*" (The last is Herskovits's second proposition.)

That stability and change are facets of the same cultural process is not a new idea, but anthropologists of late have neglected stability. Starting some twenty years ago, so-called "acculturation studies" became fashionable. They quite properly focused attention on change as process, but such studies had a common weakness—they ignored the old culture that lived in the memory of a few old people who manifested an outmoded way of life in motor habits. The new ethnology was itself a reaction against old-fashioned ethnography. The systematic ethnographer had trained himself to recover the old culture and was apt to spurn acculturation studies as superficial, as many unquestionably were, while he sought to penetrate beyond the changed aspects of culture, which showed too plainly under daily life on an Indian reserve, to get at the older, more stable patterns of life, which he could usually find. Science and years were on his side. Both schools of ethnology recognized that Indian cultures were changing rapidly. One school hastened to recover the past, while the other accepted change and studied its processes.

The recovery effort actuated Boas and his students at Columbia, who were in the tradition of science. It was not an uncommon experience and considered quite a *coup* for a student of Boas to catch the dying gasps of an American Indian language and culture. Sapir in the field of language and Speck in that of natural history exemplify the tradition. Speck, beloved by Indians and learned beyond most men, sometimes managed to reconstruct a society and its culture from the merest fragments, approaching the feasts of the psycho-analysts in his study of Delaware ceremonies, which ranks among those of the first class in American ethnology.

Trained by Wissler, Sapir, and Spier, and informally coached by

Speck (in my first field work) I was naturally drawn to the old culture. By personal inclination I preferred the Longhouse or pagan Iroquois to their progressive Christian brothers, but I soon discovered that reservation society is a going concern and that much of its economic and social activity relates to surrounding white society and culture. But I left acculturation studies to others, concentrating on a sort of social history or historical functionalism. My purpose was to understand contemporary Iroquois society in order to comprehend the past. Before coming to the field, I had read the historical and ethnographic literature, which for the Six Nations is rich indeed, but I soon found the people themselves a better vantage-point for viewing history than the library for understanding society.

Indian culture has not vanished from the American scene and some 125 Indian languages are still spoken. L. H. Morgan, a century ago, prophesied that the Indian way of life would rapidly disappear, and in 1870 J. W. Powell petitioned Congress for funds to enable his Bureau of American Ethnology to collect and compare the vocabularies of Indian languages which were rapidly approaching extinction. Happily, the tribal cultures that managed to withstand the first shock of white contact have gone to earth on reservations and give some indication of lasting a long time. The persistent Longhouse ways of Morgan's own Iroquois prove him a false prophet; the autonomy of Pueblo culture is well known; the versatility of the Navaho in embracing the world outside them while rapidly expanding the size of their society astonishes ethnographers; and if buffalo-hunting days are but a cultural memory among the Blackfoot full-bloods, band society and band values guide politics of reservation mix-bloods today and reach out to colour county and state government; but the Basin-Plateau tribes like the Klamath, whom the westward movement reached last, seem to be losing aboriginal culture most rapidly. The latter groups had the simplest political structure; the former groups the more complex, which suggests that political organization and size of society are related to stability. Such considerations seem far more important to me than documenting the introduction of the pitcher-pump on the Cattaraugus Reservation in the 19th century, or noting the advent of television among Morgan's own Tonawanda Seneca last year.

Theoretically we must explain why Indian culture has survived and just what and how. If culture is both stable and ever-changing, as Herskovits (1948, p. 20) writes, "*Cultural change can be studied only as a part of the problem of cultural stability; cultural stability can be understood only when change is measured against conservatism.*" Years ago Ogburn (1922) documented what we all know—that some aspects of culture change more rapidly than others and that changes in technology proceed most rapidly. Even in technology, motor habits are remarkably tough and their resistance to change retards the introduction of newer machines. Stability affects artistic production. Almost no one in America, for example, writes any more with pen or pencil; the typewriter is the student's vade mecum, and a few scholars even dictate their monographs; happily one can escape the clatter of typewriters in the British Museum. We are left with the hint that culture is a matter of habit, a state of mind—which it is.

Some years ago I began to suspect that strains towards internal consistency lie deep within the covert culture. How, otherwise, do fundamental patterns of Iroquois suicide appear alike over a span of three centuries? This fact struck me in pursuing cases from the field to the library, when I developed a method which I have lately called "upstreaming" (Fenton 1941, 1949). The functioning present society becomes the model for critically examining the past. It would appear that the internal structure of a society remains relatively stable over long periods of time. And so when the ethnographer turned cultural historian—or social historian, if you will—finds the same basic culture patterns functioning at both ends of the time-stream, and his own observations confirmed by earlier observers, he knows that he has found stability and he trusts the sources. The method as applied to culture-personality studies, which was pioneered by Hallowell

(1946) among the Ojibwa, has recently been validated by Wallace, his student, who, at my suggestion, repeated the method with similar results on the culture and personality of the Tuscarora, possibly the most acculturated of the Six Nations, revealing the Indian basis of their covert culture (Wallace 1952). The same process seems to be at work in the stability of political and religious institutions.

Fields for Investigation

The fields in which stability may be investigated comprise: (1) archaeology; (2) material culture, including motor habits; (3) social culture and social control; (4) religion and the ritual sanctions; (5) art, music, and the dance; and (6) language. Among criteria for detecting and measuring stability of culture I would suggest: (1) regional uniformity *v.* local diversity; (2) internal consistency *v.* variation in behaviour; (3) drift and lag—differential change, producing adhesions, tarriance, or survivals from old times; (4) the sanction of conformity, when an innovation conflicts with structure or threatens its sovereignty; (5) the nature of the contact; and (6) documentation, a control on duration of stability.

Four Societies

Confining our attention now to the social culture, and touching on religion as it sanctions conforming behaviour, let us glance briefly at how stability affects contemporary political life on Indian reservations.

Klamath. The Klamath of southern Oregon were a riverine people with a fishing and seed-gathering economy and a general material culture that linked them with Northern California and the Basin-Plateau, but the weakly-structured societies of their neighbours were overlaid by a stronger shamanism from the north (Spier 1930, pp. 224, 227, 234).

In aboriginal times, society lacked internal consistency, and social control did not reach the margins of society, for factions, comprising relatives and hangers-on who adhered to a wealthy leader, were the normal state of affairs. The leader of a faction relied on a shaman whose advice and support were essential, and only when public opinion was sufficiently aroused did someone seek out a third party to use his good offices to compose the feud. Ritual sanctions supported adherence to the ceremony of reconciliation.

Small wonder that modern politics on the Klamath Reservation run true to form. During contact, administrative policy contributed to the decline in power and prestige of the shaman with corresponding increases for the chiefs; and the "go-betweens" became "Agency Indians." Whereas observable tarriances of the old gathering economy have disappeared, the modern type of chartered business organization, by which the 1578 tribal members try to govern their affairs and manage the per capita income from one million acres of timber, is haunted by the tradition of factions and peopled by personalities adjusted to feuding. One sees the old forms shining through general council, loan-board, and enrollment committee, and meets shaman, chief, and go-between in the persons of the present key-men. The Superintendent alone occupies a panelled office in the *décor* of Indian tribal arts; the leader of the conservative faction, who holds the power statuses, has the personality of the shaman and identifies himself with big government: his austere office furniture, carpet, two telephones, "squawk-box" for communicating with secretary outside, bookcase of United States Laws and Statutes, suggest status symbols of the U.S. civil servant of the third échelon.

Briefly, Klamath culture has gone, but the social culture hangs round to haunt and distort an otherwise admirable replica of Western business organization and "democratic" government.

Blackfoot. In a similar way, the band society of the erstwhile bison-hunting Blackfoot forms the structure of reservation politics today. The old band-leaders rose and declined with the fortunes of war and the hunt, the changing loyalties of kin and hangers-on, their own generosity, and personal qualities to attract or repel followers.

Economy and government were organized in accordance with the concepts of free territory, and ecological time—the yearly round of activities assembled the tribe for a few brief weeks at the summer buffalo-hunt, when tribal organization emerged and the state delegated its functions of control to the famous soldier societies or police. Except among the Cheyenne, strong government was lacking in the area.

Confinement to reservations and disappearance of the buffalo changed the circumstances of Blackfoot political life by introducing the concept of territory. But kinship practices and old values persist. The present neighbourhoods resemble band encampments. Of nearly 6,000 people, but 800 are full-bloods and these adhere most firmly to memories of the buffalo days.

In their own minds, cultural conservatism and taking up the white man's economy and culture divide along blood-lines; but in politics there is no clear-cut division into full-blood and mixed-blood factions. The full-bloods fractionate their votes in elections, selling out for gratuities and following kin-lines. Generosity has been translated to welfare, which implies elements of graft reminiscent of politics in American cities. Blackfoot leadership has characteristically given both sheriff, who is heir of the Crazy Dogs, and clerk to the county. I predict that those Blackfoot who now control county politics, if not entirely their own, will one day send leaders to the state and nation. As it is, they are wasting their talents in local impasses, where native capacity for organization is weak and respect for tribal council, as always, is at a minimum.

Iroquois. The woodland Iroquois with their amazing talent for organization illustrate the process of stability admirably. Consistently resident in the Laurentian watershed, their present reservations are islands in their old domain. Habitat exerts a constant and continuing effect on economy: the three sisters—corn, bean, and squash— still grace their gardens and agricultural festivals; the American elm, which occupied a central place in industry, yielding dishes, canoes, and houses, and which provided a symbol for their government, now merely shades their log, frame, and tar-paper shanties. A few herbalists bespeak a vanishing knowledge of the local flora. They now work at the white man's occupations with his tools—farming and labouring; and excel in two—the construction of railroads and "high steel" (skyscrapers and bridges), since as a people they do not seem to suffer from vertigo. But the Iroquois show greatest stability in language, the Handsome Lake religion, music, and social and political structure—in about that order. These tarriances exhibit both regional uniformity and considerable local diversity at early and late historical levels. Local diversity observable in Iroquois culture today may be interpreted as change arising after separation of communities and a gradual process of drift since white contact. Modern Cayuga ceremonies in Canada differ in order if not in structure from those of the Seneca of western New York. Cayuga ceremonies resemble those of their Onondaga neighbours. But the organization and seating of the Cayuga tribal council, which is older than the order of ceremonies, contrasts markedly with that of the Onondaga and is most like that of the Seneca. We should expect the details of their ancient government to reflect former cultural situations when the Cayuga lived close to the Seneca in western New York.

Discounting for the moment problems of factionalism and the success and failure of the dual organization to control schisms from early times (a topic which I propose to discuss in another paper), I shall touch the sanction of conformity and mention one example of measuring stability historically. Resistance to change may be illustrated by my own experience with Iroquois tribal councils: any issue or innovation which comes up for group discussion and may be construed as a threat to group sovereignty will be resisted. "We rejected it," say the people, when they have thoroughly discussed a proposal on which they cannot agree, although individually a majority favour it. Advisors used to tell me to proceed without the sanction of the group, until someone made an issue of the matter and carried it to the council; by then it would be allowed to happen and would have passed into custom. If nothing was said, the innovation proceeded quietly by a process of drift to change the course of cultural history.

Stability of one institution during two hundred years can be demonstrated. The programme of the Condolence Council, by which the League of the Iroquois mourned its dead and installed new chiefs in office, is governed by a pattern of sequence comprising sixteen events of which we can trace the more conspicuous features in descriptions of the ceremony by earlier competent observers. It is a matter of some historical significance that Colonial governors, of whom several went out to Massachusetts, New York, and Virginia, after being educated at Cambridge, learned to "wipe away the tears, open the ears, and clear the throats" of the Mohawk lords before conducting the King's Business. But the relatively uneducated Colonial students of Forest Diplomacy—Conrad Weiser, Sir William and Guy Johnson, Samuel Kirkland, and Asher Wright—have given us the best accounts of the ceremony in which they were tutored by Iroquois masters.

Taos. Finally, the Pueblo area of the American South-West, which is marked by local diversity and extreme internal pressure for conformity, affords an example of cultural stability in Taos Pueblo, the northernmost Taoan-speaking village on the Rio Grande. After three hundred years of contact with Spaniards, Mexicans, and Anglo-Americans, and fifty years of daily visits from the artists and writers who have taken up living nearby—and despite the "rubber-necking" descents of 20,000 tourists each year—the old priests of Taos go on training youth for ceremonial roles, watching the sun, conscripting labour to work on irrigation ditches, and electing the civil officers of the year. Unanimity is the key to internal stability, and Laswell (1935) has characterized Taos reaction to acculturation as "autism." But the concept of "the wall," in reality a low adobe fence, enables the Taoseños to distinguish their old people "who look inward on the plaza" from the younger innovators "who look outward over the

wall." Briefly, when the hundred-odd veterans of the recent war returned home from abroad, they sought certain innovations in Pueblo
life—modern dress, safe water, electricity, and a programme of social
security and veteran's education—which the hierarchy opposed. The
Pueblo split into factions. Elsewhere I have reported the affair, and
how a single strong man emerged to subvert the democratic checks
in Pueblo political structure to "put down the boys" (Fenton N.D.).
That the forces for conservatism prevailed can be attributed to the
surprising resources of a key-man and the intense conservatism of
Pueblo culture, which the young men have been trained to respect.
Whether Taos culture disintegrates under the frustrating pressure
of stalemated factionalism remains a question for the future to decide. The malcontents may leave; but there is no place to which the
conservatives may retire (which is the history of ancient factionalism
in the South-West), except into their *kivas*. I suspect that in the long
run the basic patterns of Pueblo culture will prevail.

Summary

I have called attention to a problem which, in a way, may illustrate
some of the continuing preoccupation of American anthropologists
with Red Indians. I have noted what theory I found available relating
to cultural stability and explained how the problem attracted me, and
what has been done about it. The suggested fields for investigation of
stability remain provisional, as are the criteria for detecting its presence
and intensity. The four societies in which I have explored the problem
suggest that those which have developed religious and political institutions have resisted acculturation in North America most successfully.
Blackfoot, Iroquois, and Taos will be with us for a long time.

Note

Paper read at the XXX International Congress of Americanists (Cambridge),
August 1952.

References

Fenton, William N. 1941. Iroquois Suicide: A Study in the Stability of a Culture Pattern. *Anthropological Papers*, No. 14, pp. 80–137. Bull. Bur. Amer. Ethnol. 128.

Fenton, William N. 1949. Collecting Materials for a Political History of the Six Nations. *Proc. Amer. Phil. Soc.* 93, pp. 233–8.

Fenton, William N. ed. 1951. *Symposium on Local Diversity in Iroquois Culture.* Bull. Bur. Amer. Ethnol. 149. 187 pp.

Fenton, W. N. N.D. Factionalism at Taos Pueblo. MS.

Hallowell, A. Irving. 1947. Some Psychological Characteristics of the Northeastern Indians. In *Man in Northeastern North America*, Frederick Johnson ed., pp. 195–225. Pap. Peabody Fdn Archaeol. 3.

Herskovits, Melville J. 1948. *Man and His Works: The Science of Cultural Anthropology.* 678 pp. New York, Knopf.

Laswell, Harold Dwight. 1935. Collective Autism as a Consequence of Culture Contact: Notes on Religious Training and the Peyote Cult at Taos. *Z. Socialforsch.* 4, pp. 232–46.

Lewis, Oscar. 1942. *The Effects of White Contact upon Blackfoot Culture.* Monogr. Amer. Ethnol. Soc., No. 6. 73 pp. New York, Augustin.

Morgan, Lewis H. 1851. *League of the Ho-dé-no-sau-nee, or Iroquois*, 477 pp. Rochester NY, Sage.

Nash, Philleo. 1937. The Place of Religious Revivalism in the Formation of the Intercultural Community on Klamath Reservation. In *Social Anthropology of North American Tribes*, Fred Eggan ed., pp. 337–442. Chicago, University of Chicago Press.

Ogburn, William Fielding. 1922. *Social Change with Respect to Culture and Original Nature.* 365 pp. New York, Huebsch. [Repr. New York, Viking Press, 1928.]

Parsons, Elsie Clews. 1936. *Taos Pueblo.* Gen. Ser. Anthrop., No. 2. 121 pp. Menasha WI, Banta.

Spier, Leslie. 1930. Klamath Ethnography. *Univ. Cal. Publ. Amer. Archaeol. Ethnol.* 30. 338 pp.

Wallace, Anthony F. C. 1952. *The Model Personality Structure of the Tuscarora Indians as Revealed by the Rorschach Test.* Bull. Bur. Amer. Ethnol. 150, 120 pp.

Wissler, Clark. 1910. Material Culture of the Blackfoot Indians. *Anthrop. Pap. Amer. Mus.* 5, pp. 1–175.

Wissler, Clark. 1911. The Social Life of the Blackfoot Indians. *Anthrop. Pap. Amer. Mus.* 7, pp. 1–64.

The Hyde de Neuville Portraits of New York Savages in 1807–1808

It was only twenty-three years after Lafayette had scolded the Six Nations at the Treaty of Fort Stanwix for remaining faithful to the British in the War for Independence that Baron Hyde de Neuville and his artist wife came as royalist refugees to New York and spent nearly two years upstate, going as far as Niagara Falls. In less than a generation, while the Bourbons were being put out of empire by the French Revolution, the once-proud Iroquois, "the People of the Longhouse," had ceded all their claims to the "old Northwest" and given up all but their fireplaces in New York, reserving small tracts around their ancient settlements and some of the better fishing stations. The Mohawks had mainly followed Joseph Brant to Canada; the Oneidas and their wards the Tuscaroras who had befriended the American cause were allowed to stay; the Onondagas held on to the principal fireplace of the League at Onondaga valley, although most of the population went with the fire to Buffalo; and the Cayuga Reservation hugged the outlet and shores at the ferrying place of Cayuga Lake. The Senecas, always more numerous than the others combined, had three settlements on the Genesee: on the trail to Niagara they withheld the long riffle where spring suckers come up Tonawanda Creek; Buffalo was their big center; and south of that, the "smelly banks" of Cattaraugus Creek and the beautiful reaches of *Ohiiyo*, the Allegheny Oxbow, home of Cornplanter and his half-brother, the prophet, were to remain to this day the domain of the Seneca

Nation. The rest of New York State had been sold to the Yankees and their land agents.

The first ten years of relations between the Six Nations and the new Federal government in Philadelphia were punctuated with a series of conferences and treaties which sought to "take the hatchet out of the heads of the Six Nations" for the murder of Indian hunters on Pine Creek, "to keep them quiet in their seats" while the Army of the United States lost two Indian campaigns in Ohio, to appease them for the encroachment on their lands by veterans of the Revolution, and finally to lead them into gradual civilization and improvement. Indian policy was an official matter, but its implementation was left to the missionaries of New England and to the Society of Friends of Philadelphia. Washington entrusted the carrying out of Indian policy to General Henry Knox, Secretary of War, and the negotiations with the Six Nations fell to Col. Timothy Pickering who at last concluded the treaty of peace and friendship with the Six Nations at Canandaigua on November 11, 1794. Washington and these two New England Federalists, then, made the first national Indian policy and the Pickering Treaty was its model. When reviewing these affairs in retrospect the temptation is great to place blame one way or the other, but history holds events in the pattern of the times. The Indians had been attached to the British interest for a century and the flag of Britannia still waved over Oswego, Niagara, and Detroit. The "General Government" was weak and little understood, since typically the States had relinquished sovereignty reluctantly, so that New York commissioned its own agents to treat separately with the Six Nations, and its governor gave secret instructions to frustrate the Federal commissioners. Small wonder the Indians were confused. When they saw clearly the choice between a State government, subject to local pressures, and the consistent integrity of a general government that held its negotiations publicly under the invited scrutiny of the Society of Friends, they chose to accept the protection of Washington, their "father," an alliance which they have consistently cherished. Even though the first Federal Indian Superintendent, General Israel Chapin, was appointed with the backing of New England land interests, he reported to Knox in Philadelphia who held him strictly to account on policy.

Such was the pattern of events attending Pickering's "Treaty of Peace and Friendship" with the Six Nations. It vouchsafed the reservations, defined the lands of the Seneca Nation, freed other lands of the United States from further claim, gave the public free use of roads and rivers, and established a perpetual annuity for the "purchase of clothing, domestic animals, implements of husbandry . . ." to be paid over by the Superintendent appointed by the President. (General Chapin was succeeded by a long line of Federal agents down to recent years, when the office was abolished, but payment of the annuity and the "shares of cloth" has become an American tradition and continues to the present, though an Act of Congress now seeks to commute the treaty.) To this compact, "Timothy Pickering, and the Sachems and War-chiefs of the . . . Six Nations . . . set their hands and seals," to the number of nearly sixty. It may be alleged that the Chapins extended credit at a country saloon so that Red Jacket and his thirsty colleagues could get an odd gallon of rum (for Sir William Johnson had long ago learned that good Indian oratory flowed from a pail of punch); but it was the news of Wayne's victory at Fallen Timbers that induced the chiefs and warriors to sign. The British were going to have to quit Niagara in two years.

Once the basic legal relationship was established between the Federal government and the Six Nations, the gradual civilization of the Indians fell back upon the missionaries.

The Baron Hyde de Neuville's exile to America and his summer sojourns in central New York came just at the end of Samuel Kirkland's mission to the Oneida Indians. At the time of Kirkland's death in 1808, the Oneidas to whom he had ministered during most of his adult life, though on the winning side of the Revolution, were torn into Christian and Pagan factions; they were reduced in numbers, being neither hunters nor agriculturists; they were much addicted to drink; and they were wholly dependent on the traders for gunpowder and clothing.[1] A Quaker mission to the Oneidas, though successful for a time in operating a saw mill and a grist mill and introducing spinning and weaving, had been withdrawn, to concentrate efforts among the Senecas at Allegheny. In June of 1800, the Oneidas were "settled in six small villages, exclusive of Oneida or *Kanonwauloohaule*, their capital . . ." and their chiefs had taken an accurate census to effect "an equal distribution of their annuity. They aggregate 678 souls, exclusive of the Tuscaroras," wrote Kirkland to A. Miller, June 7, 1800. Despite superficial appearances, the Oneidas had changed very little during the forty years of Kirkland's residence, which had given him an appreciation of the stability of Indian culture. At the same time Kirkland noted:

> Striking changes in morals and manners seldom occur. The re-marks made twenty years ago upon the Indians will, with a shade of difference, be found to be true now. . . . Those who are much acquainted with the human mind might perhaps make some re-marks upon their progress in intellect, if indeed they have made any that is perceptible. To a superficial observer like myself they appear in a moral and intellectual view like a company of children. It is easy to engage their attention—to touch their hearts—but it is impossible by any reasoning to give permanence to the emo-tions you excite. No eloquence can convey to them any idea of the value of time, or persuade them to employ it to a purpose. Their condition as a nation is hopeless. Idleness, which perhaps prevailed formerly among them as much as at present, could not then produce effects so fatal as now, for all around them was as torpid and inactive as themselves. . . .[2]

But faced with disorganization, Iroquois culture was making its own attempt to restore equilibrium. Defeated in the field of battle, bereft of allies, and faced with an aggressive agrarian civilization that was pushing westward yearly, Iroquois society had to readjust to reservation life or die. It is a curious circumstance that given these conditions of cultural contact messianic cults frequently arise. The Seneca prophet, Handsome Lake, had commenced to preach his revelations in Cornplanter's town on the Allegheny as the sun set on the eighteenth century, and the new century had scarcely dawned before his influence strengthened the pagan element at Oneida, and a second prophet was reported from Grand River in Canada. Handsome Lake visited Washington where he communicated his revelation to President Jefferson and received an affidavit and passport from Secretary of War Dearborn, which his followers afterward took as open endorsement.[3] The Allegheny faction were soon to make political hay out of this endorsement at Buffalo Creek, and Handsome Lake afterward had a religious following at Tonawanda and at Canawagus on the Genesee River. The prophet was reported in the summer of 1806 to be engaged in trying to prevent the Genesee Indians from using ardent spirits, and the Indians set apart three days to confess their sins to the prophet who had become their confessor. The chiefs sent for Superintendent Jasper Parrish, soliciting his influence to close the taverns and to prevent others from selling whiskey to the Indians.[4] Contrary to the fear that such meetings threatened the peace, Parrish found little cause for alarm; and Kirkland faced searching questions from the Oneida pagans whether he thought the Seneca prophet was indeed "inspired by the spirit of God." Besides enjoining the strictest temperance and sobriety, the prophet was reported at Oneida as exhorting "to live in peace and love one another and all mankind, white people as well as Indians. He then spoke upon the duties of husbands and wives, and the great sin of divorce."[5] Handsome Lake's fame was to come after his death in 1815,[6] and in the twentieth century would all but obliterate the cultural memory of his illustrious Indian contemporaries during the time of Hyde de Neuville's visit to Buffalo Creek.

Handsome Lake, John Obeal (Cornplanter), Farmer's Brother,

Red Jacket, and Young King signed the receipt for the Federal interest money of $6,250 in May of 1803 as "Chiefs and Warriors of the
Seneca Nation of Indians." Besides, Cornplanter received an annuity
of $250; Little Billy, Young King, Red Jacket, and Farmer's Brother
$100 each; while $50 went to Capt. Pollard and $10 to Little Billy's
mother, annually, in fulfillment of an agreement with the Morris
family for signing the Treaty at Big Tree in 1797. These then were the
well-known Indians of 1807, especially Red Jacket whose speeches
against the whites were being widely printed.

The payment of annuities and goods had for twenty-five years
entailed keeping a fairly accurate count of population for the purpose of estimating the shares and making the distribution yearly by
reservations. Thus on March 26, 1800, Superintendent Chapin made
his annual return of the number of the Senecas, with estimates of
how to divide the shares of the six thousand dollars payable under the Canandaigua Treaty of 1794. There were 1,570 Senecas that
year to receive about four dollars a head.[7] They were concentrated
mainly at Allegheny, Buffalo, and Cattaraugus; Tonawanda was a
small settlement of 83, smaller than two of the Genesee towns. At
best such population figures were estimates, for a Quaker census in
1808 gives:[8]

Senecas	1920
Cayugas	600
Onondagas	500
Tuscaroras	300 (settled on Seneca lands)
Mohawks	800 (living in Canada)
Stockbridge	170 (on land given them by Oneida)
Total	4690 [The error of 400 is in the original ms.]

Of equal interest are the lists of goods desired by the Indians,
to be purchased of Philadelphia and New York merchants, bills of
lading, and the distribution lists kept by the New York Superinten-
dents. Strouds, blankets, coating, linen, calico, powder, leads, flannels,

muslins, particularly blue and scarlet, make up a typical inventory of 1805.

These background items deserve attention, for they explain in part how a French refugee could find that the noble savage of his expectations had become by 1807 rather disenchanting. Memoirs of places visited and memories of things seen become valuable as historical records when made by competent observers and written down at the time. The Baron and Madame Hyde de Neuville were scarcely qualified observers of Indians, and the Baron's letters were at best written after the fact, and finally edited and published years after his death by descendants who in all probability had never seen an Indian. Somehow in France the empirical tradition of Champlain and the *Jesuit Relations*, which were read avidly in the seventeenth century, had got diluted by the end of the eighteenth century into a pale romanticism by which the exotic noble savage reached court society in the writings of Chateaubriand. As members of the court literati the Hyde de Neuvilles were in for a shock. Their best preparation for the task of seeing Indians was Madame de Neuville's training as a watercolorist.

Arriving in New York on June 20, 1807, the de Neuvilles went up the Hudson to Albany almost immediately, and then to Ballston Spa, near Saratoga. How long they rested at the Spa is not clear, but they were soon in Utica near the Oneidas, and by September first had reached Niagara, via Cayuga, Geneva, Batavia and Buffalo. The Baron's *Mémoires et Souvenirs* leaves the reader to guess how they returned. The *Mémoires*, being neither a journal nor an accurate description of the country, would indeed scarcely merit attention as an ethnological source, were it not for the close link between it and the Baroness Hyde de Neuville's interesting watercolor portraits of Indians, recently acquired by this Society. The tribes mentioned in the *Mémoires* or represented in the Baroness's pictures are the Oneida and Seneca, the Cayuga by implication, and possibly the Mohawk; besides these New York tribes, the Osage are represented by two copies after St. Mémin and the Cherokee by one portrait, possibly a copy, dated 1820. The latter two groups are not mentioned in the Baron's memoirs.[9]

Traveling up the Hudson, Hyde de Neuville was struck with the grand scale of nature everywhere, but, he says, it was the people who really attracted his attention. While yet at Ballston Spa he declares their intention of leaving in a few days for Niagara Falls, adding that they also plan to visit some of the Indian settlements. "Some of them come here where we are sometimes, but they are of savages a little more civilized, and might not be noticed, if their copper color did not suggest their origin. Madame de Neuville sketched at this time," the Baron continues, "a big and stout girl of the country of Atala, but who has neither the charm nor the grace."[10]

The Indian girl of Ballston Spa is represented in two drawings made in July 1807: a seated figure and a head, full face (figure 1). Both are inscribed "Sauvage de Balston Spring. . . ." Judging by the location of Ballston Spa, this girl was probably a Mohawk, though from the text she might be a Stockbridge Indian. The portrait is drawn with nice feeling for the mass of her face. The earrings and typically Iroquois woman's moccasins, together with her physiognomy, are all that suggest an Indian, although the stiff hat, often with a silver band, was much in favor at Onondaga later in the century. The shawl and dress leave one to guess whether she wore the short woman's leggings above her moccasins.

The Baron and Madame Hyde de Neuville next visited Utica, where he penned a long letter to his sister, telling her about the country west of Albany where the villages were named after the cities and heroes of antiquity, though "at the first glance you would think that these lands were only inhabited by savages, or by a people in the lowest stage of civilization."[11] In the same letter the Baron wrote:

We have just come back from visiting parts of the country that five years ago were inhabited only by the bear, the beaver, and a few

FIGURE 1. "Sauvage de Balston Spring. 1807. Juillet." Watercolor portrait and pencil sketch by Baroness Hyde de Neuville. From the Baroness Hyde de Neuville Collection, courtesy of the New-York Historical Society (acc. nos. 1953.217 and 1953.216).

Sauvage de Balstou Spring. 1807. Juillet.

fugitive and savage Indians; and now you cannot go a mile without finding a house, an inn, and here and there villages, churches, schools, and even towns that begin to be worthy of the name.

We visited a few savage tribes. They are poor wretches, besotted with drink, stagnating in idleness and misery, and rejecting every effort to draw them out of it. The French missionaries did them a great deal of good, but since Canada is no longer part of France, these poor Indians have fallen back into miserable degradation. The American government treats them, however, with kindness; but in order to civilize such men, to overcome the obstacles inseparable from so charitable an enterprise, would require more than zeal of humanity, more than all the speculations of philosophy; it requires the courage of men who go through life for the sole purpose of overcoming its weaknesses; and finally it demands evangelical faith. . . .[12]

The first of the "savage tribes" visited by the de Neuvilles were the Oneidas in the vicinity of Utica, where they stopped both going to and returning from Niagara Falls. Here the Baroness made at least three drawings, of which two are identified by her own hand and the third by her husband's description of the division of labor between the sexes.

The family portrait of "an indian and his Squah," which appears on the same sheet as a view of Utica Church in 1807, illustrates well the Baron's remarks to his sister on the sloth and wretchedness of the aborigines (figure 2). These people, I judge, may be typical of Kirkland's pagan Oneidas who have come up to town for a drink. The man carries a staff, a symbol of status still affected by the old men of Iroquoia and by the maskers at the Midwinter Festival. Madame de Neuville's training as a painter shows in her handling of these subjects; the legs are too massive for Indians, although the Baron does note that "this tribe is ugly and have pockmarked, malformed legs and tawny copper colored skin, with black straight hair."[13] Though,

— an indian and his Squah —

FIGURE 2. "An Indian and his Squah" with pencil sketch of Indian at work. By Baroness Hyde de Neuville, Utica NY, 1807. From the Baroness Hyde de Neuville Collection, courtesy of the New-York Historical Society (acc. no. 1953.226).

as he points out, these people are scarcely covered by breechcloth and blanket, I am even more intrigued by the unfinished sketch on the same sheet showing an Iroquois in long shirt, leggings, and moccasins, engaged in some free-flowing activity. I speak of this because the costume anticipates the style of a generation later, so beautifully illustrated by Lewis H. Morgan.[14]

The portrait of "Mary, Squah of the oneida tribe" (figure 3) was

mary, Squab of
the oneida tribe,
utica 7ᵇʳᵉ 1807

FIGURE 3. Mary, Oneida squaw, Utica, September 1807. Watercolor and graphite on paper. From the Baroness Hyde de Neuville Collection. Courtesy of the New-York Historical Society (neg. no. 37246, acc. no. 1953.207).

sketched at Utica in September 1807 on the de Neuville's return from Niagara. Here is a typical Iroquois woman, in physical appearance much resembling her more-nearly fullblooded descendants today. I take it she was not used to sitting on a chair and possibly felt not

FIGURE 4. Indian family, probably near Utica, fall of 1807. Watercolor and graphite on paper. From the Baroness Hyde de Neuville Collection, courtesy of the New-York Historical Society (acc. no. 1953.215).

dressed for the occasion, in a mere blanket and leggings, without moccasins. Iroquois women still wear their hair parted in the middle and they still like earrings, but the nose ornament has vanished.

The third sketch, probably drawn near Utica in the late fall of 1807 and inscribed "Envoyé à Mde. Boisgrand" (figure 4), illustrates perfectly the Baron's remarks on the traditional division of labor between the sexes: "The men do nothing, while the women are always encumbered with cultivating the earth; and they carry constantly heavy burdens which they hold suspended on their backs and which a large strap of leather holds fixed on the forehead, whilst the men are loaded only with their bow and arrows."[15]

This picture holds immense ethnological interest. It belongs to the

FIGURE 5. Unidentified Indian man, 1807. Watercolor and graphite on paper. From the Baroness Hyde de Neuville Collection, courtesy of the New-York Historical Society (acc. no. 1953.206).

"they-went-to-the-woods-to-hunt-for-meat" genre and apparently depicts a family group on the autumn hunt. The attire of all ages and both sexes is illustrated. The boy and his father both wear leggings to the mid-thigh, gartered at the ankle and below the knee; the hunting shirt leaves the thigh bare. Father wears both nose- and earrings, the son only the latter; both wear the scalp lock. The father slings the deer over the left shoulder using the bow as a balance. A floral design decorates the instep of his moccasins. The woman, who appears in both front and side views, is equally interesting. Her shorter leggings are similarly tied; blanket replaces shirt and covers the head; but most unusual is the arrangement of burden-strap and pack-frame, which suggests that the cradle-board came much later.

The next of these Indian portraits, reproduced as a frontispiece to this article, presents a provoking problem of identification (figure 5). Although there is little definite to go on, the temptation is great to put a name to it. Here is an Iroquois hunter in the full vigor of manhood; probably a full blood, he sports the same distended ear lobe as the "fair-indian" pictured by the Baroness at Canisteo the following year. His right index finger takes a peculiar crook, possibly an old injury, which might show in other portraits. Note the knife sheath and powder horn worn over the buckskin shirt, the patched leggings extending to mid-thigh, the moccasins; note also the chair and drop-leaf table, which must have belonged to someone of consequence. Knife in hand, this Indian hunter appears to be holding a piece of buckskin, possibly the vamp of a moccasin. The artist has not named her subject; but the Baron tantalizes us: "The Chief *Read Jaret* [could he mean Red Jacket?] is no better housed than the rest; he was busy making foot-gear of deer skin called *mocassins*, and he readily accepted the money which we offered him."[16]

The Baron next writes: "We went to see the Cagugas [Cayugas] in their little village which is close to the side of the road. Their squalid dwellings are lined on the inside with miserable beds of which deer skins form the only mattress and covers. The fire is kindled in the middle of the cabin, and a hole made in the shingles is the only chimney, so that with any wind at all, the smoke must blind them."[17]

After commenting on the safety of the backwoods in contrast with the dangers of travel in France, the Baron mentions Kirkland's school among the Oneidas, and goes on about their appearance and dress, saying that they wear breechcloth, smock or shirt, and wrap their legs with cloth, leaving the thighs and arms nude. He never saw one smile nor did they resemble at all Atala and the warlike savages of Chateaubriand. "These poor savages," he wrote, "addicted to drunkenness and laziness, are not at all formidable, and, acting on the advice of the people of the country, we left our arms behind in setting out. . . ."[18]

In a rare burst of directions, de Neuville mentions passing what I take to be the Finger Lakes, as well as "Geneva, Batavia, Buffalo, where we found the best savages, well adorned with tin plate, silver rings, and streaked grotesquely with variegated paints. . . ." The account continues: "The first of September we at last saw the famous falls of Niagara, a sight at which we did not regret the troubles experienced in getting there. Leaving Buffalo in the early morning and favored with fair weather, after having followed for three miles a path which the sand made tiring, we reached the shore of Lake Erie, where the surf is strong and presents the look and sound of the sea when not very rough."[19]

This must have been the day that Madame de Neuville painted the watercolor inscribed: "tonaventa Peter de Bufalo dessiné en allant à Niagara" (figure 6). So far Buffalo Peter's name has not cropped up in any of the registers, and I am not certain that he was entirely Indian, though he exhibits the finest set of deformed ears of the lot.[20] Aside from the linen shirt, the usual hunting gear is augmented only by the battle axe. A string of wampum in the left hand marks him as a councillor. The artist has also attempted to picture some of the flora of New York—pine or hemlock, and Indian hemp, milkweed or perfoliate bellwort in the foreground.

FIGURE 6. Peter of Buffalo [perhaps Tall Peter, Seneca chief at Tonawanda], inscribed: "tonaventa Peter de Bufalo dessiné en allant à Niagara," watercolor, 1807. From the Baroness Hyde de Neuville Collection, courtesy of the New-York Historical Society (neg. no. 37255, acc. no. 1953.220).

The next two pictures date from a subsequent visit of the Hyde de Neuvilles to the Indian country of western New York. The "Squah of Seneca tribes with his [*sic*] papou" (figure 7), dated August 1808, is a very good likeness of a Seneca woman. Perhaps not as Mongoloid as Oneida Mary, her Seneca sister is equally unused to chairs and hides her feet similarly. I have seen Seneca women of the Handsome Lake followers carry a nursing child in a blanket in this fashion, and the dark skirt recalls the blue muslin in the lists of annuity goods. Compare the chair with that in the following sketch.

FIGURE 7. Seneca squaw and papoose (western New York),
dated August 1808. Watercolor on paper. Baroness Hyde de
Neuville Collection. Courtesy of the New-York Historical
Society (acc. no. 1953.209).

FIGURE 8. The fair Indian of the Buffalo tribe, Canisteo, October 1808. Perhaps Seneca captive Mary Jemison's half-blood son Jesse (1776/7–1812) or her grandson Jacob who entered Dartmouth College in 1816, aged 27. From the Baroness Hyde de Neuville Collection, courtesy of the New-York Historical Society (acc. no. 1953.219).

The last of the Baroness's New York State Indian portraits is inscribed: "the fair indian of the buffalo tribe drawn to canisteo 8bre 1808" (figure 8). Obviously a white captive had mothered or sired him, but which one? His age, the location, and his garb might do for one of the sons of the "White Woman of the Genesee," or the son of one of her sons, possibly Jacob Jemison who entered Dartmouth College in the spring of 1816, aged 27.[21] There is nothing to go by, however; the dress recalls the Quaker mission box, and only the slit ears and earrings betray his ethnic origin.

The three remaining Indian pictures in the Hyde de Neuville collection date from a later period, when the Baron was French Minister at Washington during the administration of James Monroe. Of these, two are obviously copies of St. Mémin's earlier portraits of Osage chiefs. The third and, ethnologically, much the most interesting, shows a Cherokee hunter with bow and long blunt arrows, pack, blanket coat, leggings, and moccasins. The picture bears the inscription: "Cherokee 1820 Mr. Martin"; but whether Martin was the subject, the artist, or the intended recipient of the picture is uncertain.

To summarize, there are in the Hyde de Neuville collection at The New-York Historical Society portraits of three Iroquois women and three Iroquois men, of whom at least one is part white. There are two family groups, and children appear with mothers in three sketches. The costumes show an admixture of Iroquois and white influence. Ear-lobe distension among the men, scalp lock, wampum beads, buckskin shirt, leggings of men and women, breechcloth and moccasins—these are traits of Indian culture, those of the children resembling the parents'. The hat, shawl, blankets, cloth (where it replaces buckskin), and the mission-box garb of the "fair Indian" may be ascribed to white influence. Apart from dress other items of ethnological importance may be noted. The persistent use of the staff by old men of rank, wampum beads as the symbol of chiefship, the pack-frame instead of the cradle-board, cast interesting lights on Iroquois cultural history. The powder horn and the wooly strap we may assume came in with the gun, but they have already gone with the muzzle-loader. The obviously medieval shape of the battle axe is puzzling.[22] The furniture is what we would expect for the period in New York.

Posture and body movements are believed by anthropologists to be culturally conditioned. These Iroquois women are not yet used to sitting in chairs. The position of the children facing forward in

FIGURE 9. Red Jacket (Sa-Go-Ye-Wat-Ha), aged seventy, by Robert W. Weir, 1828. Oil on canvas. Courtesy of the New-York Historical Society (neg. no. 6374, acc. no. 1893.1).

transport contradicts the cradle-board position aft but corresponds with the way modern Seneca women within my observation carry their children. Likewise, I could duplicate the position of the hunter's bow in relation to the deer he is carrying by reference to the modern Seneca's method of carrying a burden using an axe. Thus while cultures change they also remain remarkably stable.

How important are Madame Hyde de Neuville's Indian portraits? As the only on-the-spot pictorial record of Iroquois Indians and their activities at the beginning of the nineteenth century, they are of unusual significance to both historians and ethnologists, despite the artist's technical limitations and occasional overtones of romanticism. To be sure, well-known Indians had been portrayed before. Joseph Brant sat for his portrait twice in England, as well as to Charles Willson Peale at Philadelphia in June of 1792, while four years later Cornplanter sat to Bartoli in New York for the colorful portrait now owned by this Society. But it was nearly twenty years after the Baroness Hyde de Neuville visited Buffalo Creek that George Catlin painted his first great Indian portrait, that of Red Jacket, who much preferred his portrait by R. W. Weir, painted two years later in New York and now owned by The New-York Historical Society (figure 9). Red Jacket had a torn left ear, but a good right ear like the hunter shown in figure 5. Though we may never know for certain who the Baroness's subject was, this and her other sketches will remain an important record of the Indian scene.

Notes

Among the eighty-eight watercolors and sketches by the Baroness Hyde de Neuville, recently acquired by this Society, are twelve portrait and genre studies of American Indians. Nine of these depict Iroquois men and women encountered by the Baron and Baroness in their travels through upstate New York in 1807 and 1808.

The writer is indebted to Mr. David H. Wallace, Assistant Editor, for comparing the photographs with the originals, for checking inscriptions on the drawings against the text of the *Mémoires*, and for valuable suggestions on itinerary and chronology.

1. See the author's "A calendar of manuscript materials relating to the history of the Six Nations . . . ," *Proceedings of the American Philosophical Society*, Vol. 97, No. 5, October 30, 1953, pp. 578–595.

2. *Journal*, March 30, 1804.

3. National Archives, War Office, *Letters Sent*, A 182 ff. March, 1802; A. C. Parker, "The Life of General Ely S. Parker," Buffalo Historical Society *Publications*, XXIII (Buffalo NY, 1919), p. 250.

4. Jasper Parrish to Henry Dearborn, Canandarqua, July 29, 1806; Parrish Collection, Henry E. Huntington Library.

5. Kirkland Papers, Hamilton College Library, August 3, 1806.

6. Parker, Arthur C., "The Code of Handsome Lake, the Seneca Prophet," *New York State Museum Bulletin*, 163 (Albany: 1913).

7. Chapin's arithmetic is mysterious, but the census is interesting.—O'Reilly Papers, NYHS, 13:56, 63.

8. Sam and Susanna Emlen to Wm. Dillwyn, Westhill, January 26, 1808. Ridgeway Library, Dillwyn Coll., YI 2/7305/F 28. Courtesy of Dr. George Snyderman.

9. Jean Guillaume, Baron Hyde de Neuville, *Mémoires et souvenirs du Baron Hyde de Neuville*, 2nd edition (Paris: Librarie Plon, 1892), 3 vols.

10. Hyde de Neuville, *Mémoires*, I:454.

11. Hyde de Neuville, *Mémoires*, I:456.

12. Hyde de Neuville, *Mémoires*, I:458.

13. Hyde de Neuville, *Mémoires*, I:459.

14. *The League of the . . . Iroquois* (Rochester, 1851).

15. Hyde de Neuville, *Mémoires*, I:458.

16. Hyde de Neuville, *Mémoires*, I:459.

17. Hyde de Neuville, *Mémoires*, I:459.

18. Hyde de Neuville, *Mémoires*, I:459.

19. Hyde de Neuville, *Mémoires*, I:460.

20. He may have been Tall Peter, of Buffalo Creek, who joined the Christian Church in 1823 and was one of the chiefs most active in promoting the 1838 sale of Indian lands in northwestern New York. See Henry R. Howland, "The Seneca Mission at Buffalo Creek," *Publications of the Buffalo Historical Society*, VI (Buffalo: 1903), 136, 148; and "Journals of Henry A. S. Dearborn," *Publications of the Buffalo Historical Society*, VII (Buffalo: 1904), 194, 206.

21. *A narrative of the Life of Mary Jemison, the White Woman of the Genesee . . .* (New York: 1932), p. 102. The "fair-indian" may also have been Mary Jemison's

youngest son Jesse, who was born c. 1776/77 and was murdered in 1812 by his brother John.

22. There is, however, a similar scimitar-shaped axe in the best-known engraved portrait of "the brave old Hendrick the great Sachem or Chief of the Mohawk Indians" (published *c.* 1756), which shows that such weapons were no recent innovation among the Iroquois.

"This Island, the World
on the Turtle's Back"

The Huron and Iroquois Indians were the aboriginal inhabitants of the lands bordering the lower Great Lakes, specifically Lakes Huron, Erie, and Ontario, and the St. Lawrence River, in what are now parts of Ontario and Quebec in Canada, part of Pennsylvania, and nearly all of New York State.[1] These peoples who spoke languages of the Iroquoian family always referred to their country as "This Old Island," or *Wendat Éhen*, in Huron, which they conceived as resting on the back of a turtle swimming in the primal sea. How the earth, various plants and animals, and the several celestial bodies and forces were created and put in operation; what special duties they were assigned of benefit to man; and how the first human beings on the earth learned to adjust to the situation as they found it comprise the subject and content of a myth that is one of the great intellectual display pieces of the New World. The Iroquois Indians had three such myths by which they marked their cultural history, and these were recited by their learned men at public gatherings or in the long lodge of a family that had kindled a fire and cooked a kettle of mush for the myth-holder. The telling filled several days or nights, and great heed was paid to verbatim recall and recitation. Because of the inherent power of the myths, recitals were held only after the first frost when the earth sleeps. Though each authority claims fidelity for his version, each narrator had his own style. The published versions exhibit a remarkable consistency of plot and incident, but are nevertheless quite different in detail, and probably they differed slightly at each telling.

Our present concern is with the first of the three great myths, the Earth-grasper; the second is the Deganawi:dah epic of the founding of the League of the Longhouse people, to which we will turn momentarily; and *Kaíwi:yo:* 'the good message', which is the revelation of Handsome Lake, the Seneca prophet, and which contains the ethos of present-day Longhouse culture, will occupy the greater span of attention because we know the most about it. I mention the three now because this is how Iroquois annalists see their own culture history: they speak of a time of Sapling before Deganawi:dah; of the period of the League's formation; and of the present since Handsome Lake. Naive as it may seem to sophisticated readers to employ the mythology of a primitive people for organizing the results of scientific inquiry, this is done deliberately in order to describe the culture in its own terms, for locked up in the three Iroquoian epics are the major institutions of their culture as well as the themes that guide behavior throughout their history and illuminate certain actions even today.

The isolation of themes or motifs and their use for classification and comparison of literatures has long been the standard method of systematic folklorists for storing and retrieving a huge body of information for use in a variety of problems, such as the dissemination of tales as evidence of historical relationships. These two interests—classification and comparison—have united literary folklorists and anthropologists for some seventy years. But the application of the theory of themes to the analysis of a culture is a more recent development that sprang from the association of anthropology and psychology, and it was first carried out rigorously by Morris Edward Opler on ethnographic and folkloristic materials from the Lipan Apache, the warlike raiders of the American southwest.[2]

Opler's idea struck me at the time he submitted it to a journal I was then editing as a useful scheme for organizing the materials of

Iroquois culture, because he had succeeded in describing Apache ways in terms of their own internal consistencies, utilizing both the oral literature and his observations of their behavior. This came at a time when other ethnologists were losing interest in folklore studies, complaining that folklorists did not do anything with the tales except collect and present them. Opler's method offered a means of integrating folklore with the description of a culture; and the Iroquois have a large body of mythology, fiction, and tradition. If one could apply Opler's method, it might solve another problem: it might tell us something about the most durable aspects of culture, which are internal and are affairs of the mind. Why has Iroquois culture survived into the present century? In three hundred years of continuous contact with aggressive white people in the country's most populous state, several Iroquoian languages are still spoken from Brooklyn to Niagara. The voices of Seneca drummers rise from the swamps of Tonawanda and echo on the Allegheny hills. Masks are still carved in response to dreams, and the Falseface Society makes its spring and fall rounds. Work in high steel has replaced the adventure of the warpath. The kettle endures as a symbol of hospitality, although corn soup is cooked in aluminum ware instead of iron kettles hung over the fire, or in stone-propped earthen pots. The Seneca Nation is a republic, but at Tonawanda and Onondaga chiefs are elected by clan matrons and raised with the Condolence Council; and a fierce tradition of political independence contrasts with pride in a second generation educated in centralized schools with neighboring whites.

Besides having a rich mythology and folklore, the Iroquois have the best documented history of any primitive people; and they boast one of the largest ethnographic bibliographies. Historians have nevertheless failed in the attempt to describe Indian life from the viewpoint of the culture itself because the literature available to them was written by Europeans, and historians admit to evidence only written documents. Consequently, historians have denied the existence and questioned the authenticity of institutions like the League of the Iroquois on which the earliest sources are silent or give meager accounts of it indeed. The first full-scale description of the kinship system and of the League itself had to await the emergence of anthropology with L. H. Morgan at the mid-nineteenth century and to accompany the linguistic and folkloristic studies of Horatio Hale. By the writings of these two pioneer scientists it may be judged that the Iroquois social system, their political institutions, and their elaborate rites for installing chiefs were either invented for the amusement of anthropologists, or had eluded colonial administrators, missionaries, historians and explorers because they were too busy to write about them and because they were not trained as anthropologists. This is a perplexing problem because to admit the latter proposition is to deny change, and to deny it is contrary to the history of science. Is cultural persistence a response to boredom of nineteenth-century life on reservations? How are cultural institutions internalized in language and folklore? How can oral tradition be utilized for enriching documentary history and ethnographic observation? Do not the themes and motifs of folklore afford a model for finding analogies in other aspects of the culture? If so, what are they, how do they structure the culture, and how do they function as guides to individual behavior? What is the life of these themes? What is their role in tradition? What is their fate in culture change?

I raise these questions now in anticipation of presenting the history of Iroquois culture that will be stated in terms of its central themes and illustrated by the sketches of some typical careers of Iroquois persons who have since gone the long trail and whose lives epitomize Iroquois culture at its various periods. Before doing this, however, I propose in the present article to identify the themes that are to be found in the cosmology. So let us listen to "what our grandfathers were wont to relate."

Depending on how the tale opens, the Iroquois, like their Woodland neighbors and the Plains tribes, distinguish three types of narratives, which may be classified as myths, tales, and traditions. The first class relates of things and events "which truly happened" long ago, and in which the old people really believed; second, there is a great bag of tales which are pure fiction and open, "It is as if a man walked"; and third, there are human adventures which commence, "They went to hunt for meat." The latter often relate the experiences of individuals who founded medicine societies and may be distinguished from tribal history. It is an interesting but surprising commentary that the life of fiction is hardier than that of legendary material, but even Trickster stories have vanished since 1930, as has the cosmology which we are about to hear.[3]

The myth of the Earth-grasper, or more commonly the Woman who fell from the Sky, exists in some twenty-five versions which all adhere to the same general plot and contain most of the essential elements. There is enough structural similarity between the Huron version first recorded by the Recollect Gabriel Sagard in 1623—which was again heard in the next ten years by the Jesuit missionaries Brébeuf and Ragueneau—and the elaborate texts which Hewitt had from informants living at the close of the last century, to warrant our saying that one continuous mythological tradition confronts us, that it has three hundred years of recorded history, and that it extends into pre-Columbian times. This is no ethnological freak, nor is the relationship between early Huron versions and later Iroquois versions contrived.[4]

The essential elements in the cosmogonic myth number less than ten, but the longer versions contain fifteen or more component motifs which can be readily identified in Thompson's *Motif-Index of Folk-Literature*, 6 volumes (Bloomington, Ind., 1955–58). Martha Randle, editor of the Waugh Collection, lists nine essential points: (1) sky world; (2) uprooting of the light-giving tree; (3) casting down of the sky-woman; (4) animals diving for earth; (5) establishment of the earth on the turtle's back; (6) Sky-woman's daughter becoming mother of twins, Good- and Evil-minded; (7) Good-minded as culture hero liberating animals pent up by his brother and securing corn; (8) a cosmic duel with avowed fatal weapons—rushes or maize vs. flint or antler; and (9) the banishment of Evil-minded while Good-minded and Sky-woman retire to the sky-world, promising to return on the last day of the world.[5] This is the plot, but various episodes embellish the longer versions which include impregnation by the wind, twins quarreling in the womb, lodge-boy and thrown-away, constructive and destructive creation, a toad that hoards water until a flood issues from its belly or armpit, father search and son testing, experimental man making, and the theft of light. Peculiarly Iroquoian touches in this creation myth, which has a wide distribution in North America and Eurasia, are the dream-guessing contests in the sky-world; the struggle for power and control of the earth by a test of demonstrated mountain moving between Sky-holder or Good-minded and Hadu?i?, the hunchback mask being, who loses and becomes the Great Defender of mankind; the rite of returning thanks from the earth upward through the mid-pantheon of appointed forces to the sky-world; and the creation of the clans and moieties in the formative period of human society. When man is up against it, a fatherless boy from the fringe of the bush emerges to define the situation, propose a solution, and lead the community out of its dilemma. One senses that in this culture tradition has attuned the society to listen to the prophet.[6]

The prophet who would succeed among the Iroquois must speak in ancient tongues, he must use the old words, and he must relate his program to old ways. He is a conservator at the same time that he is a reformer. It will become apparent as one traverses the course of Iroquois culture history that its several reformations have been accomplished by such prophets. This is one of the reasons that Iroquois culture has endured so long; theirs is a tough tradition and a remarkably stable one. None enjoy greater prestige in this society than the men of intellect who perform feats of prodigious memory by relating the myths. These old men "who know everything" single out the young men who are seriously interested and able to learn and instruct them. Soon these young men are marked by the community. In recent years the ethnologist who sits at the feet of the professors of the tribal lore may soon find himself cast in this role. This is how Chief John A. Gibson became keeper of the lore of the Longhouse, and it is how J. N. B. Hewitt, himself a native Tuscarora, came to write it down. Because I succeeded Hewitt as ethnologist to the Iroquois at the Smithsonian Institution, I know something of both men.[7]

Chief John A. Gibson, who died in 1912, a lifelong resident of the Grand River Reservation in Canada, was unquestionably the greatest mind of his generation among the Six Nations. A young man when he was first installed as one of the eight Seneca chiefs to sit in the council of the Confederacy, as the League of the Iroquois tribes is called on the Grand River, this wide-awake and keen-witted Seneca chief attracted the notice of the senior member, one of the Onondaga fire-keepers. (It was the Onondaga chiefs who had taken the lead in rekindling the council fire that had burned for generations on the hills of central New York after they had removed to Canada following the American Revolution.) To keep the lore of the Longhouse alive, the elder Onondaga councilor decided to tutor his promising Seneca younger brother. Consequently the customs, traditions, and ceremonies that Gibson mastered were the ways of ancient Onondaga; and when the old man realized that he must lay aside his antlers of office and prepare to take up the long trail, he asked Gibson to stand in his place and lead the ceremonies at Onondaga Longhouse. This meant that for the rest of his life Gibson spoke Onondaga, although he occasionally preached in Seneca, his mother tongue. He was multilingual, his wife addressed him in Cayuga, he spoke to her in Onondaga, and they used these languages to their children who also learned Seneca from a grandmother. There were times when Chief Gibson performed rituals in Mohawk, he could converse with visiting Oneida chiefs, and he knew some Tuscarora. Besides, his English was excellent. Small wonder that the Gibson family were sought out by ethnologists and linguists as informants and as interpreters! The opportunities for learning Iroquoian languages on the Grand River before 1900 were better than they had ever been when the Six Nations were living scattered across New York State. This circumstance, coupled with real intellectual curiosity and a keen mind, enabled Gibson, who was not satisfied until he had traced a custom or a belief back to its earliest remembered antecedents, to become the greatest living source on Iroquois culture at the turn of the century when field ethnology commenced in earnest. His work with Hewitt on mythology and rituals and with Goldenweiser on social organization and political structure is unapproached by any other Iroquois informant.[8]

At the time that Hewitt worked with him, Chief Gibson had been totally blind for some twenty-six years as the result of a lacrosse injury at the age of thirty-one, an affliction which possibly freed his remarkable powers of memory and comprehension for intellectual pursuits. His version of the cosmology, which he dictated in Onondaga and which Hewitt wrote down in phonetic script in 1900 and afterward published,[9] is certainly one of the longest Iroquois texts extant, running to over 20,000 words and taking up some 145 pages in print. It is the best of the five versions that Hewitt collected and the one that I will follow, both because it is most complete and because Gibson's Onondaga deserves better treatment than Hewitt's pseudoscientific, biblical English. In making my own version for the general reader I will dip into the mush pots of Hewitt's other informants, if only to sample the flavor of their styles. But first a word about Hewitt himself.

I remember John Napoleon Brinton Hewitt, who died in October, 1937 at seventy-eight, because I had been to see him twice in the Smithsonian tower office I was later to occupy. Then I was a graduate student seeking help after my first fieldwork and Hewitt was an old man. He had married again late in life, and his wife, who claimed dowager rights in old Washington society, had gotten him up to look like a Smithsonian scientist: wing collar, Oxford gray coat, striped trousers, and white piping to his vest. He was the last of a notable group of self-taught students of the American Indian whom Major J. W. Powell had assembled soon after founding the Bureau of American Ethnology in 1879. Hewitt shared the added distinction with La Flesche, the Osage, of being a native Indian by Iroquois reckoning, since his mother was part Tuscarora; and he had grown up close to her tribal reservation near Niagara. Though he had planned to follow his Scottish father into medicine, by a series of mishaps, in 1880 at twenty-one he ended up working as secretary to Erminnie A. Smith, a Jersey socialite and folklorist, who employed him to assist her in collecting myths and interpreting among the Iroquoian tribes. Upon her death in 1886, Major Powell, who had already commissioned Erminnie Smith as temporary ethnologist, called Hewitt to the Bureau where he was to serve for fifty-one years. Hewitt soon added Mohawk, Onondaga, and Seneca to his quiver of Iroquoian tongues; and these and Tuscarora he recorded with painstaking accuracy in a phonetic orthography that, without the least difficulty, can be read back to native speakers today. He also became the leading authority on the League and its rituals. Being neither a trained linguist nor a schooled scientist, he had the good sense to concentrate on collecting texts, which is just as well, considering the state of theory in his day. His voluminous manuscripts, which are still largely in the original languages which he knew, are available for study today. The old men of the Seneca Nation and of Six Nations Reserve may be gone, but Hewitt wrote down their words for all time.[10]

It is not that Hewitt lacked a philosophical turn of mind, for he was much interested in philosophy and in comparative religions, and his own justification for taking texts, or recording myths in the original languages, reveals this flair. He prefaced the *Cosmology* with this remark: "Upon the concepts evolved from their impression of things and from their experience with . . . their environment rest the authority of men's doctrines and the reasons for their rites and ceremonies. Hence arises the great importance of recording . . . [texts]."[11]

With this in mind I have gone through the four published versions of Hewitt's *Iroquoian Cosmology* looking for the concepts and
themes which characterize the culture as I have come to know it from
extensive fieldwork and reading. I have also noted literary devices
by which the narrator leads his listeners. The versions differ to the
extent that the narrators have different personal histories segmenting
cultural history at earlier and later points of time, and close scrutiny
tells us something about their personalities, as well as about culture
change. Old John Skanawaati Buck in 1889 was closer to sources on
the old culture than Gibson, but Gibson is far more complete and
incorporates all the system of his teacher without some of the cultural
niceties. It is apparent from John Armstrong's short Seneca version of
1896 that the Senecas were mighty hunters and excellent naturalists
familiar with habits of game on which they had recently depended.
They knew star lore; he himself was an herbalist. The Seneca cast
the patron of the Falsefaces in a more friendly role than the Onondaga, who emphasize the power struggle between the Creator and
Haduʔiʔ. Seneca versions may be expected to show tribal differences
from Onondaga in detail and in literary devices but not in plot, and
Armstrong's version is foreshortened and ends midcourse, raising
questions of rapport between informant and folklorist. The Mohawk version of the cosmology comes from Seth Newhouse, the self-
appointed chronicler of custom and law on the Six Nations Reserve,
with whom Hewitt worked in 1897; it contains a number of Christian
elements and manifests a passion for legitimacy notable in Canada
today, as might be expected, since his people had been in contact with
Anglican missionaries from the early eighteenth century. But it also
illustrates and explains Mohawk usages not found elsewhere. I infer
from Hewitt's papers that Newhouse was an opinionated person, that
fancying himself an author he regarded Hewitt as competition, and
hence the two savants had some disagreements.[12]

The longest version in Onondaga between Gibson and Hewitt—
which comprises the *Iroquoian Cosmology; Second Part*, which I

have analyzed into its constituent plots, incidents, and themes—incorporates most of the detail from the three earlier versions. What escapes us in this analysis and what I spare the reader can be used later "to shingle the bare poles of the longhouse" as chapter heads and illustrations. Notes and marginalia in my books say that I first read these myths in 1932 and 1933, as a fresh graduate student. But manifestly what I have now attempted was impossible then, and I shall try to convey to readers some of the thrill of rediscovery. In the years between, the whole field of Iroquois studies has expanded; and those of us who have done fieldwork have met to share experiences and ideas in the Conference on Iroquois Research, which has sent up its smoke when the leaves turn on the hills and on the fifth night of the new moon at Red House, New York.[13]

Hewitt was inclined, like many of the folklorists of his day, to derive myths from phenomena in nature; and he spent himself in the futile search for the original and ideal myth. But this commentary on his career, which was taken after I had personally reviewed traditions with informants and translated texts relating to the founding of the Iroquois League, nevertheless seems odd in the light of his own early realization that myths are composite cultural pieces and that they have varied histories in time and space. It is odder still, viewing what he wrote in 1903, that he did not follow Boas' lead and study their dissemination: "the great and fundamental fact [is] that all legends are the gradual result of combination from many sources by many minds in many generations."[14]

As among the factors that enter into myth formation—distribution and diffusion, the role of the narrator, and cultural drift between generations—the last two have greatest significance for a discussion of the cultural history of a single people. We can regard the myth of the Earth-grasper as a mirror of Iroquoian culture without denying that its principal motifs—celestial tree of light, the woman who fell from the sky, primeval water, earth diver, earth from the turtle's back, twins quarrel before birth, and lodge-boy and thrown-away—are at home in the mythology of neighboring Woodland peoples. Two of these—earth diver and rival twins—are known the breadth of the continent.[15] And indeed the notion of a primal sea out of which a diver fetches material for making dry land is among the most widespread concepts held by man, having a distribution, according to Earl W. Count, stretching from Finland across Eurasia, including India and southeastern Asia, and covering most of North America, suggesting that it diffused eastward to America when people settled the New World.[16] I am confident that as guardians of the lore of the Iroquois Longhouse, Chief John Gibson and Seth Newhouse would have been intrigued but not amazed to learn that their myth of the beginning of the world has such a distinguished world history; but they would claim priority for it in America, where they were certainly its greatest systematists. This drive toward synthesis which is so evident in the culture of the nineteenth-century Iroquois and which characterizes their two greatest myths, the Myth of the Earth-grasper and the Deganawi:dah epic, represents in my opinion a response to the threat of the dominant culture by these narrators of ancient myths who seek to conserve as much of the old culture as possible within an ancient matrix. This is the whole history of the Longhouse movement, and it is exemplified among the Six Nations of Grand River by the career of Chief John A. Gibson, who was its greatest advocate.

The myth of the Sky-holder or Earth-grasper, according to Gibson and Hewitt, has three main parts which correspond to epochs. The first describes society of the Sky-world; the creation of the Earth upon the Turtle's back forms the second cosmical epoch; and the third is the World of Sapling, the period of primitive human society.

The sky-world is the upper surface of the visible sky. Here live manlike gods who have a culture like that of pre-Columbian woodland Indians who as persons manifest the emotional strengths and weaknesses of the Iroquois people of later times. In a clearing stands their village of typical bark-covered lodges which are extended to accommodate single maternal families. Newhouse said the lodges faced the rising sun and extended toward the sunset, a nice detail, but there was no sun yet. The only illumination is furnished by flowers on the tree of light which stands at the center beside the chief's lodge and for which he is named. Otherwise the environment consists of the familiar flora and fauna, specified or not, depending on the interest of the narrator. Entering the end doors, one finds along the interior walls of the lodges beds of rough bark where the occupants spread their mats to sleep and where they sit by day, each family having its own fire and compartment; these extend the length of the hallway to the opposite door.

After the morning meal the housemates go forth to their appointed tasks. The warriors are in the habit of going out to hunt in the mornings and of returning in the evenings. The older versions imply that this routine afforded the opportunity for a girl and a boy, who had been secluded or "downfended" after the old puberty custom, to get together: she goes over and combs his hair and somehow gets pregnant. The women of the family question her, but she refuses to tell. The lad meanwhile sickens and dies in a couvade over the birth of their daughter. He is buried on a scaffold in a spare room.

Gibson cleans up this incident and elaborates the plot by making the secluded youngsters siblings and putting them under the avuncular authority of the old man of the Sky-people, their mother's brother. Uncle becomes ill over some imagined omen, discloses the nature of death, and asks the Old Woman, his sister, to have him put up in a tree. The Iroquois love their dead, and the daughter or niece spends hours visiting the corpse and receives in one instance a wampum bracelet in token of paternity and in two instances instructions as to her marriage to the owner of the tree of light who is chief of a distant village.

The old wedding custom where the bride-to-be carries a basket of boiled bread by the forehead strap through the woods to the house of the groom, speaking to no one on the path, never ceases to fascinate Iroquois listeners, who thrill at the most detailed description. The bread, of sodden-corn flavored with berries, is a symbol of woman's skillful labor in raising and grinding corn in a wooden mortar. The forehead strap or tump line was as essential to woodland women for a variety of transport as her suburbanite sister's automobile is today. The directions for her journey, the hazards of getting lost and crossing a stream over a floating maple log, and the tabu on speaking to strangers on the path all heighten her anxiety of leaving home to qualify as a woman in her husband's settlement. Distant patrilocal residence poses a theoretical problem for the ethnologist as well as for the bride, since the later theory of this society is matrilineal and matrilocal (the daughters should bring spouses home to mother's longhouse), a dilemma to which I will return. On arriving at the grassy clearing surrounding the village, etiquette prescribes that she shall go directly to his house and go right on in through the door to where the fire burns in the center of the lodge. There before the owner of the celestial tree she puts down her basket at his feet where he lies in his bunk, saying, "We two marry," and then sits opposite with the fire between them. He will lay down a string of white corn and say, "Soak it and make mush." This was all standard bridal custom for the Iroquois until the middle of the last century.

But the mush-making proves an ordeal. The bride is expected to strip and without flinching endure the pain of having her naked body spattered with boiling mush. Then she suffers the added indignity of having the blistered skin licked off by ferocious white dogs with abrasive tongues. She thus earns the admiration of her torture-loving listeners by surviving the test, and then is persuaded to engage in the most intriguing footsie gambit of aboriginal literature, in which she makes up her bed at the foot of his, and they sleep *pied à pied*. Only the soles of their feet touch, yet in some unexplained way, they sit up, their breaths mingle, and she becomes pregnant. Rather than seeking a sanctimonious interpretation of the act, as Hewitt was inclined, I am confident that many Iroquois would think this funny. To complete the bridal contract, the groom sends back dried venison, of which he has an inexhaustible supply; this he compresses by shaking it down in her packbasket. Despite its density, she is enjoined not to readjust her forehead strap going home. She reports his message to the town council, instructing them to remove the mats from their houses so that it may rain corn and fill them; and they distribute the magic meat which expands to fill the council house. Then she goes back to his village to live.

If the marriage of Awenha:ih 'fertile flower' or 'Sky-woman' to Hodahe⁊ 'Standing tree', proprietor of the celestial tree and chief of the Sky-world, was not an unqualified success, at least it was not dull, and as an example of brittle monogamy, as Elsie Clews Parsons used to characterize the society of Hollywood, it is quite familiar to Iroquois listeners for whom the family means the maternal lineage. Confronted with the solid chain that runs from the eldest woman to the umbilical cord of the youngest infant-to-be, Iroquois spouses react sometimes as Sky-chief. A justifiable suspicion is augmented by jealousy, and it manifests itself in tests and in compulsive behavior. These ordeals are more or less reassuring, but since peace and domestic tranquility are always threatened and then broken by this strain of paranoia in the culture, individuals end in brooding and depression. Society employs several devices for diverting their minds: a game of ball, or a little dance, perhaps, while people try at random to guess his soul's desire as revealed in a dream. The other channel is active witchcraft. So when Sky-chief manifests symptoms of jealousy over his wife's blooming pregnancy, the community attempts to relieve his disturbed mind by guessing the word his soul desires. The dream feast, of which we read so much in the *Relations* of the Jesuit Fathers from Huronia, is held beneath the Tree of Light and attended by all the supernaturals of the pantheon except Wind. It has been foretold to Sky-woman what will be the verdict, so she counsels with her brother Earthquake, before returning to her spouse.

In myths of this length the sequence of events is not always clear. Part of the confusion arises from a device which narrators employ to post their listeners in advance of what is going to happen by letting them in on revelations that clairvoyants divulge to actors. It also builds up suspense. Thus in the Gibson version, Sky-chief has been holding a continuous dream feast dating back before his union with Sky-woman; she learns from her uncle's corpse, on a visit home, the nature of the dream which ordains and specifies her involvement. The dream that nobody has yet guessed, though they have diverted his mind, is a model of paranoid destruction: growing things shall wither, especially the flowers on the tree of light, which shall be uprooted so that he can shove them into the hole where he and his wife shall sit down on the brink, hang their feet over, and eat together. She is cautioned not to hesitate. Her name Awenha:ih 'Ripe blossom' makes her an acceptable bride because it fits into his plans. In the Onondaga versions the key word is "Tooth," a reference to the flowers on the tree; and Fire-dragon or meteor guesses it. In one Seneca variant the key word is "excrement." The satisfied dreamer cries *Kuh!* (Onondaga) or *Gwah!* (Seneca), as he still does at the Midwinter Festival. Since it is a cardinal principle of Iroquois culture that the consequences of revealed dreams must be carried out, they proceed to fulfill them. They uproot the tree, and Sky-woman and Sky-chief sit down as directed to eat the food that she has placed beside them. Standing suddenly, he takes her by the nape of the neck and shoves her into space into which she is peering. Versions differ as to her curiosity or his rage, or whether he takes her by the left leg or shoves her with his foot. Life in the Sky-world ends with the casting down of Sky-woman and the resetting of the tree.

The second epoch, which is concerned with the creation of the world on the turtle's back, consists of some eighteen episodes and opens with the fall of Sky-woman, who becomes Earth-mother, the Old Woman, and the wicked Grandmother. She falls through the sky's crust into darkness. Old John Buck (Onondaga) said that she went provisioned for her journey into space with three ears of corn, dried meat, and firewood stuffed in her bosom and carrying her child on her back; but Gibson and Armstrong (Seneca) say that these cultural gifts were presented by Meteor and included miniature mortar and pestle, a small pot, and a soup bone, and that in falling she brought her own earth scraped from the sides of the hole.

The spectacle of the Sky-woman falling through space, assisted by waterfowl, to the back of the turtle swimming in the primal sea is a favorite subject with Iroquois artists, with notable examples of Jesse Cornplanter and Ernest Smith of the Seneca, and Tom Dorsey of Onondaga. Loon notices her; Bittern, whose eyes are ever on the top of his head, remarks that she indeed is not coming from the depths of the water; the ducks go up to guide her landing, while the council of animals sends various divers to fetch up mud from the depths. Muskrat alone succeeds, but comes up dead, paws and mouth full of mud; Turtle volunteers, and Beaver with assistants plasters the mud on Turtle's carapace. Here Sky-woman is brought to rest, and immediately the earth starts expanding as she moves about and vegetation sprouts in her tracks. The process of the expanding earth will continue throughout creation. This cosmological notion of superimposed worlds from the tree of life, the sky-dome, and the first vegetation springing from the earth on the turtle's back has been reduced to curvilinear symbolism by generations of Iroquois women working in moosehair and quill embroidery and afterward in beads for decorating clothing.[17]

A daughter born to Sky-woman grows up rapidly and has a succession of animal suitors. On her mother's advice she accepts the fourth, the one with the dirty body who wears a deeply escalloped robe and leggings, who, naturally, is Turtle. He has several magic arrows, one having no point attached, which he keeps straightening, a characteristic motor habit of Iroquois arrow makers, and this one he leaves alongside of her body as she sleeps. In the Seneca version she is impregnated by the west wind while swinging at play on an uprooted tree; she descends to kneel on the grass, is entered by the wind, and is delighted. It does not take the old woman long to discover that her happy daughter is going to have a child. In this most unusual pregnancy she hears male voices quarreling within her body.

Of the twins who converse in the womb, the elder is born normally and becomes Sky-holder, alias Good-minded, Thrown-away, Sapling, the Creator, whose every act will symbolize and promote growth and fertility. The younger twin, the ugly one who is covered with warts and has a sharp comb of flint on his forehead, a motif that is memorialized in Seneca Falsefaces, seeks daylight and erupts through his mother's armpit, killing her. He is Flint (Ice), the Evil-minded, patron of winter, and author of monstrosities, bad luck and disaster. Flint becomes the favorite of his grandmother when he lies to her about cutting up his own dead mother, whom they bury in the doorway, and whose head they put up a tree for light. The theme of sibling rivalry dominates this period.

That grandmothers can be wicked and reject their grandsons is a hazard of growing up in a society that subscribes to the theory of matrilineal descent, inheritance, and succession. When Sky-woman tosses the elder twin into the brush to find shelter in a hollow tree, accepts the lying younger twin into her lodge, conspires against his elder brother, and then refuses to make bow and arrows for him, Thrown-away is driven to seek his father. As we shall see, the theme of the fatherless boy who becomes the hero permeates Iroquois folk history. One's father's line is always a second choice, after mother's brother, but father does impart certain culture gifts. Using a second magic arrow, which father has left, and a borrowed bow, Sky-holder shoots at a passing bird and parts the waters, revealing at the bottom of a lake his father's lodge, which he visits. Father Turtle, who holds-the-earth-in-his-two-hands, teaches the hero the arts of husbandry, the chase, and housebuilding; how to make fire; how to spit maize for roasting; and he gives the son several ears. In Seneca versions the father who is Wind offers as prize a flute and a heavy bag containing game animals to the winner among his four sons of a race around the earth. "So now the youth took up the bundle and packed it home by means of a burden strap." On arrival he announces having changed his name to "Maple Sprout" or "Sapling," in the Mohawk version. Sky-holder has also acquired a third magic arrow as proof against the water serpent and meteor, but it is not clear what use he made of it.

Sky-holder's acts of creation form the climax of this section. They are opposed and hindered by the evil grandmother, and they are offset by contrary acts of Flint. Here the growth principle is thwarted by frost, a dualism which symbolizes the alternation of seasons, and the contest goes on building up into a cosmic struggle for control of the earth. First comes the flora, starting with red osier for medicine, the grasses, shrubs, trees, and cultivated plants, including the sunflower for oil; Flint counters with thistle, poison ivy and other noxious weeds. Next come the birds, starting with Bluebird, the now extinct Passenger Pigeon that got immersed in bear oil so that afterward its squabs were fat. Handfuls of earth were cast into game animals. Flint makes a cosmic mistake by creating the bat which is, as an old Feather Dance song says, "the only animal that has teeth and yet flies." Rivers were created with two-way currents for man's convenience in travel; but Flint put in rapids and falls. Overcome by jealousy at the great ears of corn in Sky-holder's garden, Flint stunts them because many should not have it so good. Meanwhile Sky-holder is busy at man-making; and for the sake of balance, Old John Buck and Gibson have Flint making several species of apes which they obviously must have seen in zoological gardens but which quite enhance the narrative. When Sky-holder next looks around to view his creations, the game animals have disappeared, and only when Deermouse tells him does he discover where Flint has impounded them in a cave. Moving the rock, Sky-holder frees the game animals pent up by Flint, who tricks him afterward into releasing some monsters that might better have remained beneath the ground. Those that escaped in a thundering herd are the familiar game animals, but most of Flint's dangerously large animals remain imprisoned and are propitiated by the medicine societies of later times. This alternate impounding and release symbolizes hibernation and spring, as annually the animals go to earth and then reappear with young.

The climax is reached in a cosmic struggle of two phases between Sky-holder and his enemies to which the uncommitted game animals and humans are witnesses. In the first half he contends with his grandmother in the game of peach pits for which the "great bet" is the control of the earth. Each summons and exerts his *orenda* or magic power; each uses his own dice. For Sky-holder the dice are the heads of six volunteer chickadees who score for him "a clear field" (all of a color). Even today the duality of nature in the procession of summer and winter is dramatized at Green Corn and Midwinter festivals when the two halves of the longhouse community alternately symbolize the Master of Life (Sky-holder) and Sky-woman, one taking the eastern position, since east is life, and the other sitting west, which is winter and death, to contend in the Bowl Game.

In the second half, Sky-holder and Flint struggle to the death with avowed fatal weapons. Flint confesses that antler and flint will do him in and elicits from Sky-holder the secret that maize and rushes are his weakness. (Every Indian knew that antler would chip flint.) So Sky-holder goes around putting these objects up high and handy. Round the world they go heaving rocks and flinging mountains until, in some versions, nothing is left but their bones to be gathered by grandmother.

At this point occur two interruptions in most versions. A contest of power with the mask being, and the theft of light by Sky-holder and assisting animals, forestall the banishment of Flint and Sky-holder's return to the Sky-world.

The episode of the encounter between the Creator who is out inspecting his works and Haduʔiʔ, the hunch-backed master of winds, patron of disease, gamekeeper and tutelary of the Falseface Society of later times, is deeply rooted in mythology and is evidently ancient. The dramatic incident underscores the importance that the

Iroquois attach to this grotesque character who occupies a central place in their supernatural world, who is memorialized by hundreds of masks in museums, and who is celebrated by ceremonies among the Longhouse Iroquois today. A test of power evokes the familiar incident of moving a mountain while holding the breath, in which impetuous Haduʔiʔ smashes his nose in avid curiosity to see Sky-holder's success, thereby losing the contest. The forfeit is a promise not to harm the people but to rid the earth of disease, to dwell on the margins of the earth, and to coach the Falseface Society whose members shall call him "our dear grandfather." Power to cure disease is given to those who wear masks and impersonate him, compensating for man's gift of tobacco in perpetual contract. He leagues with Sky-holder to rid the earth of Flint's monsters and promises not to harm the people. The ritual detail that is projected on mythology belongs to the description of later ceremonies. Here also belongs the use of tobacco "to send up one's words" to the supernaturals as in White Dog Sacrifice.[18]

The theft of light by Sky-holder and his animal helpers is a separate mythological episode having no contemporary counterpart. The plot is to secure the head of Earth-mother from a treetop where Sky-woman hung it, or put it in orbit for the use of man. Small mammals work together at canoe building, in voyaging, in guarding the boat, and in escape. Sky-holder makes his debut as Sapling in one version, but having no instep, uses antlers for climbing hooks; but Gibson has the Creator, Sapling's alter ego, manipulate his feet for shinning. Sapling's sudden descent with the head explains how the Sycamore tree got its scabs. Fox gets away with the sun in his mouth, and Black squirrel takes it over the treetops to the landing where the magic flight continues, Muskrat or Otter being clobbered with a paddle for talking back to the pursuing grandmother. Enormous variation in detail, in characters, and in episode indicate that this by no means uniquely Iroquoian motif is widespread in North America.

The epoch of creation closes by rapidly assigning roles to the actors in the mid-pantheon of service to mankind and returning others to the Sky-world. Earth-mother becomes "grandmother moon" and regulates women's affairs. Father Turtle, the Earth-grasper, becomes morning star, the Day-bringer. Sky-woman returns home, but her brother becomes "Elder brother the Day-Sun." Monsters are relegated to the mountains, and Thunders, "Our grandfathers whose voices reverberate from toward the sunset," keep an eye on them and bring rain to water crops until the end of time when they shall come from the east, foretelling the end of the world. The two brothers return to the Sky-world via the Milky Way, afterward the path of souls, which is forked to accommodate divergent careers and divided minds.

Sapling's world is the epoch of human society in the first times, which are described in some sixty pages, the final third of Gibson's text. It is a long period of enormous growth and expansion. Sapling, who in the older versions is an alias for the Creator, is the first man and culture hero; but various crises occur for which there are no traditional solutions, and this requires the Creator to make four returns in the guise of Sapling or the fatherless boy, a young man who proposes the clan system. The proposals draw heavily on the cultural memory of Gibson's sources, and I think that this explains the length of the myth and the compulsive character of its contents, which makes it a more rigid document than shorter, freer versions of John Buck and Armstrong, who were themselves, together with their audience, nearer to the old life. Gibson felt that his hearers needed to know.

I propose to reserve these rich cultural materials for appropriate use later on and confine the discussion here to structural, literary, and thematic considerations. Eight episodes are telescoped in as many paragraphs.

Odendonniha 'Sapling' and *Awenhaniyonda* 'Hanging Flower' are the first couple. They beget offspring and the people multiply. The Thunders water their crops when appealed to with tobacco.

The second coming of the Creator is occasioned by the need to teach the people the Four Ceremonies of thanksgiving which are sacred to the Creator and are the house-posts of later Longhouse festivals. The order of celebration and the content of the specified rituals is naturally that of Onondaga on Grand River. In general, the ceremonial cycle is balanced between a summer in-gathering of crops and a midwinter festival, coming after the hunt, marked by stirring cold ashes, kindling a new fire, dream guessing and renewal, and climaxed by the White Dog Sacrifice. Between festivals, it is the matron's duty to return thanks at dawn and dusk. Etiquette of hospitality or greeting and of departing is prescribed. The address of greeting and thanks to all the spirit-forces of the pantheon, the familiar Iroquois *Kanonyonk*, which opens all public gatherings and prefaces every day of religious celebrations to this day, enumerates gifts that the Creator left on earth for man's use and enjoyment from the grass to the Sky-world.

The third coming of Sky-holder is occasioned by a typically Indian division of kindred into factions. Persons disappear; murder eclipses the sun. The elaborate ceremony for compounding murders and quickening the dead appears much later. Sapling seizes this opportunity to teach the first fruits ceremonies.

"For some time," we read, "the ceremonies were carried on correctly, and then again, there began to be disagreements." Disphoria over gossip becomes intense. The fourth, and since this is the magic number, the last appearance of the Creator is occupied by formal teaching of values afterward stressed in the Handsome Lake doctrine. Two aspects of ethnobotany receive attention. Herbal medicine, in which the Iroquois have a continuing interest, because they constantly suffer from real and imagined illnesses, depends on the necessity of botanical accuracy and must be imparted systematically, whereas symptomatology can remain vague as in their concept of "Disease, the faceless." The introduction of maize horticulture and the cycle of ceremonies attending its growth and maturation is accomplished by sending a pubescent boy and girl to find the "three sisters" (maize, beans, and squash) growing in the footprints of the gods, leading to the grave of Earth-mother and then having them report their discoveries to the town council. Inhumation has succeeded scaffold burial. Communal agriculture and mutual aid commence. From this episode two themes may be stated: only the pure may seek and find medicine and other cultural gifts; there shall be regular ways of organizing group activity, and these will become set in ritual.

A human being dies and the elders put the problem to the town council. An unknown young man, fulfilling the classic "no father" theme, proposes that they bury him. It is decided that in such events the elders shall choose a speaker to address the relatives, review with thanks the Creator's gifts, especially for herbal medicines that are used in sickness; and he shall anticipate that with the formation of clans the moieties shall function in turn to "lift up the minds" of the bereaved relatives. These things shall be the responsibility of elders.

Similarly woman's priority in matters affecting continuity of life is affirmed by placing control of these affairs in the hands of the matron of the *Ohwachira*, i.e., matrilineage. The Iroquois feel that this is consistent with the forces of nature. This statement is bound to provoke an argument among ethnologists and historians; indeed Gibson may have projected his own view on the past. In the legend of clan origin, a young man leads half of the families into crossing the river on a vine, the other half being left on the near shore. Camps on both banks are instructed that when their women go at dawn to water always to dip with the stream and to observe carefully and remember the behavior or character of the first bird or animal seen. These creatures become the eponyms of the familiar Iroquois clans, and, as we shall see, clan sets of personal names evolve.

A related problem that has to be settled by the elders is the establishment of a regular place of council, a concern that will crop up throughout history. The seating of the clans and their function in government occasions some movement across the council fire.

This long creation myth ends on two notes that provide the themes for understanding the stability and persistence of Iroquois culture during three centuries. The culture as ordained shall endure as long as does human society, the earth, its resources, and its products. This sentiment we shall encounter again and again throughout history, particularly in the Iroquois view of their agreements with the whites. "As long as the sun shines, the waters flow, and the grass grows"—so runs the line in the treaties. Related to it is the ending: "There shall always be tribes of people living on either side of the river."

The second note is the theme that culture is an affair of the mind: they thank the young man for the most important work that he has accomplished, in the creation of clan society, and they commemorate his contribution by giving him a new name, "He of the great mind."

A word about literary devices and style. The most conspicuous device that Gibson employs is the use of opening and closing lines for transition. "So-and-so began to travel from place to place" is the usual opening line of a fable, and Gibson employs it to introduce an incident. Another form of transition, which gives pause, after a series of actions, is: "So-and-so thought many things"; or "So-and-so returned to where his lodge stood." Typical ending lines are: "Now at that time they two went home"; or "Then he went elsewhere." Certain other connectors bind society to the future, as we have seen, as, for example, when after the Bowl Game the narrative concludes: "Human beings who dwell on the earth shall continue to relate it." Most of these devices refer to time and movement.

As Hewitt himself points out, the myth "is told partly in the language of tradition and of ceremony, which is formal, sometimes quaint, sometimes archaic, frequently mystical, and largely metaphorical." What this means is that when narrated in council or before a public gathering, the speaker would lapse into the high, intoned preaching style of council oratory which is an art in itself and which would markedly affect the impact if not the form of the myth. (A more intimate style of delivery characterizes the telling of tales by the fireside when a native folklorist impersonates the characters, and he and his audience live out the plot and incidents.) The figures of speech become concrete in the thought patterns of the Iroquois who regard the metaphors as fact. "Floating foam" is a figure that must have caught the fancy of some early storyteller. Rivermen know the flecks of foam beneath rapids; herbalists see it well to the surface when boiling roots; and women by the stream side observe it in dipping water. The "path" has many uses, referring to a course of action, to one's career, to the route of souls to the hereafter, as when the Creator says: "Where my path will have ended, there shall you find corn, beans, and squash growing from the grave of Earth-mother." I remember as a boy being entranced by Thornton W. Burgess's "bluebird that whistles off the snow"; but it is indeed bluebird in the *Iroquoian Cosmology* that gives the death cry—*Ko:weh!* (five times)—and frightens off the glacier, breaking up Flint's winter.

One final example. The ever-growing tree stands for life, status, and authority—for society itself. Uprooting the tree of peace and casting all evil weapons of war into a bottomless pit to be carried away by the stream, and then replanting the tree represents a kind of denial of reality so that life may go on. Thus we saw Sky-chief push all living things including his pregnant wife beneath the sky's crust and then replant the tree of heaven. Indian oratory is replete with this metaphor. Likewise a pine tree symbolizes chiefship, and the tree falls with the death of a chief; but the office continues, so the tree is raised up again with his successor. And finally, there is thought to be a giant elm at the center of the earth where the Masker rubs his rattle and derives his strength. We will find it again in art forms.[19]

We have seen that four is the magic number, imposing four tasks, so the listener always knows which will be the last. Suspense is created in other ways. Sky-holder directs Sapling, his alter ego, to go around and pick up antlers or flints as he sees them lying about and put them up handy. There is going to be a fight. Irony is conveyed when the wicked grandmother addresses Thrown-away, whom she hates, as "my dear grandson."

I will now summarize, as "Papa Franz" Boas used to say, by

enumerating the main themes in Iroquois life as drawn from concepts in the cosmology. I have reduced these to twenty.

1. *The native earth*: the earth, our mother, is living and expanding constantly, imparting its life-giving force to all growing things on which our lives depend.

2. *Renewal*: the alternation of seasons and tasks is attuned to ecological time as are the lives of plants and animals that rest when the earth sleeps.

3. *"It is us women that count"*: a chain of kinship connects all members of society running from the dead through our mothers to the smallest child whose life is separated from the spirit world as the thinness of a maple leaf, and even those yet unborn whose faces turn this way from beneath the ground. Consequently the Iroquois love their dead and cherish their children.

4. *Paternity is a secondary consideration*: *Agadoni* comes after *Ohwachira*. The fatherless boy becomes hero, but the boy rejected by his matrilineage may seek his father and learn.

5. *Twins are lucky*, and creative, but siblings fight. Only the pure who have been downfended or secluded succeed.

6. *The law of the kettle*: hospitality is a right and a duty to share. Throwing ashes is the negation of sharing, hospitality, friendship, peace, harmony and accord; but it is typically paranoid behavior that occurs all of the time in the culture.

7. *Home is where one customarily sits*. The bench or bed is the place of reflection and of council.

8. *Do not oppose the forces of nature*: going to water, traveling, making medicine, participating in ceremonial circuits.

9. *There is a regular way*: life and customary procedures are fairly established.

10. *Orenda* (supernatural power) adheres to animate and inanimate things, to aspects of the environment, and to sequences of behavior.

11. *Restraint is important*: one must not exert too much power and "spoil it." The equable person succeeds.

12. Acting the role by impersonation is a means of taking on power.

13. *Kanonyonk*: By continual and repeated greeting and thanks, the hierarchy of spirit-forces between the earth and sky that the Creator appointed to assist man in the enjoyment of the earth must be remembered and balanced in the fulfillment of their tasks.

14. *Dreams compel fulfillment*: Seeking the "word" that the soul desires, which once discovered must be fulfilled, involves diverting the mind by games, dances, and so on, and these prescribed ceremonies are subject to annual renewal for life.

15. The column of smoke, which carried the gods back to the sky-world, is a vehicle for sending up words. Smoke itself symbolizes thought, desire, community, and government. Tobacco is the "word" and closes the contract.

16. Earth-shakers are friendly spirits to be awed and propitiated: Turtle, Thunder, Haduʔiʔ, the Bigheads.

17. A man never refuses when asked, and he never shows fear.

18. *Things go by twos and fours*: forked path, divided mind, sex, seasons, moieties, life-death, balance of forces.

19. A pattern of reciprocity obtains between moieties for quickening life and faculties, for restoring society, and for all ceremonial associations of renewal.

20. Culture is an affair of the mind.

Notes

1. This paper was given as the address of the retiring president of the American Folklore Society in Philadelphia on 28 December 1960. *The People of the Longhouse* is the title of a general book on the Iroquois Indians of New York which the writer has in preparation for Farrar, Straus and Cudahy of New York.

2. Morris E. Opler, "An Application of the Theory of Themes in Culture," *Journal of the Washington Academy of Sciences*, XXXVI (1946), 137–166.

3. This is becoming true throughout the continent. See the author's "Folklore (American Indian)," *Encyclopaedia Britannica* (1960).

4. The cosmogonic myth is reported in detail in an account of Gallinée's visit to the Seneca towns in 1670 (see *Découvertes et Établissements des Français dans l'ouest et dans le sud de l'Amérique Septentrionale . . .* , ed. Pierre Margry, I [Paris, 1876], 360–362). Descendants of the Huron who were afterward called Wyandot were living at Detroit in 1872, when Horatio Hale of Clinton, Ontario, visited them and collected their ancient traditions (see Horatio Hale, "Huron Folk-Lore," *Journal of American Folklore*, 1 [1888], 177–183). Later Marius Barbeau confirmed Hale's findings in his *Huron and Wyandot Mythology, Geological Survey Memoir* 80 (Ottawa, 1915), collated earlier variants from Sagard and the Jesuits to recent sources, and has recently published the Huron-Wyandot texts which he recorded phonetically from the last speakers of the language in Oklahoma in 1912 in his *Huron-Wyandot Traditional Narratives*, National Museum of Canada, Bulletin 165 (Ottawa, 1960). In his "Sketches of the Ancient History of the Six Nations," published in *The Iroquois Trail, or Foot-prints of the Six Nations*, ed. William M. Beauchamp (Fayetteville NY, 1892), David Cusick prefaces his sketches with "A tale of the foundation of the Great Island (now North America), the two infants born, and the creation of the universe." To the same genre, if not to the same source, belong Elias Johnson, *Legends, Traditions, and Laws of the Iroquois, of Six Nations . . .* (Lockport NY, 1881); Henry R. Schoolcraft, *Notes on the Iroquois, Proceedings of the American Philosophical Society*, IV (1846), 611–633; Erminnie A. Smith, *Myths of the Iroquois*, 2nd Annual Report, *Bureau of American Ethnology* (1881), pp. 47–116; and the twentieth-century author and artist Jesse J. Cornplanter, *Legends of the Longhouse* (New York, 1938).

In addition to the latter three versions, for the Iroquois proper there are Seneca variants which were written down by New England missionaries at Buffalo Creek (see William N. Fenton, ed., "Seneca Indians by Asher Wright (1859)," *Ethnohistory*, IV [1957], 305–307), and folklorists Jeremiah Curtin (see *Seneca Fiction, Legends, and Myths*, ed. Jeremiah Curtin and J. N. B. Hewitt, 32nd Annual Report, *BAE* [1918], p. 460); Harriet Maxwell Converse (see *Myths and Legends of the New York State Iroquois*, ed. Harriet M. Converse and Arthur C. Parker, New York State Museum, Bulletin 125 [Albany, 1908] pp. 31–38), and Arthur C. Parker, who was himself of Seneca descent (see Arthur C. Parker, *Seneca Myths and Folk Tales, Buffalo Historical Society Publications*, No. 27 [1923] pp. 59–73). And to complete the roster of Iroquoianists who collected the cosmogonic myth, F. W. Waugh found Oneida, Cayuga, and Tuscarora variants on the Six Nations Reserve (see Martha C. Randle, *The Waugh Collection of Iroquois Folktales, Proceedings of the American Philosophical Society*, XCVII [1953], 629); and Reverend William M. Beauchamp, who with Hale was a charter member of this society, collected it at Onondaga (see William M. Beauchamp, *Iroquois Folk Lore Gathered from the Six Nations of New York*, Onondaga Historical Association, Syracuse NY, [1922]). Not excerpted are the four versions—Mohawk, Seneca, and two Onondaga— which comprise J. N. B. Hewitt's *Iroquoian Cosmology; First Part*, 21st Annual Report, BAE (1900), pp. 127–339; and *Iroquoian Cosmology; Second Part, with Introduction and Notes*, 43rd Annual Report, BAE (1928), pp. 449–819, which are my principal sources.

5. Randle, *The Waugh Collection of Iroquois Folktales*, p. 629.

6. Stith Thompson, *Tales of the North American Indians* (Cambridge MA, 1929); Thompson, *Motif-Index*; Earl W. Count, "The Earth-Diver and the Rival Twins: a Clue to the Time Correlation in North-Eurasiatic and North American Mythology," in *Selected Papers of the 29th International Congress of Americanists. Indian Tribes of Aboriginal America*, ed. Sol Tax (Chicago, 1952), pp. 55–62; Anthony F. C. Wallace, "Revitalization Movements," *American Anthropologist*, LVIII (1955), 264–281; Anthony F. C. Wallace, "The Dekanawideh Myth Analyzed as the Record of a Revitalization Movement," *Ethnohistory*, V (1958), 118–130.

7. A. A. Goldenweiser, "The Death of Chief John A. Gibson," AA, XIV (1912), 692–694; William N. Fenton, "Simeon Gibson: Iroquois Informant (1889–1943)," AA, XLVI (1944), 231–234; John R. Swanton, "John Napoleon Brinton Hewitt," AA, XL (1938), 286–290.

8. Goldenweiser; Hewitt, *Iroquoian Cosmology; Second Part*, pp. 453–454.

9. Hewitt, *Iroquoian Cosmology; Second Part*.

10. See Swanton.

11. Hewitt, *Iroquoian Cosmology; First Part*, p. 134.

12. William N. Fenton, *Seth Newhouse's Traditional History and Constitution of the Iroquois Confederacy*, Proceedings of the American Philosophical Society, XCIII (1949), 153–157.

13. The history of the Conference on Iroquois Research, which has been held annually at Red House NY since 1945, is recorded in two places: William N. Fenton, *Symposium on Local Diversity in Iroquois Culture*, BAE, Bulletin 149 (1961), p. 4; and *Symposium on Cherokee and Iroquois Culture*, ed. William N. Fenton and John Gulick, BAE, Bulletin 180 (1961).

14. Hewitt, *Iroquoian Cosmology; First Part*, p. 139.

15. Thompson, *Tales of the North American Indians*, pp. 279–280.

16. Count (see fn. 7).

17. Following the lead of Frank G. Speck, who undoubtedly discovered the

double-curved motif, Arthur C. Parker demonstrated among the Iroquois an even richer oral and decorative art involving symbolic trees and growing plants; cf. Arthur C. Parker, "Certain Iroquois Tree Myths and Symbols," *AA*, XIV (1913), 608–620.

18. J. N. B. Hewitt, "White Dog Sacrifice," in *Handbook of American Indians*, ed. F. W. Hodge, *BAE*, Bulletin 30 (1912), II, 939–944.

19. Parker, "Certain Iroquois Tree Myths and Symbols."

"Anthropology and the University"

An Inaugural Lecture

I

President Collins, Dean Perlmutter, Associate Dean Wheeler, colleagues, fellow students, ladies and gentlemen: were one to do this properly in the idiom of the ancient speakers of this country whenever they kindled a fire and raised a column of smoke for all mankind to witness their proceedings, one should properly say: Swayanéshon, Swásendagéhde, Swatíno?en?, Swadiksa?son?onh heyo:dak—that is, "You who are of chiefly lineage, You who are warriors, You matrons, and even You Children." We are met here today to light a fire for a new kind of learning in this university, and perhaps to establish a way of doing it that fulfills both the great tradition of Old World learning and conforms to a custom of the New World. When at the Moon of Midwinter I quit the duties of tending the council fire that smolders a few miles east toward the River and came out here and put down my bundles at the edge of the Pine Bush, near what the old people called Skanéhtate, "Beyond the pines," I was greeted by a charming colleague and led by the arm to this place. At first I was a little confused as to what was expected of me, not knowing the customs of this place, but I was told that the Old World custom of the Salon had recently been established here and I was invited to address it. But when I demurred, saying "next year," since I was on the point of leaving to attend the Seneca Midwinter Festival, it was suggested that there was yet a higher form of ceremony at European universities: when a new professor takes up his duties he is expected to give an inaugural lecture. My persuasive colleague further suggested that this custom ought to be introduced at SUNYA, and because it appealed to my sense of the fitness of things, I accepted. Especially since I was given this spring semester to think and to write and was not expected to teach until fall, I welcomed the opportunity to speak to the university community on how anthropology fits into the scheme of things. I do this because I thoroughly believe that teaching is the first responsibility of a university professor. Communicating what one has learned by reading, observing, interviewing, and other forms of original investigation is but part of the continuum of "increase and diffusion of knowledge among men," to borrow James Smithson's prophetic words, of which teaching is one stage and publication is merely the terminal stage. Some of my ideas are yet in the formative stage and some of my examples are drawn from publications.

Having made this commitment, I decided that if I were to be a research professor I had best renew my craft. So I did two things: I immediately went to the field to revisit my Seneca friends whose grandparents had guided my pre-doctoral training and then afforded me a post-doctoral education in politics during the New Deal, and then I went out to the Henry E. Huntington Library, in San Marino, California, to read with the humanists. Both were liberalizing experiences of different sorts. While it would be nice to report some discovery among the manuscripts and rare books I examined in the library, I must confess that it was an incident which climaxes the Seneca Midwinter Festival which afforded the motif for the poster advertising this lecture and which gave me the theme for outlining my topic.

The Husk Faces or "Bushy Heads," in Seneca, make their appearance on the fifth and sixth days of the Midwinter Festival at Coldspring Longhouse. These mute maskers with straw or corn husk faces race over snow-covered fields between houses to warn the people that the proper False Faces, who wear wooden masks, are on the way to blow ashes on the heads of all who have dreamed of them or have been cured by them in the past. The Husk Face heralds carry peeled hickory poles with which they knock down anything that gets in their way, be they dogs or persons. They too have the power of curing by blowing ashes on the head, shoulders and elbows of their hosts. And they have a special song and a dance of their own. One of them hands a pole to an old man who raps out the rhythm on the floor and intones their song of nonsense vocables to which each Husk masker dances around his pole. Their reward is popcorn, which bespeaks their association with cultivated crops.

But it is on the sixth evening of the festival during the haste to discharge all ceremonial obligations incurred through dreams that the Husk Faces appear en masse and dominate the ceremony. Before they arrive they send their messengers racing through the longhouse from opposite ends three times; at each pass of the heralds the main body is known to be getting closer. They slam the doors as they enter and leave and dancers scurry for the benches to avoid them. This year the second pass interrupted the activity of False Face beggars and clowns— mostly small boys who beg for gum or tobacco, but also young men who compete at dancing. There is always one memorable beggar. This year it was a visitor from Newton Longhouse on Cattaraugus who impersonated "Sumo," the Japanese wrestler. Wearing Karate dress, he bounded barefoot into the women's end of the longhouse, combining Karate postures with classic False Face antics. He wore a mask of lemon-colored wood with crooked mouth, but hairless. All the youngsters in one voice mouthed, "Sumo!" (presumably some TV character from the new folklore). Sumo stayed for a half hour, preempting the attention of the best singers whom the women sent the master of ceremonies to fetch, and he was still there near the men's stove at the second romp of the Husk Face heralds. One of them rushed him over toward the stove, cross-checking with his stave, and they both kicked at each other Karate style. This exchange produced much laughter.

The people of Coldspring have a new longhouse that was built for them after the compensation was received for the Kinzua Dam which extinguished their old fire. At the old longhouse, which was clapboarded, the Husk Faces used to announce their arrival by drumming on the outside of the building with their staves, or rubbing them like a rasp down the boards. But they no longer do this, I discovered, because it would mar the new paint. But this ritual casualty aside, they have preserved the main feature of the ceremony: at the third passage of the messengers, they capture some old man and take him outside where he is briefed on the purpose of their visit. He always says certain standard things, ending with a prophecy. "These people say that they have come from the east and they are hurrying westward to their homes where it is summer to till their crops which they plant amid great stumps in a ravine." At this point, the interpreter pretends to forget and says: "Because a year has passed since I have seen their chief matrons,—who are named Great Ears of Corn, Giant String Beans, and Many Squash who tell me that they have left some of the women at home to tend to many crying babies—I forget, so I shall have to go out again to find out what else they have to say." All of this portends a good harvest for the people of the earth. It also means that society will continue. The prophet usually returns and ends by making some predictions about how it is going to be in the next year: "that hopefully the war will end and your sons will be returned to see the ceremonies once again."

Casting myself in the role of the public interpreter, and having explained the poster which announced this lecture, I shall speak on the nature of anthropology and what we may expect from it in this university.

II

Anthropology at the State University of New York at Albany, as at many universities, is placed with the social sciences where it is lodged momentarily with sociology at the west end of the Academic Podium.

This arrangement is convenient because it is partly based on kinship but its logic is mainly administrative and conforms to the recent history of the discipline. Anthropology, however, is interested in the whole of human behavior, which it views in the context of social and historical reality, and studies in the manner of the natural sciences; and anthropology is therefore equally at home in the humanities and in the natural sciences, out of which it emerged. But anthropology is not all things to all men and it is not a new form of academic imperialism; however, it has developed specialties in each of the three major areas of human learning and its few remaining generalists range all over the academic lot. And even those of us who are deeply committed to a specialty, whether it is human genetics, which is a natural science, or ethnohistory or linguistics, which are humanities, maintain a sense of kinship with all the rest. The reason for this holism lies in the culture concept to which we shall return momentarily.

But a lot of younger people act as if they were ignorant of this. It must have come as somewhat of a shock to younger anthropologists when, in 1954, Kroeber inquired into the placement of anthropology in American universities, and discovered what he knew all along: that its ascription to the social sciences is relatively recent. Its former ties were with the natural sciences, which is evident in the fact that both the American Association for the Advancement of Science and the National Academy of Sciences originally linked anthropology to psychology because both were thought to be marginal to biology. Kroeber writes: "As a matter of fact, even beyond its frankly biological constituent, anthropology is in part natural science, in part humanity, only secondarily social science. And so far as it has a social science ingredient, it prevalently treats the data of this historically, which the core social sciences do only to a minor degree" (Kroeber, 1954:765).

Kroeber then made a chart on which he scaled the learned fields, starting on the left with "Wholly Natural Science," then "Social and Natural," at the center "Core of Social Sciences," then to the right, "Social and Humanities," and at the extreme right, "Wholly Humanities."

Anthropology finds two modal points and a median point within this scale. Modal Point I of Anthropology lies between "Wholly Natural Science" and "Social and Natural"; it comprises Physical Anthropology and Cultural Anthropology (Ethnology). At the midpoint, falls Social Anthropology beneath the "Core Social Sciences." To the right, Model Point II lies between "Social and Humanities (History)" and "Wholly Humanities" and comprises Linguistic Anthropology and Archaeology. The centralizing tendency of all of these fields, it may be pointed out, again may be ascribed to the focal concept of culture.

Kroeber makes four sets of observations on his chart. These relate to features of anthropology which distinguish between it and the more typical social sciences. (1) "The natural sciences utilize museums as research apparatus in their natural history aspects, and the humanities have art museums. Anthropology grew out of expeditions and museums; teaching of the subject began quite hesitantly a full generation later. But there have never been any museums of sociology." (2) Comparative linguists and anthropologists understand each other's work, and anthropology has had some really distinguished linguists. There is a similar sharing of views and work in archaeology with specialists in the high civilizations. Culture history, moreover, is shared with the latter, with historians of ideas and of science, and by anthropologists. (3) Several diagnostic practices and concerns of anthropological research—individual bodily measures, face-to-face intimate inquiry from individuals, learning a language both as a tool and as an end, and first-hand discovery of concrete remainders of people's pasts—have not been characteristic practices of sociology, which is "the nearest analog to anthropology in the core social sciences." (4) Kroeber's fourth point related to the use of the comparative approach, which emphasizes the remote equally with the familiar, and which may be open to argument, but the stress on fundamental findings before immediately practical ones does align anthropology" with biology, geology, and astronomy rather than with sociology, economics, and government" (Ibid., 765).

The close nexus between anthropology and museums is documented by the careers of the more famous old departments of anthropology here and in Europe. At the leading universities on both continents, the teaching of the subject has grown "up alongside or out of a museum of anthropology," or the department has maintained a close liaison by exchange of teachers and students with a great independent museum, usually a natural history museum, as is the case in New York, Chicago, London, Paris, and Berlin.

"Anthropology" then, according to this view, "may be defined as basically a science concerned with the natural history of the totality of those human activities whose higher achievements in civilized societies have long been the domain of the humanities; though the anthropological intent and approach are naturalistic even when applied to humanistic and subhumanistic data" (Ibid., 766). The addition in recent decades of "a social science component and some degree of social science orientation" and the history of joint-tenancy with sociology in many institutions has given anthropology the complexion of a social science.

The real cause of this, however, was the moving out from the museum to the university and the subsequent concentration on research problems related to teaching that emphasized non-material culture—social organization, ceremonialism, and the newer fields such as culture and personality. Already in 1920 the book-minded and the verbal-minded had been exposed to the subject, and the object-minded had all passed into archaeology, until there were few ethnographers in the 1930's with an interest in material culture and no longer did professors bring objects into class for demonstration or require any familiarity with collections of their students. We now have anthropologists who have never worked in a museum in any capacity, and who have never made a collection in the field.

Having dispelled some of the illusions about anthropology being a social science, I should perhaps agree with Kroeber and Lévi-Strauss that the added social science ingredient has broadened and balanced anthropology and that it is here to stay. But as Kroeber comments in a later paper, when anthropology and sociology are placed side by side, they exhibit a duality and a paradox: how diverse they are in what they specifically do and yet how alike they are in assumptions and basic theory (Kroeber, 1959:398).

When anthropologists are counting coup, which is the widespread American Indian custom of striking a post, a drum, or a shield and then reciting one's exploits on the warpath, they customarily brag of their recognition and participation in all three learned councils: The National Academy of Sciences—National Research Council, The Social Science Research Council, and the American Council of Learned Societies. This span of learned fields has occasioned much comment both within and without the discipline, since anthropology beat the other social sciences into the National Science Foundation; but it might be added that anthropology should be regarded as a field *sui generis* and that its devotees are bound together around the globe in "a common interest in the total history of man and in his nature as both a biological and social creature" (Casagrande *in* Mandelbaum, Lasker and Albert, 1963:462). These common interests find their expression in the International Union of Anthropological and Ethnological Sciences. Inasmuch as I have been involved in all of these organizations in some way, perhaps a few comments are in order.

When anthropologists are wearing their social science feathers, they are wont to recall their participation in World War II, when most of us were in Washington. Specifically, they recall the joint efforts of a number of disciplines working on a common problem or to compile and interpret the cultural resources of a particular world area. Having witnessed this development myself from the vantage point of the Ethnogeographic Board (this was a clearing house for the three learned councils that was set up at the Smithsonian Institution to mediate between the community of scholars and the urgent needs of the intelligence services), and then having myself gone out and visited the nascent area programs in selected universities across the country, which I reported on individually before publishing the results of the survey, I must acknowledge that the initial impetus for area studies came from the humanists at the American Council of Learned Societies, where the intensive language training program started (Bennett, 1947). It was Mortimer Graves who asked the Ethnogeographic Board to send an anthropologist around to the universities to see what kind of a job was being done on the cultural aspects of the areas to fulfill a common directive which had issued from the War Department. I found that in each college and university the directive was being interpreted according to the local way of doing things. In effect, each of the programs could be understood only as manifestations of the local academic culture. Often enough, however, social scientists and humanists put aside departmental loyalties to pool their disciplines during the war, and it was they who returned afterward to advance area studies as part of the continuing curriculum. Only then did the Social Science Research Council commission several thoughtful appraisals of its potentialities for education (Fenton, 1947; Seward, 1950; Casagrande, 1963).

One other comment on the participation of anthropologists and other social scientists in government may be in order. That is on the problem of communicating research to the policy-making level. I fear that this problem is still with us and that we have learned nothing from history in this regard. Time and again during World War II, teams of specialists were assigned a task. They wrote their reports, they defended their recommendations in panels, only to have the policy makers who received their reports and recommendations turn to the old China hands or to some military officer who had done his service within a military installation in the country and who naturally thought that he knew all about the people in question. More often than not, the panel's advice was ignored. Important decisions went this way contrary to the findings of social scientists, contrary to the welfare of the United States, and detrimental to the welfare of the people in the affected area. If the truth were known, the decision to drop the bomb was of this sort (Leighton, 1949). Political decisions go on being made without the direct participation of social scientists, and our present tragic involvement in Vietnam rests on a misreading of the situation, an ignorance of history, and a failure to realize that Vietnamese nationalism, if we can speak of it at all, depends on the strength of villages and the confidence in headmen elected by these villagers, while the constitutional fiction of representative government which has been conjured in our image seemingly has no validity in the local culture.

Despite its many ramifications and liaisons with its sister disciplines, the urge toward autonomy runs strong in anthropology. While we anthropologists at Albany are content for the moment to dwell in the same house with sociology, if not in the same room, I am happy that this university plans that anthropology should make its way toward separate departmental status within the social sciences in the near future. I regard this as essential.

Perhaps I may end this part of the discussion with a comment from a colleague who participated in an appraisal of anthropology today and who has written a definitive paper for UNESCO on "The Place of Anthropology in the Social Sciences and Problems raised in teaching it," and whom I regard as the wisest prophet of the moment. Professor Claude Lévi-Strauss of the Collège de France, speaking at the bi-centennial of the birth of James Smithson, remarked:

There has been much question lately as to whether anthropology belonged among the humanities or among the natural sciences. In my opinion this is a false problem, since anthropology has the unique feature of not lending itself to such a distinction. It has the same subject matter as history, but for the lack of time perspective it cannot use the same methods. Its own methods tend rather toward those of the sciences not devoted to the study of man, though synchronically oriented like anthropology itself. As in every other scientific undertaking, these methods aim at discovering invariant properties beneath the apparent particularity and diversity of observed phenomena. (Lévi-Strauss, 1966:119)

III

It is the concept of culture which unifies all of anthropology. Sometimes the diversity of things—and this is as true of the branches of anthropology as it is of diverse ways of life which anthropologists study—leads to the unity of a field. The study of man and of his ways of life, of all that he has learned during the million years that human societies have inhabited this planet, occupies the working time of a number of specialists and exists at several levels of integration. But specialists all acknowledge that man is a self-domesticated creature, they are all concerned at some point with the totality of his behavior, they all study and seek to explain the behavior of individuals living in societies, and they all face the fact that for most men the proper ways are the manners of his society, and these ways have synchronic as well as diachronic aspects.

Of all of the definitions of culture, which more or less stress the totality of man's activities, I prefer the original of E. B. Tylor, an Oxonian of the last century: "Culture or Civilization, taken in its wide ethnographic sense, is that complex whole which includes knowledge, belief, art, morals, law, custom, and any other capabilities and habits acquired by man as a member of society" (Tylor, 1889, I:1).

Even man's physical evolution is governed by the rules that he has laid down for himself for life in society—rules of incest, exogamy, food habits, the state of the economy, the size of his society and the rules for the distribution of goods and of authority. We look like what we are because of the way we live. This affects the gene pool and it operates on natural selection. Because of this the physical anthropologist cannot operate simply as a biologist; he must constantly study man as an animal in his social and cultural setting. Indeed the more primatologists observe the society of man's nearest relatives among the higher apes and their behavior the less there remains to tell us apart.

If man's culture does not spring from his biological heritage but is learned behavior transmitted from generation to generation through the medium of language, how is it to be studied, and what are the levels of integration in our understanding of it?

The science of the study of living cultures is cultural anthropology or ethnology. The latter term originally had a different meaning when it was thought that man's cultural behavior was transmitted in the blood stream and that race determined culture, which it does not, as we now know. But old meanings die hard.

The description of living cultures in time and in space is what we call ethnography. The relationships among ethnography, ethnology and cultural anthropology are best understood as levels of integration. These understandings and their formulation I owe to Lévi-Strauss.

Stage I. Ethnography comprises the initial activities of fieldwork, observation and the description of activities engaged in by the society under study. Ethnographers constantly refine their methods; this is the thrust of the ethno-science movement, which seeks to find the basis of its models in native systems of thought. The description, classification, and analysis of material objects continues in the museum, from whence the ethnographer returns to the field with new problems for solution by questioning native informants, and, in this sense, the museum represents an extension of fieldwork (Lévi-Strauss, 1963:355).

Stage II. Ethnology represents a first step toward synthesis. Three kinds of synthesis are possible: (1) geographical (distribution of cultural forms and relationships to neighboring cultures); (2) historical (to which I shall return under *ethnohistory*); and (3) systematic (where a topical, or comparative treatment of a single activity is undertaken).

Stage III. Cultural anthropology and social anthropology belong to a higher and final stage of synthesis, using ethnographical and ethnological findings. It is important to understand that the three stages comprise but one discipline, a single line of investigation, in which concepts from a higher level enable the ethnographer at the first level to make more sophisticated observations. It is a maxim of fieldwork that one finds out what he already knows. Intensive work at any stage in the process never excludes the data of ethnography or ideas about it.

There is no mystique about social anthropology. It is simply the study of a single topic in ethnology—social organization which, in Britain, is developed to a level of sophistication and is probed in such depth that its practitioners seldom get around to material culture. Lévi-Strauss, again, points out that cultural anthropology and social anthropology cover the same ground, but that the former starts from techniques and material things and proceeds to social and political activities, while the latter "begins with social life and works down to the things on which social life leaves its mark and the activities through which it manifests itself" (Ibid., 357). Whatever the doctrinaire differences, however, between the offspring of Malinowski and Radcliffe-Brown and the American cultural anthropologists whose tradition stems from Franz Boas (and this is where I belong), we all stress the holism of man and his works or his representations.

There is a model for expressing the totality of human culture that I owe to the late Ruth Benedict, which relates ego to his universe and summarizes all of the mutual relationships with which he had to deal and which we as anthropologists study in our various specialties (Benedict, *in* Boas, 1938:627). Ego is at the center of a circle having four axes and four polar positions midway of the quadrants of a circle. The circle is divided on a vertical axis between personal relations (right) and relations with material things and impersonal forces (left). Horizontally, the circle represents natural phenomena and relations with them (lower half), and all things and relations supernatural (upper half). The four polar positions on the circle are "Gods" at two o'clock and Man at four o'clock (on the personal side); the Environment at eight o'clock, and Impersonal Power at ten o'clock. Returning to the center, all relations between ego and man, i.e., between man and man, comprise the area of social relations and the subject matter of social anthropology; and relations between ego and man, and man and the environment—which seek to discover the attributes and properties of objects, the exploitive techniques for gaining subsistence from them, and the mechanical principles on which discovery and invention rest—comprise the area of technology or material culture. Organized reciprocal relations between man and the environment for ensuring subsistence and distribution of goods and services are in the area of economic anthropology. Now the upper half of this universe represents a projection of the lower half: reality is projected on surreality. Man's rapport with the Gods and the techniques of communicating with them, such as prayer, ritual and sacrifice, the endowment of these supernaturals with animate personalities, and the ascription to them of power may be viewed as a projection of, and is seldom inconsistent with, social relations and expected behavior on earth. Likewise on the impersonal or material side, principles of mechanistic manipulation when projected become techniques of magic; and just as objects have their attributes so supernatural power is attributed to objects, which acquire properties not inconsistent with cognitive systems on earth. Religion thus balances relations between the Gods and Impersonal Power.

Language, oral literature, music, dance and liturgy, and graphic and plastic arts that communicate, sustain, symbolize and increase man's conception of his universe are the areas of inquiry in which linguistics, folklore, musicology, art and religion engage. As we have seen earlier, this whole philosophical construct links the anthropologist to the humanist and to the humanistic disciplines in the university.

All of those ecological relationships such as subsistence patterns, primitive medicine, ethno-botany, ethno-zoology and the like, and the methods that the ethnographer devises for studying them, lie very close to natural history branches of the sciences.

Studies of social organization, of political organization and law-ways borrow heavily from related social science disciplines and contribute comparative information.

Still other studies of perception and cognitive systems link anthropology to the behavioral sciences.

The virtue of the Benedict model is that it is synchronic or functional and explains the totality of social and cultural relations at a given point of time. Like the configuration in a kaleidoscope, it is of the moment and is subject to change with a completely new pattern at the flick of the wrist. Its defect is that it fails to account for change and history, since cultures are changing constantly. Now if anthropology is anything, it is an historical discipline. In its concern with the totality of human experience on earth, it must be diachronic as well as synchronic. In regarding the pattern of a culture, we must constantly ask how it came into being and what it is likely to become. If the anthropologist has anything to say to the historian on this problem, it is in the application of ethnological concepts to historical criticism, and to the historiography of native peoples. This is mainly what ethnohistory is about.

Two examples may make this clear. Certain patterns of culture that govern modes of behavior tend to persist over long periods of time. Iroquois suicides follow two classic forms during three centuries: middle-aged women abandoned by their husbands take and eat *Cicuta maculata* L., a violent alkaloid, and die a miserable death, which invokes sanctions on the kindred. Second, men who have failed on a mission of trust or who cannot face torture hang themselves or cut their own throats. It was only when I collected modern cases of suicide that I was able to explain the earlier cases reported in the *Jesuit Relations* for the seventeenth century (Fenton, 1941).

The second example is an even more puzzling historical problem.

From late seventeenth century sources onward we read of the Five Nations who have a central fire at Onondaga and of their constituting but one household. Yet this league or confederacy is nowhere described in detail by any of the colonial writers. Lafitau describes the nature of local government, Cadwallader Colden speaks of the genius of the Five Nations and cites some of its metaphors, but not even Sir William Johnson who made it operate to fulfill the British interests left a systematic description of Iroquois politics. Not until the middle of the nineteenth century, when L. H. Morgan in youthful enthusiasm set out to gather material for creating a fraternal order on the model of the Iroquois Longhouse, does the system begin to emerge from the all but extinguished fires of the cultural past, and only when Horatio Hale discovered and published the *Iroquois Book of Rites* (1883) do we have the native Iroquoian texts for the great ceremony of the condoling council, which like a university convocation mourns the dead chiefs, lauds their accomplishments, and installs their successors in office. Was it there all of the time? Or was it something that the then living chiefs made up to amuse ethnologists? Actually a structure and a process which has small basis in the historical records and would be missed completely by proceeding chronologically can be recovered in considerable detail by proceeding against the stream of time using the fuller accounts recovered by ethnologists as a basis for finding the same constructs in the earlier records of council procedure. Thus, I have been able to trace the paradigm of the condoling council back to the early colonial period.

Both of these examples of ethnohistorical research employ an approach which I have termed "upstreaming" because the investigation proceeds from the ethnological present to the historical past, from the known and observable to the unknown, and the criteria for identification are derived from the culture under study. Such reconstructions are at best approximations as is all historical interpretation (Fenton, 1957).

IV

Anthropology offers a model for understanding the present. Human societies walk about on the earth locally, and in time they acquire or create unique cultures. These local societies with cultures of their own exist as communities with definable limits. A model for the study of a community is built out of the following comparative terms, which, according to Arensberg, apply to all human and animal communities: (1) of individuals, (2) of space, (3) of times, (4) of functions, and (5) of structure and process (Arensberg, 1955:1146). Let me illustrate this with a couple of anecdotes and some recent observations.

The first term answers the question *who?* But *where* is also involved. One summer while attending an anthropological congress at Cambridge University, which is an ancient society that has developed some unique and diverse customs, I was invited to take supper with the resident dons of King's College by Professor Meyer Fortes, the social anthropologist, who is a Fellow at King's. It being August and the university in recess, the Fellows were not "dining in Hall," but in the Master's dining room, which made it a less formal occasion. As we entered the cloakroom various Fellows were donning robes which they took down from rows of pegs around the room. As my host robed, it was apparent that I must do likewise, for he admonished me: "Watch what the old men do! That is the way to succeed at fieldwork in Africa, and as a new professor and one of the 'boys' in Cambridge society, I can assure you that it works here too." Having no robe, I was asked: "What is your university," while someone glanced around the pegs and discovered an unused robe hanging at the far end where it was left long ago by some absentee Fellow whose university was now forgotten. "This will do for Yale," I was told, "and I assure you no one here has ever seen a Yale gown." Having conformed to local custom, I was ushered into the Master's presence, introduced, and seated far down the table with the "Boys," where the conversation was excellent. I recall that we retired afterward to drink port in the Combination

Room, but I no longer remember the placement of people nor the ritual sequence. One can read C. P. Snow for that.

One other Cambridge anecdote. I was lodged in John's College up the street. My window looked out on a court. Here was a beautiful lawn that was raised perhaps a foot above the walkways which were cobbled with glacial pebbles of local flint. The walks and drains were being repaired by an old man and his helper who trundled sand in a low wheelbarrow of wood. The whole scene reminded me of a plate from an early edition of the *Canterbury Tales*. The work habits of these artisans, their tools, and their speech, which I could barely follow, belonged to a preindustrial era of British civilization. I never saw anyone walk on that lawn but the gardener and I heard the stock answer that it takes centuries to make a lawn. As I look out my office window toward the bus stop and the parking lot, today, I believe it.

As a newcomer to the State University of New York at Albany community and as a trained anthropologist, I am curious about the movements of people, who they are, and the spaces that they occupy or traverse. Albany has some interesting spatial patterns. It is an old city and it has old ways. It gives every appearance of being a stratified society, and that is understandable considering the long history of the place and the succession of people and regimes from the Indians to the Dutch to the English and Americans. The Dutch never did give in to the English, and a pattern of civil disobedience developed early in connection with the fur trade and the traffic in firearms, powder, and rum. English governors made laws regulating the trade and the Dutch disobeyed them. This spirit of lawlessness carries over today into traffic patterns. There seems to be a point of honor in being the last car through the traffic light. But the solution to the parking problem is even more interesting. Here the double-parkers look down their noses at the triple-parkers, and there seems to be a direct correlation between how far one parks from the curb and the prestige system. The arbiter of all this is the cop on the beat who seems never to make a mistake and ticket the wrong car. Low license numbers and initials help, but there is also a whole series of bogus totemic devices which are variants on official shields that are supposed to convey immunity.

Having removed my point of observation from State Street hill, where the smoke of the council fire has risen for centuries, to the edge of the Pine barrens toward Schenectady, I would venture a few observations on a formative culture. Here the planners laid out the dimensions of the academic community in rectangles of perfect symmetry. They provided walkways between parking lots, residential quadrangles, and an academic podium. Between there are open spaces planted to trees, shrubs and grass. Then the parking lot was segregated into green numbered areas and fewer purple numbered areas closer to the buildings. Permits were issued to faculty and to staff, and to students, for a modest fee (not forty dollars a semester or even one hundred as at some California campuses), and seemingly there is some color resemblance between permits and preferential parking places. But the planners failed to take into account what the people of this formative society would do. Within my limited observation and without an adequate sample, preferential spaces are disregarded, and the faculty who need the exercise are made to walk longer distances to their offices. They should be grateful. But only a few old men walk on the walks, and since the elders enjoy no particular prestige in this society, younger members of the society ignore their example. Some people even drive on the walks, but I can't learn who they are. I hear that an intelligent grounds keeper would be one who puts the walks where people naturally go. This is not the way to make an English lawn, but it might be the way to plan a university. Turn the people loose and watch where they go. Put the buildings where they sit down or camp for the night. Perhaps this is how it should have been done, but now it is too late.

Societies with cultures sooner or later develop symbols of identity. These serve to guide everyone on matters of placement, of times, of functions on which the welfare of society depends, and on the proper way to do it. The Cheyenne had their camp circle, the Trobrianders their Kula ring, and the Iroquois their Roll Call of the Chiefs. Perhaps this society at the State University at Albany will find some device that stands for the arrangement of academic rankings, the hierarchy of students, and yet symbolize the unity of the whole academic community. For as long as we admit students and employ faculty, offer courses, learn together, and grant degrees, there are bound to be age grades in this society and reciprocal roles of relative status. We hear much of student power, these days, but many more have to be Indians than the few who accept chiefship, and it helps if the chiefs have skins "seven thumbs thick," in the idiom of the old Iroquois, so that they can take criticism. Perhaps an example from my own fieldwork will inspire someone to invent something.

This is the famous Roll Call of the Founders of the Confederacy of the Five Nations. On it are listed the titles of the then village chiefs who joined with Dekanawidah to form and ratify the Great Peace before the Dutch came to these parts. Morgan first published this list in his classic *The League of the Ho-de-no-sau-nee* (1851) and thirty years later Hale translated the ritual poetry which commemorates the event. Since there are fifty titles to be remembered and they are distributed unequally among five tribes, and they bear relationship as siblings or cousins to each other, the problem for the ritual holder in reciting the Roll Call is to keep it all straight in his head. Various mnemonics have been devised to remind the singer of his place. Kernels of corn, wampum-strings, and a stick carved with pictographs and having 50 pegs. The last of these devices seems appropriate in this center of public administration where organization charts are a virtual mania. For indeed this is a primitive chart for a confederate government, which is a kinship state.

Some years ago, the prototype of the copy that I own came to rest in the Cranbrook Institute of Science near Detroit, and the then director asked me to identify and describe it. The original had been collected about 1917 on the Six Nations Reserve, near Brantford, Ontario, from one of the ritual holders of the ceremony of the Condolence Council. I was then occupied translating the texts of this ceremony from the manuscripts of J. N. B. Hewitt who preceded me at the Smithsonian Institution. I was aware of other mnemonic devices for remembering the order of ceremony and so this was one more clue to unlock the past. But I was completely unprepared for what happened.

Because the museum was reluctant to let the specimen out of its possession, we had drawings made of the markings on both sides of the stick, and we had these blue printed in copies sufficient for all of the chiefs. When I distributed these prints, the response was electric. The cane, or stick, was the key piece in their thinking about their ancient political structure, second only to the great wampum belts already in museums, and "it should never have left the reserve." As if to convince me that it ought to be recovered, chants that I was after were recorded, lists were compiled and compared, and alternate systems were produced and discussed. I found myself in the midst of a movable seminar. Moreover, they insisted, I must see the great ceremony of condolence to understand it. This is how it happened, and my report on the specimen and my observations on the ceremony are now available in print to my Indian collaborators (Fenton, 1950; 1946).

But my publications had a chain effect that I had not anticipated. Between field trips to observe the ceremony several ritual holders reproduced the cane replete with pegs and pictographs, as if to endow their rite with ancient symbol. The new canes are faithful reproductions of the original relic and several of them show distinct improvements: handles of antler, elaborately carved eagle heads. Later, one of the copies was advanced as the original from which the maker of the museum specimen had taken his copy. Today the manufacture of Roll Call canes is a native art: every proper Iroquois chief has one, they are made to sell to collectors, to museums, and to shops across Canada that specialize in Iroquois crafts. For this much, I am responsible.

Along with this diffusion of reproductions has gone an awakened interest among educated Iroquois who grew up learning an Iroquoian tongue but became detribalized by education, successful careers, and long residence outside of the reserve. Several such educated Iroquois have read the writings of anthropologists and have returned to relearn their first language and cultivate the arts and customs of the old culture. Such was the origin of the specimen which was made as a present to me by Dr. T. J. Jamieson who practiced medicine in Detroit and only late in life reasserted an interest in the ancient ritual and political structure of his ancestors. Indeed his grandfather was a Mohawk chief. Dr. Jamieson has even prepared a completely new translation of the ritual text that was originally published by Hale. I have this token to keep with the understanding that I don't give it to any museum (see Fenton, 1966:78–81).

The Cane with its arrangement of 50 pegs is a model of statuses; they are arranged according to rank by committees and tribal delegations, and the tribes are spatially seated so as to form two moieties the length of the Longhouse. The time for its use is when a chief dies, then a peg is removed, until the other side of the confederacy forms a condoling party and approaches over the road to the house of the mourners whose minds are depressed. In the recitation of the Roll Call with its laudatory chant, and its supporting cries of antiphony, everyone is reminded of the greatness of the League, and the minds of the depressed brothers are lifted up. Ultimately, as in the installation of a university president, the one who will wear the name about his neck is stood up before the crowd and charged with the responsibilities of his ancient office. Only then is the missing peg put back. So with this process the structure of the League is reconstituted. Society is restored and the community goes about its daily life.

V

While I have been talking the Husk Face messenger has been quietly waiting by the door for me to say what kind of a ceremony we shall have in this new longhouse. I sense that he is getting restive. What then should be the program in anthropology at the State University of New York at Albany?

First, I shall address myself to programs and requirements for research, and then I shall turn to teaching.

By this time, several things should be apparent. The first is that anthropology, more like the natural sciences than the related social science and humanistic disciplines, is field and laboratory oriented. The second is that anthropology has a field of its own. The study of man and his cultures, or ways of life, which is the essential subject matter of anthropology, runs the gamut from biologically oriented physical anthropology through archaeology and ethnology to linguistics and folklore. These are the unique specialties of anthropology that are not preempted by other social sciences and are shared in part with the humanities. I regard the rest of the hyphenated specialties—ethno-botany, ethno-science, ethno-musicology—as variants of the preceding or as bridges to other specialties. The same may be said of political anthropology, economic anthropology, and other obviously named relatives of social science disciplines. Their unique aspect is an inter-cultural point of view. Third, anthropology, at least at Albany, has no territorial ambitions: it will not replace history as queen of the humanities and social sciences; but it does have something to contribute toward a liberal education today. Hopefully it will draw students from many academic disciplines and return them enlightened men. Anthropology has always derived its strength from other disciplines, the most famous anthropologists of the generation who taught me started in other fields, and I myself do not regard an undergraduate major in anthropology as the best route to graduate work in the same curriculum. Better that students first learn history, languages, philosophy, or one of the sciences.

There is a huge literature in anthropology and we at Albany are making a late start to collect it. All branches of anthropology have library requirements, and every effort should be (and I believe is being) made to build up the collections of the university library. Its holdings must contain complete runs of the major anthropological periodicals in the original volumes where available. The library should also acquire the major classics in ethnography, both in book and monographic form. Students cannot be educated from text books and readers alone; they must have familiarity with the sources. The ethnologist or cultural anthropologist is most dependent on the library for his research and teaching, the ethno-historian most of all, and the linguist least. Having read in the major libraries of the world, I am reassured by the presence and expanding future of the State Library, but I am equally convinced that the university must do for itself.

Physical anthropology is a laboratory discipline. Adequate laboratories are essential to research and for the training of both undergraduate and graduate students. Upperclassmen should have the opportunity to demonstrate their capabilities in the laboratory, both as a learning experience and as research assistants. We have the beginnings of staff and program in this area.

A university department of anthropology usually operates research and teaching programs in archaeology both locally and far afield. We look forward to welcoming prehistorians to our staff. A summer program of local archaeology for the training of students, in cooperation with the Anthropological Survey of the State Museum and Science Service, is in its second year. After the field season, while writing up the results of excavations, archaeologists attached to a university require a range for the storage and retrieval of collections. Here on long trestle tables collections are laid out while they are being washed, catalogued, and arranged systematically and chronologically by students working under faculty supervision. There is no better way for a student to get acquainted with archaeology than by handling materials collected by himself and others in the field. Ultimately the archaeologist is dependent on museum collections for comparative work. I am not advocating a university museum at the State University of New York at Albany because collections can often be borrowed for study or one can go to the museum. I rather favor strengthening ties to the State Museum locally and to the other great research museums of the region.

Similarly, the linguist and the musicologist, having collected original tapes and texts from informants in the field, works between field trips at the university listening to and transcribing his recordings. The ideal facility for this purpose is an acoustically treated interior room adjacent to a sound studio. It may also be desirable to bring informants to the campus for further work on field collected texts and for supplementary interviews. In my experience informants who make good interpreters also make good teaching assistants or demonstrators in seminar. Thus students may learn to transcribe and analyze a language on campus before going to the field.

But the ultimate source of all such materials and persons is the field. Fieldwork is the sine qua non of anthropological research; it is the proving ground for the training of doctoral candidates and the primary resource to which the mature anthropologist returns again and again to get new material and to renew his craft. The field is to the cultural anthropologist what the library is for the humanist, and what the laboratory is for the scientist. The field is where he seeks new information, where he tests theories, and where new ideas are generated. There is a continuous feedback effect that runs from seminar and library to the field, to writing, and back to teaching. No one should be allowed to teach anthropology in a university who has not done original fieldwork. Fieldwork, moreover, is a life-long commitment.

In the light of these considerations, here is what I think that we should do at Albany:

1. We should start with Iroquois studies. In the Iroquois of New York and Ontario there are field resources that touch every essential branch of anthropological inquiry. With over three hundred years of continuous and uninterrupted culture contact, there are rich and

extensive archival and library resources for ethnohistory. We have the staff in both history and anthropology faculties to train graduate students.

2. The major outlines of New York prehistory have been established largely by the work of Dr. William A. Ritchie of the State Museum (Ritchie, 1965). But the one segment of time that now needs attention spans recent proto-historic and historic periods on sites just prior to white contact, and just afterward. The nearby Mohawk valley contains a number of such sites, several of which are to be explored by the SUNYA summer field party this summer, again under the direction of Dr. Robert E. Funk of the State Museum and Science Service. The possibilities of future collaboration with other branches of the State University and with the University of Toronto, and with McGill University would broaden our horizons considerably. But there is more to anthropology than digging up dead Indians!

3. There are at least twenty thousand living descendants of the Iroquois Confederacy today. They occupy six reservations in New York State and four in Canada, all within a day's drive of Albany. With the exception of Oneida, which is spoken in Wisconsin and possibly near London, Ontario, five Iroquoian dialects—Mohawk, Onondaga, Seneca, Tuscarora, and Cayuga—still have language communities between Montreal, Syracuse, the Niagara frontier and Brantford, Canada. All of these dialects are more or less known, and Seneca has recently been thoroughly worked (Chafe, 1963, 1967), but comparative work remains to be done.

The Longhouse Iroquois are notably conservative. As followers of the teachings of Handsome Lake, the prophet, they have kept alive ceremonial cycles which are patterned differently in each longhouse where they are celebrated, and these observances have perpetuated old folkways, food habits, and knowledge of the plant and animal worlds that are still worthy of investigation. It was in these communities that I commenced fieldwork in the thirties and where I still work when opportunity affords. There are experienced informants in each of these communities who are quite used to ethnological inquiry, and who are certainly capable of coping with students. I would value their opinion of future field workers. I look forward to taking some students to the field and to working with colleagues on some of these problems.

4. Several colleagues regularly work in Mexico and Latin America, where the costs are increased by the distance traveled to the field and the longer field season. We must anticipate that our staff will be working is such distant lands as Africa, India, and ultimately Southeast Asia. In these far places, it is uneconomical for the student to spend less than a year in the field. Moreover, there are language problems which only training, time, and intensive effort can overcome. Competence in the language and culture of a foreign area is essential to the training of the nature anthropologist. This is how he acquires the cross-cultural view that is so helpful later in critically appraising the work of others, in approaching new research of his own, and in teaching. This is what distinguishes anthropology from other disciplines that are essentially culture bound in the civilization of the west.

If we succeed in attracting and holding a distinguished faculty in anthropology who will offer a balanced sequence of courses on the major cultural areas of the world, or if we are to have strength in any one world area, we will have brought to Albany a staff who are committed to fieldwork abroad and who will expect to return to the field periodically, and they will expect to send their students there. Some of these students will have received preliminary training in the Iroquois field program.

5. Anthropologists have not shirked their duty to society. The record of British anthropologists in Africa and India, who returned advice on the administration of native peoples to the Colonial Office which assisted their travel, rivals that of Dutch anthropologists in the Netherlands East Indians before World War II. On their model an applied anthropology unit was formed in the U.S. Indian Field Service in the

early days of the New Deal and several of us were attracted both from a sense of duty and for the opportunity of studying cultures in transition when there were no other jobs. Since then, the developments in applied anthropology have been extensive and varied, touching a broad span of fields in government, industry, and medicine. Just now urban anthropology is emerging from these developments, but it remains to be seen whether the application of anthropological techniques to problems of the ghetto will yield answers beyond the methods, viewpoints and techniques of related social science disciplines.

6. I have said that the museum is the traditional home of anthropology and that collections are an extension of the field. While studies of technology and material culture have not been popular among university anthropologists, of late there has been a rising interest in primitive art. Recently the profession has manifest an increasing interest in museums as resources for research, and the Committee on Anthropological Research in Museums of the American Anthropological Association, with the support of the Wenner-Gren Foundation, has set up a fellowship program to enable graduate students to select as a dissertation problem a topic that combines the study of ethnographic collections in museums with fieldwork. The experiment has also demonstrated that upper level undergraduates can perform assigned tasks and even carry out research on their own in a museum. Museum curators are most enthusiastic about the work of these interns. It has been a means of catching bright people before they are committed to graduate work and giving them a chance to find out what anthropology in museums is about.

There are several tasks that we could advance by providing undergraduate interns to the State Museum. They could inventory the ethnographic collections of New York State. They could make a register of extant Iroquois material culture. Hopefully one of them as a graduate student will write a dissertation on the arts and industries of the New York Iroquois, a topic which L. H. Morgan introduced to the Regents in 1849.

The Husk Faces are now stirring and I hear them banging their sticks. They want to hear what I am going to teach in this longhouse and then they will leave.

In this year and in this place it seems important for the anthropologist to tell what he knows about comparative politics. The League of the Iroquois was a kinship state, but as such it was not unique in the world, for it is one of a type called segmentary societies. So I shall begin with societies without government and without law and then look at societies around the world having greater degrees of complexity. Having once studied factionalism in four American Indian societies, I am aware that factions are nascent political parties, in Friedrich's theory (Friedrich 1937:298), and we should be able to find some data to support or deny such theories in the current scene. Related to this is the phenomenon of age-grading and the difficulties of communication between generations, which should interest advocates of student power.

Another thing that I would like to do in seminar is to explore the history of ethnological theory. Clark Wissler first made me aware of the history of anthropology. While editing Lafitau's *Moeurs des sauvages ameriquains...* (1724), I have sought to place Lafitau in the thought of his day, at the beginning of the Enlightenment, by tracing his sources and his influences, particularly in the use of the comparative method. The roots of anthropology go back to the Renaissance when gentlemen began to collect everything, including the manners and customs of the then known world.

To prepare students for fieldwork, I shall have to review Iroquois culture in a systematic way.

VI

The leader of the Husk Faces has just signaled to me: "This is it. We are in a hurry to get to the West. But we shall return next year to see how the people of this clearing are doing."

Dáneʔho nigaihwanonge; Dáneʔho.
"So this is the sum of my words; that is all."

Bibliography

Arensberg, Conrad M.

1955 American Communities. American Anthropologist, 57: 1143–1162.

Benedict, Ruth

1938 Religion, in F. Boas, ed. General Anthropology, 627–665. New York: D. C. Heath & Co.

Bennett, Wendell G.

1947 The Ethnogeographic Board, Smithsonian Miscellaneous Collections, Vol. 107, No. 1. Washington DC.

Casagrande, Joseph B.

1963 The relations of Anthropology with the Social Sciences, *in* Mandelbaum, Lasker, and Albert, 461–474.

Chafe, Wallace L.

1963 Handbook of the Seneca Language. New York State Museum & Science Service Bulletin 388. Albany NY.

1967 Seneca Morphology and Dictionary. Smithsonian Institution, Contributions to Anthropology, IV. Washington DC.

Colden, Cadwallader

1866 The History of the Five Indian Nations depending on the Province of New-York, ed., John Gilmary Shea. New York. (Originally published New York, 1727, and reprinted London, 1747 and 1750, and available in later editions.)

Fenton, William N.

1941 Iroquois suicide: a study in the stability of a culture pattern. Smithsonian Institution, Bureau of American Ethnology, Bulletin 128, Anthropological Paper, No. 14: 79–137. Washington DC.

1947 Area studies in American universities. American Council on Education, Commission on Implications, Armed Services Educational Programs, Washington DC.

1950 The Roll Call of the Iroquois Chiefs: a study of a mnemonic cane from the Six Nations Reserve. Smithsonian Miscellaneous Collections, Vol. 111, No. 15. 75 pp., 12 plates. Washington DC.

1957   American Indian and White Relations to 1830: needs & opportunities for study. With a bibliography by L. H. Butterfield, Wilcomb E. Washburn, and William N. Fenton. Chapel Hill: The University of North Carolina Press.

1966   Field Work, Museum Studies, and Ethnohistorical Research. Ethnohistory, 13: 71–85.

Friedrich, Carl Joachim

1937   Constitutional Government and politics. New York and London: Harper and Brothers.

Kroeber, A. L.

1954   The place of Anthropology in Universities. American Anthropologist, 56: 764–767.

1959   The history and personality of Anthropology. American Anthropologist, 61: 398–404.

Hale, Horatio E.

1883   The Iroquois Book of Rites. Philadelphia. Reprinted with an Introduction by William N. Fenton. University of Toronto Press, 1963.

Lafitau, J. F.

1724   Moeurs des sauvages amériquains, comparées aux moeurs des premiers temps. 2 Vols. Paris.

Leighton, Alexander H.

1949   Human Relations in a Changing World: Observations on the use of the Social Sciences. New York: E. P. Dutton.

Lévi-Strauss, Claude

1963   The Place of Anthropology in the Social Sciences and Problems raised in teaching it. Structural Anthropology: 346–381.

1963   Structural Anthropology. New York: Basic Books.

1966   Anthropology: its Achievements and Future. Knowledge among Men, Paul H. Oehser, Ed. New York: Simon and Schuster, in cooperation with the Smithsonian Institution, 109–122.

Mandelbaum, David G., Gabriel W. Lasker and Ethel M. Albert.

1963   The Teaching of Anthropology. American Anthropological Association, Memoir 94.

Morgan, L. H.
1851   The League of the Ho-dé-no-sau-nee, or Iroquois. Rochester: Sage. Re-
       printed: American Experience Series AE 12. New York: Corinth Books,
       1962.

Ritchie, William A.
1965   The Archaeology of New York State. Garden City NY: The Natural History
       Press.

Steward, Julian H.
1950   Area research: theory and practice. New York, Social Science Research
       Council, Bulletin 63.

Tylor, Edward B.
1889   Primitive Culture. 2 Vols. New York: Henry Holt.

Return to the Longhouse

"The One Who Slept in a Tent"

At the moon of midwinter, 1968, I revisited my Seneca friends of Coldspring Longhouse, on the Allegany Reservation near Salamanca, New York, where I had commenced ethnological field work in the summer of 1933. Now, some thirty-five years later, I was hoping to see once again the ceremonies that mark the Indian New Year. From time to time I had returned, and in particular I had followed the affairs of the Seneca nation during their tragic struggle against the building of the Kinzua Dam on the Allegheny River, and I had chaired an advisory committee to the nation. I had described the rebuilding of their homes, but I had not attended the doings at the new longhouse where recently they removed their fire. This modern structure near Steamburg was built with funds received from the United States Congress in partial compensation for 9,000 acres taken for the reservoir. The old settlement at Coldspring which I had known was obliterated. Not since Sullivan's army destroyed their towns and crops during the American Revolution had the Seneca people suffered such cultural loss. I wondered how the shock of being uprooted would affect the performance of their ceremonies.

I reached "New Coldspring" on the morning that "Our Uncles, the Bigheads" traditionally go out at dawn, progressing from house to house, hailing the men as nephews, and urging them to renew all

MAP 1. Iroquois communities of western New York and western Ontario

obligations revealed through dreams. I immediately learned that the Uncles did not go out that dawn, and I inferred that they no longer made the circuit of houses and that I could probably expect other radical changes. Ed Coury, the speaker of the longhouse, confirmed my first inference. "There was no one at home to receive them," he said; "their nephews were either at the longhouse or at work."

It was good, nevertheless, to see familiar faces among the small crowd assembled in the longhouse. For a moment seeing these old friends diverted me from the startlingly modern surroundings. Among the people were some I had known from the first summer I had spent in the community, thirty-five years earlier when I slept in a tent at Jonas Snow's. Somehow I felt reassured: with these experienced persons on hand things would go about as usual.

Except that the doors opened westward toward the road, the interior arrangements of the new building and the placement of the windows recalled the old longhouse. There was still a stove for each sex at opposite ends, and there was even a ladder at the men's end giving access through a hatch to the attic for storing and retrieving ritual gear. I recognized the old benches, and a higher bank that circled the room providing elevated seats behind the benches had been reproduced.

But the building contained some strange innovations for a longhouse. To be sure, it was a frame structure, clapboarded and painted white, but the cement-block foundation afforded a complete basement. The doors were doubled and there was a hardwood floor, perfect for dancing. The architect thought the old ladies would appreciate a basement kitchen, but they had insisted on a separate cookhouse—equipped with gas. At an outdoor fire where the kettles hung on wooden poles, I heard Alta Cloud complain that she missed the crane in Jake Logan's brick fireplace at the old cookhouse. Inside fluorescent lighting from a false ceiling contrasted favorably with the bare bulbs or kerosene lamps I had known. The room was paneled with birch plywood in which electrical outlets were spaced at regular intervals. I thought these would be ideal for tape recorders now owned by several singers; but Dorothy Jimerson told me that the outlets were for the old ladies to plug in hotplates for warming corn soup at socials. The final touch was a fresh set of corn pestles which the Uncles carry, made as replacements for the old pestles, which were given to a museum. Besides having unfamiliar, new equipment, the Uncles did not know their lines and mumbled the chants.

Presently Ed Coury stood, removed his hat, spat in the nearest can, and commenced the thanksgiving address which greets and thanks the Creator for all of the things that he has left on earth for man's use and enjoyment. Then he announced the opening of the Midwinter Festival and the dressing of the Uncles. Although Ed has more white genes than red, he had mastered the speaking style of Seneca preachers just as earlier he had learned the ritual songs. As I closed my eyes to concentrate on the old words, for a moment there was the illusion of the old longhouse and Henry Redeye speaking.

The midwinter ceremony deals with both halves of the subsistence cycle: hunting and meat, which ends at midwinter; and the maize cycle, to which the people look forward after a period of hunger. The other concern is with "good luck" and health—both physical and mental—and this is why the ceremony persists today. The next four days are devoted to ceremonies of friendship and to renewal of the medicine-society's dream obligations. The obligation to fulfill these rites and the ties of joint participation bind the generations, age-mates, and persons of opposite sex in Seneca society as long as either partner lives, helping to keep the ceremonies themselves alive.

On the fifth morning the speaker announced that the door now stood open to admit all kinds of ceremonies revealed through dreams—Bear, Buffalo, False Face, which he mentioned, and others. The bear dance has always been the most popular of the dream dances. During the opening songs, as the words of the invocation rise on the smoke of burning tobacco begging the bear spirits to listen, the conductor passes a small pipe to the members and then throws a spoon of berry juice out of doors. The saying is: "The bears will come and get it at night."

At dusk several performances of the False Faces disclosed substantial changes in the rite. In their new ranch-style houses people objected to the maskers' scraping their rattles on the varnished doors, marring the woodwork, and tracking in mud. The two head women thereupon quit because this objection meant that the circuit of houses at midwinter would no longer be observed, and they had to abandon spring and fall "housecleaning" throughout the settlement. The rites of the maskers now centered at the longhouse.

As the False Faces crawled and stooped toward the women's fire, I noted that their behavior lacked enthusiasm. Only Herb Dowdy, who was properly raucous, and Ham Jimerson, who danced while scooping hot ashes, moved the patient's head on its axis, and pumped her arms, came up to expectations. At the men's end one could scarcely hear the invocation by Art Johnny John. One lady sponsor was wearing curlers, which embarrassed her, since under the old rules she would have left the ashes in her hair for three days. I thought audience participation was quite limited: I saw no frightened children and no cases of hysterical possession; nor did anyone crawl to the fire. When the doorkeepers cleared the benches, requiring everyone to join the dances, only the older people knew the steps. But it was too early in the festival to form a judgment.

The sixth day is the climax. Events had started that morning before I arrived. The Bowl Game, now also confined to the longhouse, had gone rapidly and was over, save for the announcements, and the rest of the morning was free. People came and went. Four restless boys of thirteen chattered in English and wriggled on the bank behind me. Ed Coury announced that the Great Feather Dance in honor of the Creator would take place the following day. I have to concentrate to follow such discourse, and the distraction was such that, partly as an experiment, I turned to the noisy lads and remarked in Seneca, as the old people sometimes do when conversation is loud, "Swadáonkdiyos!"

("All of you, listen!") This quieted them for a moment, but presently I felt a finger in my shoulder and then in English the taunt: "You can't understand him anyway. Tell us what he is saying." I then related the gist of the announcements. This was too much. Unable to contain themselves, they went outside and caucused. Soon they were back in again. By then the men around me were aware of what was happening, and I sensed their amused approval. Quiet lasted only a moment, when again I was nudged. "We got you figured out. You must be the one the old people tell about. Long ago you came here and slept in a tent."

That the grandchildren who impersonated "Our Grandfathers," the maskers, would have something further in store for me had not occurred to me as I reached the longhouse that evening for Husk Face night. The benches were beginning to fill with visitors from Steamburg and Jimersontown; then contingents of Seneca arrived from Cattaraugus and Tonawanda, among whom I recognized old faces, and a carload came from Six Nations Reserve in Canada. Soon every seat was occupied. A dozen white people attended. I felt part of the homecoming to Coldspring since every community in Iroquois where I had lived and made friends was represented. It was interesting to meet the new generation because I had always been curious about the learning process in this society that afforded so few formal teaching situations. I recalled how anxious Johnson Jimerson was to learn everything of importance concerning the Coldspring ceremonies, how he constantly practiced his songs, and I was anxious to see how being a speaker at Newtown had affected him. I was also fascinated to witness the learning that had been transmitted to his son, who proved the winner by acclaim in the False Face beggar contest. Johnson had indeed, to use his words, "raised him right." The power of symbols and of certain stereotypes, much of it nonverbal, must be operative in this process. The masks are impressive enough when seen in museum collections, but they really come to life when worn by impersonators of the spirits that they represent.

The False Faces, as everyone expected, led the program. Small boys meanwhile went out to the cookhouse in twos and threes to return as masked beggars. Among them were my new friends who had challenged me that morning. The first beggar was dressed in white coveralls and wore a Negro mask. Crossing the room to where I was seated, he thrust his stick at me and demanded that I sing for him to dance. Such a confrontation is a recognized contest between the generations, between singer and dancer, and I had obviously made myself liable by exercising moral authority that morning. Now it was their turn to test me. Years ago someone had taught me a simple False Face song, and I recalled one other from my recordings. The beat was easy, and Clifford Crouse of my generation urged me to keep it going to tire the dancer. Accomplished singers try odd beats to throw the dancer off. Dancers prefer a fast tempo and short songs, so the game is to stretch the beat, keeping the dancer at it until he tires and begs for his stick, at which the singer may speed up the beat again. This byplay appeals to the Iroquois sense of humor, in which an element of kindly torture persists, and these contests are looked forward to and are remembered long afterward. Surely having contributed another incident to local legend, the lad and I were both glad when I ran out of songs.

Snow Street 1933

The friendship between the Fenton and Snow families in western New York goes back several generations. There is a hemlock ridge at the back of the Fenton farm in Conewango Valley, which is halfway between Cattaraugus and Allegany. Here for generations Seneca hunters stopped to camp in the fall on the way to the big woods of Pennsylvania, and they frequently paused with their families on the return trip. One winter day in the 1860's my grandfather, then in his twenties, who was running the farm with his widowed mother, saw smoke rising from the ridge in the swamp. It was bitter cold and the snow was deep. His mother suggested that he go down and see how the Indians were faring. He took an ax and went afoot, thinking that he might split up some firewood that he had felled. He found an Indian family encamped in a hemlock leanto: a man, an old woman, and a young girl with a newborn baby. When he came back to the farm for dinner, he reported what he had seen to his mother, who insisted that he hitch the team to the pung, fill the bed with straw, and go fetch that family to the warm farmhouse. By suppertime the Indian family was installed in the hired girl's room off the kitchen. They stayed for a week until the weather improved. When they left, the old lady thanked my great-grandmother for shelter, sustenance, and hospitality, saying that it was the first time they had been invited to sleep and eat in a white home. It was the Indian custom, she said, to return thanks. It was also the Indian custom to bind friendship with a present, whereupon she produced an old burden strap, an obvious heirloom, decorated with dyed deer hair and porcupine-quill embroidery worked in a geometric pattern, and handed it to my great-grandmother.

The Indian hunter was stout, jovial Amos Snow, who became a lifelong friend of my grandfather: companions on squirrel- and pigeon-shooting expeditions, trotting-horse fanciers, and good for some shared labor on the farm. Amos used to show up with his young family. At one point he entrusted to my grandfather two wooden False Faces, both very old, which he produced from under the wagon seat in a wooden cheese box. Later it was a string of wampum that recalled an alliance of war with some tribes in the old Northwest. These items, however they came to us, were the nucleus of a growing family ethnological collection that was kept "up attic" in a special museum room which I was privileged to visit on rainy summer days. Often there were visiting collectors present—sometimes Indians. It was then that Jonas, a son of Amos's, and my father discovered a common interest in the arts—the one a painter and the other a gifted carver of masks. Going to the reservation to visit the Snows and their neighbors were summer outings that we particularly cherished during my childhood. It was only natural that I should remember Snow Street years later when I was about to do my first field work in ethnology.

For a year I had prepared by going through F. W. Waugh's notebooks on Iroquois medicines, which Diamond Jenness sent me from the National Museum of Canada. Ethnobotany seemed a good opening subject, being close enough to everyday life not to arouse anxiety. It involved linguistic terminology, and it might be expected to survive. At a more difficult level I might do something to extend Arthur C. Parker's sketches of the medicine societies. Before I left New Haven, Professor Sapir, who had procured $500 for my field fund, advised finding a field of concentration early so that I should have a subject for a dissertation and not just field notes. He recommended religion and ceremonialism, with asides in material culture. He advised avoiding negative leading questions, which invariably evoke monosyllabic answers. I was urged to make a census to get acquainted and for the data it would afford on social organization, which I might then use in observing ceremonial usages. Sapir also loaned me a book on the phonetic transcription of American Indian languages. George Herzog, for whom I had agreed to make some recordings of music, produced an old Edison mechanical recorder, instructed me in its use, and told me where to write for wax cylinders. These hints to the novice field worker proved a boon. I was soon to learn, however, that the Seneca would control my learning and that my success would be governed by their interests.

Snow Street was a dirt road connecting Highway 17 toward Steamburg with a north-south road running past the longhouse, parallel to the Allegheny River, toward Quaker Bridge. That summer when I camped in the dooryard of Jonas Snow's household yielded entries for a journal which is a miscellany of family life, medicines, rattlesnakes, turtles, drunks, feuds, friends, ball games, singing societies, mutual aid, adoption into the Hawk clan, and socials at the longhouse—far too long a list to detail here. One or two incidents will serve to show how my progress was affected, not by any of the good advice I was given by my professors nor any strategy that I had devised for my field work, but by being annexed to a family and participating as well as I could. It was all quite confusing at first because everything kept coming at me in bits and pieces, and I lacked a scheme for sorting it out and putting it together. The Snow family were helpful enough, but they were engaged in activities of their own that they scarcely had time to explain.

Although I soon commenced formal work on medicines with an informant, and I took genealogies as opportunity afforded, it was not these systematic efforts at ethnology that were most rewarding, nor did they introduce me to Seneca society. It was the informal, after-hours activities that I engaged in with members of my "family" that brought me in touch with the culture as a going concern. Mornings, from the vantage point of my umbrella tent, I watched the comings and goings of the community along Snow Street as I wrote up my journal. Evenings, with the Snow boys, I traversed the network of paths that cut through the brush to the ballground where we fielded grounders or practiced lacrosse. Beyond was the river crossing where we poled over to Crick's Run in a john boat or went "torching" at night, to the gravel pit to swim, or to some house where people met to play games, sing, or just gossip. Inevitably we stopped somewhere.

On the first Sunday of my visit I was told that the group of men and women who had passed on the road that morning were members of a "society" on the way to hoe an old lady's garden. That evening Windsor Snow and I stopped to see Amos Redeye (Windsor's "friend") about borrowing his boat for fishing. Going on through the brush to Ed Coury's, Windsor volunteered that rattlesnakes were hunted for their oil, that the fried-out fat made an excellent liniment, but that it was no good if the snake was mad when killed.

Returning, we stopped at Sarah Armstrong's, because we heard singing from inside. At the back of the house, six men sat facing each other on two rows of chairs. One, who held the small water-keg drum, closed his eyes and lined out a verse while the others kept time by bumping their heels and beating cow-horn rattles in the palms of their left hands. Then they repeated the song together, drum and rattles vibrato, simultaneously maintaining the slower, measured tempo with their heels. Youngsters sat on a nearby bench, hands clasped between their knees, gently moving their heels and humming; they were learning the song. Someone told me, "This is 'The Women Shuffle Their Feet'; these songs belong to the Women's Dance. The men like to sing them. They are a society who meet to help one another, and when they have finished working, they sing for pleasure."

Presently the speaker stood. He thanked the men and women who had helped Sarah Armstrong, our hostess. In return, she had set down a kettle of corn soup for the society. While the women served first the singers and then the women and children with bowls of steaming corn soup which Mrs. Armstrong ladled from the kettle, the speaker continued: next time they would meet across the river. He asked the men to assemble the following week to cut brush in the tribal cemetery. After that, they would go in a body to put roofing paper on Alice White's house. The hostess passed me a brimming bowl of soup, a spoon, and a salt shaker, saying: "His face is white, but maybe he likes soup. Perhaps later he may learn to sing." Soon after, the leader gathered the cow-horn rattles and the drum, put them in a hand basket, and paused at the door to say to me, "We are glad that you came. You are welcome to sit with us. We will let you know where we meet next Tuesday."

At midnight Jonas Snow, his son Linnus, and I walked back along Snow Street. The night sky was brilliant. I had found the Seneca, as described, a charitable people. What was more, the singing society was common to all of Iroquois, and through that summer of learning to sing at Coldspring I would find a passport that would give me entry at Tonawanda, and later at Six Nations, for the drum is to the Iroquois what the violin is to the gypsy.

So it turned out that these evenings of listening to the Coldspring singers had consequences for my field work that were only gradually apparent. I was told to listen and hum the songs, not to worry about the words—"They don't mean anything"—though I discovered that these nonsense vocables ran in distinct patterns. The singers liked the idea of my recording them because they were constantly composing new songs which they wanted preserved. The women attended and wanted to dance. On Sunday nights we joined the rest of the community at the longhouse, where the social dances started "when they turn the lamps up" if the people were in the mood.

These social occasions were also the setting for much conversation. For example, I was asked which clan I was going to join. It was assumed that the Hawks, the family of Jonas Snow, his sister Emma Turkey, and her daughter Clara Redeye, was the logical choice, although the question came from two members of Snipe clan who were married to Hawks. I would only gradually come to understand that the clan functionally includes a fringe of spouses.

These same people wanted to visit their relatives at Cattaraugus. Of a Sunday Jonas Snow, his daughter and son, and Jonas's current drinking companion (the village villain), and I set out for the lacrosse match at Pine Woods. After stops at the back of taverns to visit bootleggers in Randolph and Lawtons, our progress included calls on Jonas's maternal relatives. In the pauses my vehicle served as a taxi between drinks and the ballground for various friends and relatives, introducing me to the elite of Seneca informants.

On a visit one stops with one's clansmen. We paused at a log house, the home of Hanover Bennett and his wife, who was Jonas's mother's sister. The old lady, bedridden, had had several strokes, but she was especially glad to see me when Jonas explained who I was. Her face brightened. She was the one, she told me, who was born in the shanty on the hemlock ridge in the big swamp and who had been brought to my great-grandmother's house. Before we sat down to dinner she insisted that I read from the Bible. At the time I thought she was a Christian, but later I realized that her request had been a courtesy to me, for she was later buried from the longhouse. The old log house (which was spotless), the grounds with their fine garden, and the reunion of Hawk and Bear clan lineages presented subjects for my camera. Whatever the reunion might mean to the real members of Jonas's mother's family, to me it was a symbolic reinforcement of my own family's link to the Seneca. I was beginning to encounter difficulty in sorting out my role of anthropologist from my role in my adoptive family.

After this bright moment I was to see a darker side of Seneca character. The afternoon nearly ended in disaster when the lacrosse game turned into a brawl in which my host and his now drunken companions joined. The bloodshed was fortunately cut short by a violent thunderstorm which cooled tempers rapidly, after which we made tracks for Coldspring.

That Sunday visit to Newtown provided both prelude and climax to a summer's field work. In the next two months I became more involved in the affairs and concerns of the Hawk clan. They did not get around to giving me a name at the Green Corn Festival, which postponed my formal adoption until I returned at midwinter. The bereaved relatives turned to me, nevertheless, when the old lady I had met died in September. This was my first opportunity as an anthropologist to attend and observe a longhouse funeral and surely under rather unique circumstances. When we drove the forty miles to Newtown that evening, I suddenly realized that the people riding with me regarded me as next of kin. And that is how I was treated when we arrived. I sat with the mourners half the night, and after the midnight meal we went aloft to sleep. I was assigned a bed near the wall, and I still have the vision of "my family" bedding down on the floor around me. Once we were awakened by drunks, who were dismissed by the women. And toward dawn I awoke to see not three feet away the beautiful face of the young woman who, throughout the long illness, had cared for her grandmother and was now snatching a few moments of sleep before the funeral, secure in the taboos of exogamy, in the common bed of the Hawk clan.

A Messenger of the Tonawanda Chiefs

I was introduced at Tonawanda, which is the central hearth of the Handsome Lake religion, under the best of auspices by the Coldspring "Keepers of the Good Message," as they call the prophet's words, whom I drove from Quaker Bridge to Akron for an annual convention of their peers. They introduced me to the local leaders and to the great ritualists and chiefs from Six Nations Reserve where I was afterward to work. I did not then anticipate spending two and a half years at Tonawanda as Community Worker for the United States Indian Service, which gave me daily contact with the Seneca and constant practice in the language. I seldom missed any of the events at the longhouse, so that it seemed natural for me to be appointed to go with Chief Eddie Black to carry the message sticks to Canada announcing the next convention of Handsome Lake preaching at Tonawanda. This embassy gave me entree to the chiefs of Onondaga Longhouse, where Hewitt and Goldenweiser had preceded me and where I was to feel at home after 1939 when I took up Hewitt's work at the Bureau of American Ethnology until 1951. Hewitt's texts, which I learned to read and translate, contained the words of the old men, and I was welcomed by the next younger generation who wanted to learn with me. With the advent of electronic recording machines, we put down the sacred words for posterity. These were of a quality that lent themselves to published albums by the Library of Congress.

Considering the publicity in the media to the fortunes that popular singers reap from hit recordings, one can understand why questions arise about earnings from my Iroquois recordings. The Iroquois all have television sets, and they visit and participate in various tourist attractions. They occasionally hear my recordings of their grandfathers being played under circumstances that are hardly educational, although the Library of Congress intended that they be limited to educational use by museums, libraries, schools, and television. Who is to prevent the proprietor of a roadside alligator park in Florida, who hires a Seminole Indian to wrestle a 'gator, from playing them as background music? I have heard that one Canadian station uses the Medicine Song as the theme song for a cartoon series. If these allegations are true, both the Iroquois and the collector are being damaged. Such incidents contribute to the decline of rapport between one ethnologist and the grandchildren of informants with whom he once enjoyed excellent relations.

The Heads of Our Grandfathers Are beneath the Ground

One would scarcely expect the reentry to field work among a people with whom an ethnologist had previously worked to be more difficult than his first field trip. Nearly eighteen years elapsed between my last field trip to the Six Nations Reserve in 1951 and my return in 1969. My first brief trip, in January, coincided with the midwinter ceremonies at the Onondaga Longhouse, and I asked whether I would be welcome to attend, as I had in the past. To my dismay I learned that Onondaga Longhouse was closed to white people, including anthropologists! I found myself in the odd situation where research is possible but field work no longer feasible.

To be sure, admission to Iroquois "doings" had always been a privilege granted by the local longhouse officers, never a right. And over the years at Six Nations Reserve there were irritations, particularly with certain journalists, some of whom, from the Indian standpoint, wrote without sympathy or understanding and even with ridicule. For the latter reason, the Lower Cayuga Longhouse had been closed since the late 1930's. Nevertheless, the chiefs admitted me in 1945 to observe a Condolence Council, of which I published an account (Fenton, 1946). I honored their invitation to a repeat performance at

Onondaga Longhouse in 1951 and was received under most cordial circumstances, although I was unable to attend on later occasions. So it did not seem to me inevitable that I should be excluded at Onondaga, even if the longhouse were closed to the general public.

Possibly Six Nations Reserve has had a surfeit of anthropologists. The list is as long as it is illustrious, beginning a century ago with Lewis Henry Morgan, Horatio Hale, and J. N. B. Hewitt and running on through Alexander A. Goldenweiser, Frederick W. Waugh, and Frank Speck. Upper Cayuga, where Speck observed, is still open; but Onondaga, where I succeeded Hewitt and Goldenweiser, is now closed. This anomaly may not be unrelated to the fact that at least seven anthropologists later spent from a summer or two up to three years on the reserve, collecting material for doctoral dissertations at major universities here and abroad. In the course of their researches many aspects and details of Iroquois life were subjected to examination and published—mythology, foods, law, factionalism, the longhouse ceremonies, conservatism, public health, the emerging elite, language, and so on. Like the Navaho, therefore, the Iroquois may have come to feel that they scarcely had a breather from being "studied," and perhaps they tired of answering questions or trying to guess the ulterior purposes of seemingly well-heeled, middle-class white observers. They protested that continued study made them self-conscious and that their privacy was being invaded. They suspected that investigators would go home and write books about them and make a lot of money. It did not escape the Iroquois that several anthropologists who first came as poor graduate students had gone on to remunerative jobs in universities and museums. Others seemingly forgot all about the Iroquois and never wrote. There was once a comfortable collaboration, based on mutual respect for a valued heritage, between older Iroquois who still knew and appreciated their traditions and the often eminent scholars who came to record and discuss them. For the new generation the importance—even the recognition—of this intellectual collaboration has become quite negligible.

Although my former sponsors were in favor of my gate-crashing the longhouse assembly and facing down any opposition, I decided not to attend any ceremonies unless and until I was invited. I did, however, offer to show for a longhouse audience, during my next visit, slides of objects that I had found in European museums, which had aroused considerable interest among the educated public.

During my courtesy call on the superintendent of the Six Nations Reserve, he suggested that the council would like to hear from me. I therefore arranged to appear at their monthly meeting in April to seek permission to reside and carry on my work during the next twelve months. Addressing the chief, the councillors, the superintendent, and the public present, when my turn came, I stated that my appearance before them was more in the nature of a report than a request. It was then more than thirty years since I had first visited the reserve. I reiterated the times and the conditions of my residence among them and observed that I had always been made to feel welcome. I explained my present position as a university professor, which enabled me to resume my former work among them. I recalled that in 1955 I had appeared before them in the interest of borrowing the Queen Anne communion service for an exhibition in Albany at the state museum, of which I was then assistant commissioner, and that three councillors (whom I named) had come with me to watch the service. A lady councillor at the center table interrupted, "That was my late husband, who died two years ago. He always spoke well of you and of that visit to Albany where he said the councillors were royally treated." (This was a most fortunate break, as I later learned, because this woman had recently objected to studies proposed by other anthropologists.) I went on to reassure them that recovering old texts in no way concerned present conditions on the reserve. I was not making a survey and I would not pry into their business. I would be concerned with their affairs to the extent that they wished me to know about them, and I would be of what limited service I could as a guest among them. (This was a good plea.) Later, if they approved, I hoped to return with students who I thought might be trained among them as I had learned to be an anthropologist while working among their old men. Indeed, I acknowledged, as was so often alleged—"Fenton has made his living off us Indians"—that I owed my whole career to them. I mentioned a portrait of a Seneca which hangs in my office at the university—how I tell inquiring visitors that he was my mentor under whom I wrote my doctoral dissertation. (This brought a laugh.) I said that what I was really asking for was "a hunting license for the year 1969." And this was substantially what I was granted.

Within ten days I fulfilled my promise to show the pictures of collections in European museums. We met in the dining room at the Onondaga Longhouse after supper. As might be expected, the audience kept straggling in during the showing, which progressed until, toward the end, a slide jammed, one of several old pictures of local personages I had inserted. I could hear a sudden inspiration of breath among some of the audience as each image had appeared, and it occurred to me that someone might construe it as an omen that the projector jammed just then. The incident brought my talk to an abrupt halt in any case and prevented reshowing the first tray that latecomers had missed. I offered to hold a second showing another night. Then the meeting was opened to questions.

None of the questions related to the pictures or to my remarks. The questions came from younger people who had come in last and they all related to my role as an anthropologist. "What is your work?" "Are you not the one who made recordings of Indian songs here twenty years ago?" Then my young inquisitor leveled the charge that I had not paid the singers, yet had made a lot of money from the recordings. I explained that I had always paid the prevailing wage rates. "I suppose it was then about sixty cents an hour," the young man retorted. "Anyway you should know how much you paid." No one admitted knowing that payments had been made by the Library of Congress for releases, and my explanation of a nonprofit cultural institution was greeted with disbelief.

Then a young matron seated on the floor to my right accused me of selling her grandfather's sacred songs to some television program. She said that she had heard his voice as background music to some cartoon that her son was watching, although she could not identify the song or the program. "I shall never forgive what you have done to my grandfather." She stormed out of the room, saying, "I don't want to hear any more from your or see those pictures. You are just like all the others." But her mother, the daughter of the old chief, who was seated before me where I could see her face, questioned me quietly and at length about the releases. At first she did not believe that he had received any such payment, but at the end she shook my hand and thanked me, saying, "My father always spoke well of you."

It is not difficult to understand the frustration that adherents to the old system of "life chiefs" must feel, when something they know and respect is not acceptable to a large segment of their own people and is completely misunderstood by Canadian society at large. The longhouse warriors (the young men of the Handsome Lake faith) abhor the elected council, the official government of the reserve, and they have twice locked it out of the council house in Ohsweken. My first questioner had read the report in the *Brantford Expositor* that I had appeared before the elected council and requested permission to reside and work on the reserve. "Why if you know so much about us," he asked, "did you go to that council? You should know that it does not represent most of the people. Why didn't you go to the proper council of the Confederacy?" Touché! There was no use explaining that I was locked up in official protocol, being an American in Canada. And my offer to appear before the life chiefs was never taken up.

So what I had hoped might be a pleasurable evening turned into a confrontation. Only afterward did people come up to me, one by one, and express interest in my remarks and in the pictures. Perhaps some regarded the photographs as another proof of the white man using the Indian. In any event, the occasion was exploited for venting aggression and hostility toward a representative of the white race.

The Iroquois enjoy cutting someone down to size. Characteristically, when criticism arises, no one stands to defend. Only men of
prestige among the chiefs, men who spoke with confidence, and dared
to do so, used to assume the role of public defender. I thought of this
as I was being attacked, and when one of my accusers interrupted
me, I reminded him that in all of my experience in councils of their
grandfathers no man ever spoke while another was still talking. And
this remark ended the attack.

One cannot be objective about such an experience. In writing
about it, my tendency is to make it look better than it probably was.
Howard Sky, an informant from my early work, consoled me next
day. "I was really disappointed in the people last night. Those young
people are trying desperately to be Indians, and they don't know quite
how. They don't succeed in making their viewpoint clear because they
don't know how to speak. Young men like the secretary of the council
who questioned you last night get so mad when they go anywhere to
speak that no reasonable body will listen to them for long." When I
commented that I recognized in the disturbed young people what
we face in the young militants in the universities, he replied, "Yes, I
think you are right. These people don't know really what they want.
But they are against all whites."

Hearing of my experience, one of the elected councillors who had
formerly been with the old chiefs showed little surprise. To him the
impatience and intolerance of the young crowd were an old story,
which he said went back to a previous "do" (as he called the counter-
revolt of some years ago); then he pleaded for moderation, saying
that there was a proper way to raise objections. "They are the same
hotheads," he went on. "Then they would not listen. That is when
they started putting white people out of the longhouse. And there
has been trouble ever since." The councillor went on to outline his
policy of religious tolerance. "I believe in letting the white people
in because we go to their affairs off the reserve. Sometimes we don't
understand what is going on, but we go anyway. Serious people should

be admitted [to Seneca Longhouse, where he is speaker], and if they want to write about it, they could request permission. I believe in what you are doing because that is the only way that we are going to preserve the old words. Those young people won't listen to anyone— not even to the old people—so they will not listen to you."

Twenty years and a new generation had brought changes in attitude with dimensions and intensity that I had not foreseen; unwittingly, I had walked into a hornet's nest. Field work is difficult now, yet research is still possible. The ethnologist's work matters to people who care about preserving the old lore. As my friend and colleague Howard Sky put it, "There are people down below who are waiting for you to finish this work in which we are engaged. They need it. And they cannot get it anywhere else. No one can recite Dekanawidah clear through."

References

Fenton, W. N.

1936 "An Outline of Seneca Ceremonies at Coldspring Longhouse." Yale University Publications in Anthropology, No. 9. 23 pp.

1936a "Some Social Customs of the Modern Senecas." *Social Welfare Bulletin*, 7:4–7. Albany: New York State Department of Social Welfare.

1941 "Masked Medicine Societies of the Iroquois." *Smithsonian Institution Annual Report, 1940*. Pp. 397–429, 25 pl. Washington DC.

1941a "Tonawanda Longhouse Ceremonies: Ninety Years after Lewis Henry Morgan." Bureau of American Ethnology, Anthropological Paper 15, Bulletin 128, pp. 139–145, pls. 9–18. Washington DC.

1942 "Songs from the Iroquois Longhouse: Program Notes for an Album of American Indian Music from the Eastern Woodlands." Smithsonian Institution Publication No. 3691, Library of Congress, *Folk Music of the United States*, vol. 6.

1946 "An Iroquois Condolence Council for Installing Cayuga Chiefs." *Journal of the Washington Academy of Sciences*, 36:110–127.

1950 "The Roll Call of the Iroquois Chiefs: A Study of a Mnemonic Cave from the Six Nations Reserve." Smithsonian Miscellaneous Collections 111, No. 15. 75 pp., 12 pls. Washington DC.

1953   "The Iroquois Eagle Dance: An Offshoot of the Calumet Dance ..." Bureau
       of American Ethnology Bulletin 156.
1967   "From Longhouse to Ranch-Type House, the Second Housing Revolu-
       tion of the Seneca Nation." In Elisabeth Tooker, ed., *Iroquois Culture, His-*
       tory and Prehistory. Albany: University of the State of New York, State
       Education Department, New York State Museum and Science Service.

Fenton, W. N., Ed.
1944   "The Requickening Address of the Iroquois Condolence Council" by
       J. N. B. Hewitt. *Journal of the Washington Academy of Sciences*, 34:65–85.
1968   *Parker on the Iroquois*. Syracuse NY: Syracuse University Press.

The Advancement of Material Culture Studies in Modern Anthropological Research

Abstract

Despite living in a gadget-, thing-oriented culture, American anthropologists since at least 1920 have written relatively little about material culture. This decline in interest is related to the reduced status of the research museum in ethnological investigation. Most modern ethnologists in the United States have never collected for a museum or worked with museum specimens. Yet studies of material culture have not vanished, and a surprising number appear under such rubrics as technology, primitive art, and cognition.

Theoretical treatment of material culture goes back at least to the works of O. T. Mason who wrote about the origins of invention before the turn of the century. Also at this time Franz Boas was beginning his important and voluminous writings on the material culture of the Eskimo and of the Northwest Coast. This early tradition was continued and amplified by Wissler and Dixon. Other important works that came before World War II were those of Leslie Spier, Peter Buck, Ralph Linton, and Cornelius Osgood. Although the research began in the thirties, Kluckhohn and Hill's important work on Navaho material culture was not completed until 1971. Among other works appearing since World War II are those of Weltfish, Sayce, and Robert Spier.

In 1965 the Committee on Anthropological Research in Museums

(CARM) was appointed by the American Anthropological Association. This committee, with financial support from the Wenner-Gren Foundation for Anthropological Research, has recommended endowing nearly forty museum research fellowships. Partially supported by CARM, several guides to collecting and inventorying museum objects have appeared recently.

The future of material culture studies is linked to the future of the museums of man. Anthropological museums will have to break from the Victorian mold of the natural history museum and identify more closely with history and art. Museums will need to expand from being places designed to preserve objects to being centers where men, through the study of artifacts, can better understand other men.

A decade ago several of us who had museum connections became concerned about the decline in material culture studies generally and set out to put museums back into the mainstream of anthropological research. We were particularly aware that the ethnographical collections for which we were responsible were not being consulted by our colleagues and their students, that the few students who came to look at collections were devotees of primitive art, and that, while collecting was proceeding in Africa and Melanesia where native cultures were rapidly disappearing, these activities were not resulting in documented collections. We knew too that documentation was poor on older collections in our care, and with few exceptions the same situation prevailed in European museums where much of the best of older North American material is to be found. We decided that the best way to improve a bad situation and to accomplish our aims was to train a new generation of scholars who would use collections as resources for research both in the museum and in the field. Our representations to the Executive Board of the American Anthropological Association (AAA) resulted in the appointment of the Committee on Anthropological Research in Museums (CARM) in 1965, which has been supported entirely by the Wenner-Gren Foundation for Anthropological Research. The program and accomplishments of CARM have been summarized in the annual reports of the AAA (Frantz 1968, *et seq.*) and in the 1969 annual report of the foundation (Wenner-Gren Foundation 1969 [and subsequent years], pp. 22–24). In the words of one of its members, this ongoing program of research fellowships represents "a response to the conviction that hope lies in the increase of quantity, quality, and prestige of ethnological research based on museum collections" (Sturtevant 1969, p. 637). Examples of CARM's accomplishments will be discussed subsequently.

The Present Status of Material Culture Studies

The present minimal participation by anthropologists in studies of material culture is paradoxical when one considers that a principal theme in American culture is the dominance of technology. In a society that turns out and accepts eight million automobiles per year, there is a definite relationship between our technology and the artifacts that it produces and which the society accepts and incorporates into daily life. These artifacts require for their production a certain know-how of assembly, supporting skills for their maintenance and repair, and a complete understanding, if not created demand, for the place of the artifact in the cultural activity in which it is employed.

But somehow the American tradition of mechanical ingenuity has not reached anthropology as a profession. If it has, it operates at a level other than research. What has happened to the American handiman whose motto was: "Don't buy it, if you can make it!" Most of us have been touched in some way by the how-to-do-it mania, which has swept the country in recent years, and evidence of our participation in it always amazes and sometimes alarms colleagues visiting from abroad. I am at a loss to explain this seeming paradox between anthropologists and their culture, unless most of the object-minded individuals have gone into archaeology.

Material culture studies, nevertheless, have stayed alive at a generally consistent level during the present century. The hue and cry of a decade ago, when several of us contributed some ten papers to the literature deploring the decline in such studies since 1900, is evidently not warranted according to Sturtevant's recent findings (1969, pp. 623, 625, 632). Such studies have never bulked very large in the literature of anthropology, so they have never really died, although fewer individuals proportionately contribute them. Considering the whole profession, relatively fewer anthropologists are employed in museums. Most of the jobs are now in universities. Anthropology, nevertheless, still has a huge responsibility for collections, although the rewards for taking care of them enjoy a priority beneath teaching and publishing. Ethnology, which is the central field of cultural anthropology, is the least dependent on collections for its researches and therefore enjoys an ambiguous relation to museums. Indeed, as Sturtevant maintains, research on material culture has always been less important in ethnology than research on social and mental culture. This is not as it should be, since true material culture studies seek to identify cognitive patterns. At any rate only 7.7 percent (five out of sixty-five) of the papers published in the journals of the United States, England, and France in 1967 dealt with material culture, and several of these could have been done without reference to museum collections (Sturtevant 1969, p. 632).

In recent years there has been a noticeable trend away from research responsibilities in museums having major collections. In several instances collections are separated widely from curatorial staff—a move that was begun years ago in New York by George Heye when he built the annex to the Museum of the American Indian at Pelham Bay at a considerable distance from Broadway and 155th Street. Where the staff are university professors who do not use collections to illustrate their teaching and do no research on them, the objects take up valuable space. Where the emphasis is on exhibits which can be justified for educational purposes (although no one knows how effectively the exhibits teach) and where public relations become the predominant interest of the director, research collections are bound to suffer and become less important. They cease to illustrate concepts worthy of modern anthropology, and when the director succumbs to the temptation to sell important pieces on the art market, first-rate curators leave and second-rate curators are hired. By this time the museum has ceased to encourage field collection of documented specimens and takes in undocumented collections which are useless for research purposes and which only compound the problem.

The gloomy picture that I have painted of the crisis now faced by our ethnographic museums is illuminated by a few bright spots, which have recurred about once in a decade during the past seventy years, suggesting that interest in material culture studies has not always been at such a low ebb and that our major museums may survive for the next generation. Hope for material culture studies lies in studies now only beginning; the solution to the plight of museums having research responsibilities awaits massive federal and state aid, which is not likely to be forthcoming for a decade at least. Meanwhile they must hold out as best they can. History affords some perspective on these trends.

Historical Trends

It is now commonplace to observe that anthropology was nurtured in museums and has matured in universities. The *rite de passage* occurred after World War I. Until then jobs were in museums or in research bureaus (Bureau of American Ethnology) connected with institutions having museums. Early teaching posts—at Harvard, California, and Pennsylvania—were conducted in museums or were split appointments between curatorial and teaching duties. For a few years Boas divided his time between the American Museum of Natural History and Columbia University before relinquishing the former, and afterward Wissler went the other route. Since much teaching went on in museums, students grew up with ethnographic collections and did their first research on problems in material culture; and their fieldwork was commonly supported for the purpose of increasing the museum's collections with documented specimens. Field notes were demanded for the accession records and for the museum catalog, and the need for this documentation often led to the exploration of other topics related to the specimens.

Gradually interest shifted away from objects and problems of invention and diffusion to topics and problems less amenable to museum treatment. Kroeber's early work was on the decorative arts of the Arapaho and their neighbors; Wissler's early work on the material culture of the Blackfoot and the Dakota Sioux pioneered a series of historical and distributional studies; but Lowie concentrated on kinship and age grades, and Leslie Spier wrote his dissertation on the Sun Dance (Kroeber 1900, 1902; Wissler 1904, 1910; Lowie 1916, 1920, 1929; Spier 1921). As anthropology ceased to be object minded, anthropologists no longer felt compelled to care for collections. They lost interest in putting up exhibits to fulfill some systematic plan, to illustrate some ecological concept, or for teaching purposes. Wissler alone retained his original interest (stemming from psychology) in the museum as an educational instrument. Others, like Lowie, who first lectured at the American Museum and afterward went to the University of California at Berkeley, drifted away from museum responsibilities. Sapir, long before teaching at Chicago and Yale, first built up the collections of the National Museum of Canada, where one finds pages of catalog entries in his meticulous hand. He directed a major program of field research, which sponsored both Speck's work on northeastern Algonquian art (Speck 1914), and Waugh's studies of Iroquois subsistence, technology, and medicine (Waugh 1916, and ms. field notes). It was then that he wrote what is undoubtedly the most famous methodological paper in American ethnology (1916) and his widely known book on language (1921).

Articles and monographs devoted to material culture topics were quite popular in the United States at the turn of the century. W. H.

Holmes, O. T. Mason, and Frank H. Cushing were contributing papers to the *American Anthropologist* on decorative arts, the origins of inventions, on basketry, and on weapons treated systematically. Studies of this genre, which reflect the theoretical interests of the day, fall off sharply after Wissler's landmark paper in 1914 on the material cultures of the American Indian. Indeed, Wissler then lamented that "for some years the study of material culture has been quite out of fashion" (1914, p. 447; de Laguna 1960, pp. 801, 519–20). Wissler's remark set me to wondering just when the break had occurred. Apparently, the decline commenced in 1900, leveled off in 1910, and fell off sharply after 1920 (Sturtevant 1969, p. 626).

The decennial indices of the *American Anthropologist* tell the story. For the years 1928–1938, there are nine entries to articles under "material culture" and sixteen under "technology." For the next decade, 1939–1948, Greenman's article, "Material Culture and the Organism" (1945, pp. 211–29), stands alone, and there is one reference under "technology." At the mid-century (1949–1958), "material culture" has become "technology," under which perhaps better indexing discloses thirteen entries ranging from canoe-making on Truk to textiles. Of promise is "Implications of Technological Change for Folk and Scientific Medicine" (Gould 1957, pp. 507–16), which portends a search for system. In the most recent cumulative index, 1959–1969, I note in Volume 66 an exchange of views between Amesbury and Ehrich on the validity of "material culture" as a concept. (To the former it is totally unacceptable, since "all culture is nonmaterial.") One finds an encouraging number of articles on technology in relation to some systematic exploration of cultural ecology, such as "Material Culture and Cognition" (Robbins 1966, pp. 745–48), and as material for cross-cultural comparisons.

But as Sturtevant points out, most of these articles seem unrelated to the existence of ethnographic museum collections, and he concludes: "Most modern ethnologists have never studied museum specimens, have never collected for a museum, have never been in a museum storage area. Yet I suppose that at least 90 percent of museum ethnological specimens have never been studied" (1969, p. 632).

As a control I looked at the *Southwestern Journal of Anthropology*, which was founded in 1945 by Spier. Inasmuch as he gave material culture a high priority in his own ethnographic fieldwork, it is not surprising that he rounded up four articles, which are indexed under "material culture," including Foster's important study of Mexican mold-made pottery (1948, pp. 356–70). Other titles occur under topical headings—blow gun, cloth, textiles, etc.

To summarize, although material culture studies are not what they once were, studies of technological subjects have never really gone out of fashion and they persist in new guises and serve different ends. The commonplace that one hears in the profession—"there isn't much interest in material culture studies any more"—really says that fewer anthropologists proportionately are involved with materials per se; but the remark overlooks the important fact that other anthropologists are interested in the ideas that lie behind the objects and are searching for data to analyze systematically and to treat statistically. Material culture offers them the longest sequence and the broadest distributions, and as an area it is most amenable to evolutionary inference.

Theoretical Interest

Technology and its artifacts, inventions, and subsistence comprised much of the earlier theoretical works in ethnology. Between 1894 and 1904, Otis T. Mason of the U.S. National Museum was turning out his great monographs: "North American Bows, Arrows, and Quivers" (1894), *The Origins of Invention* (1966, first published 1895), and "Aboriginal American Basketry" (1902). His approach was systematic, analytical, and he foresaw the idea of the culture area, which was utilized by Boas in arranging exhibits, first in Chicago in 1893 and afterward at the American Museum—an idea which Wissler later developed into a theoretical concept.

No one, however, was more problem oriented than Boas. From his first fieldwork among the Eskimo (1888), and afterward on the Northwest Coast, he observed, sketched, collected, and described a vast array of materials both as technology and as art. Of all his writings the most succinct statement of his views on technology is contained in the chapter, "Invention," in his *General Anthropology* (Boas *et al.* 1938, pp. 238–81). The stress is on mechanical principles—gravity, the lever, torsion, disturbance of equilibrium, the resisting power of hard surfaces, the roller, the pulley—and the application of these to implements—the hammer, weighted projectiles, centrifugal force (bola), increasing the velocity by lengthening the arc (atlatl), the spring (snare), propulsion (blow gun), fire by friction (drill), float, and others. I might add that the mechanical knowledge required in canoeing—the leverage of paddling versus poling—can only be appreciated by learning to handle small boats in different ethnographic settings, and yet these motor techniques are nowhere described. They are most amenable to motion picture techniques.

Wissler, between 1904 and 1914, when he was conducting field and museum studies that produced a series of landmark monographs on the material culture of the northern Plains (1904, 1910, 1914, and 1934), was keenly aware of motor habits as they related to productive processes of material culture (1914, p. 123). As a trained psychologist he distinguished between psychological and cultural phenomena and concluded that "culture differentiation and psychological differentiation run in relatively independent cycles" (1914, p. 130). Wissler is perhaps better known for bringing a system to listing data, for mapping distributions, locating culture centers, defining areas, noting trait associations, inferring history where direct history failed, and for discovering a common denominator for all cultures—his "universal culture pattern" (1923).

Dixon wrote *The Building of Cultures* (1928) in criticism of Wissler's environmentalism, especially the age and area hypothesis. Dixon himself had done important work on the elaborate basketry of the

Indians of northern California (1902) and was thoroughly familiar with the ethnographic collections at the Peabody Museum at Harvard. In his critique of Wissler he makes a valuable distinction between discovery and invention, the latter being "purposeful discovery" (1928, p. 34).

No one made better use of this argument than Leslie Spier, who in a few brief years produced important comparative ethnographies on the Wisslerian model, but with great sophistication, on the Havasupai (1928), Klamath (1930), and the Yuman tribes of the Gila River (1933). In Spier's fieldwork, material culture received detailed consideration, as he believed that the ethnographer's drawings and his explanations should enable the reader to reconstruct the objects.

Of comparable virtuosity are the studies, *Samoan Material Culture* (1930) and *Material Culture of Kapinga-Marangi* (1950), by Peter H. Buck (Te Rangi Hiroa), who brought into his Yale seminar examples of the objects he was analyzing and describing and then projected his field observations to the search for older specimens that navigators had carried off to museums in Europe. The dividends of that seminar have appeared in strange guises among the Navaho and the Iroquois. Those of us who knew the late Ralph Linton are aware of how deeply he identified with the world of artifacts from his early fieldwork on the material culture of the Marquesas (1923), his long association with the Field Museum, and his sustained interest in primitive art (1955).

We see the influence of Malinowski in the H. S. Harrison article on material culture in the 1930 edition of the *Encyclopaedia Britannica*. Harrison wrote about invention, environmental influences, diffusion, and the implications for cultural evolution. In his treatment, he revealed himself to be an "instrumentalist," like Malinowski, and favored the "opportunist" factor in innovation. Thirty-eight years later, in 1968, George Quimby rewrote the article and made the discussion fit the system of L. A. White, for whom evolution is the dominant theory of development. In this view, "material culture consists of tools, weapons, utensils, machines, ornaments, religious images, clothing, and any other ponderable object produced or used by humans." These objects have an enduring quality and they often outlast the societies and cultures that produce them. And the instrumental character of much of man's material culture, to the extent that it satisfies primary needs of subsistence, shelter, clothing, etc., posits a functional relationship of technology to environment, and of man to a secondary environment which his culture creates. Indeed, as Harrison reminds us, "a great part of man's material culture is directly associated with his primary need . . . of procuring foods." It follows that studies of subsistence embrace much of material culture (Parker 1910; Waugh 1916).

The "materialistic" view of material culture by White and Quimby contrasts with the "idealistic" definition of objects. Thoreau was possibly the first to question whether objects themselves are really part of culture when he characterized an arrowhead as a "fossil thought" (Journals, March 28, 1859, in Shepard 1927, p. 318). Cornelius Osgood, in his work on the northern Athabaskan cultures, defines the field as comprising *ideas* "about objects external to the mind resulting from human behavior as well as ideas about human behavior required to manufacture these objects" (1940, p. 26). Perhaps Osgood's conceptualizations of material culture remain better known than the definitive character of the monographs. In themselves, they are important landmarks in the field of material culture studies.

The last person whom most students of anthropology would identify with material culture studies is the late Clyde Kluckhohn who contributed to many theoretical insights to cultural anthropology; but when I last called on him in 1960 during a survey of ethnological research in museums he showed me the notes he was preparing for a work on Navaho material culture (Kluckhohn, Hill, and Kluckhohn 1971), which has now appeared posthumously. This gorgeous book sets a standard and provides hope for a renaissance of studies by ethnologists of man's arts and industries. The material culture is set

over and against its environment; how it varies and relates region-
ally; how it is learned; how it sustains the value system, the roles of
kinship, the fit between ecology and economy; how it affects political structure, and its vital place in religion and ceremonialism. Its
authors have achieved a definition adapted from Osgood and others:
"Our descriptive criteria include actions and technical knowledge
associated with the manufacture and use of the product, and ideas,
both secular and religious, that promote or inhibit the manufacture
and use of the product as well as place it in the Navaho cosmos." The
fieldwork, which was begun by W. W. Hill in the thirties while still
a student of Buck and Spier at Yale, has been carried on and greatly
extended by his students and those of Kluckhohn.

Anticipating the new ethnography, Gene Weltfish, a student of
Boas, studied the distribution of basketry techniques both in the
museum and in the field and sought through linguistic methods to
learn the conceptual categories of material culture which serve as
tribal and temporal indicators (1958, 1960).

Of general works on material culture, three deserve mention. For
the old-fashioned quality of the thought and its rhetoric, I admire
Sayce's *Primitive Arts and Crafts* (1933, 1963), which takes off from
Dixon and draws its main examples from European and classical
prehistory, from Africa, as well as the Americas, and the areas that are
strongly represented in the ethnographic collections of the British
Museum. Sayce makes numerous suggestions of problems awaiting
research, and his book affords a vista of British cultural anthropology
before social anthropology broke away (see also Forde 1937).

The content of technologies has been best handled by European
workers—the Danes and Germans. A notable statement of the relation of material cultures to culture history is Birket-Smith's *The
Paths of Culture* (1965), which I reviewed in the *American Anthropologist* (Fenton 1966*b*); but my second example is the comprehensive
treatment of technology in relation to the cultural ecology of native
peoples by a team of Austrian museum ethnologists (Hirschberg *et*

al. 1966), a handbook that is both systematic and well documented by museum specimens and bibliography. Until an English edition is available, the work contains an English-German glossary.

The third example is the works of Robert F. G. Spier in which he restates the relation of technology to material culture (1968, 1970). His analysis leads to a series of mathematical functions for which the following rules may be written:

> I. *M.C.* < *T.*: "Material culture is a product of man's technology."
>
> II. *T/m* or *T/a* > genre *t/a*: "The technology of a medium or activity produces a genre of techniques and artifacts." Here *t* is a specific mode of *T*, where *t* = technique, and *T* = technology.
>
> III. *A* is a sequence of coordinated *t*'s. Here *A* = an activity.

In terms of the operation of these rules a whole series of problems become researchable through material culture: problems of time and space, of learning, retention and recall, of utilization, and of the relation of the objects and techniques for using them to other major activities of culture. One recalls Malinowski's famous canoe-building episode, the wampum records and mnemonic systems of the Iroquois confederacy, and the symbolism and use of masks in various cultures, the cases in point where the object is the key to a whole cultural realm.

Ethnological Research and Museum Collections

In a recent paper on the interrelatedness of fieldwork, museum studies, and ethnohistorical research, I indicated how dated specimens could be made to serve the interests of culture history (1966*a*). Using examples from my own fieldwork, I further suggested that concepts derived from living culture supplement other techniques of historical interpretation, and when applied to historical documents, may yield insights which in turn exert a feedback effect on further fieldwork and on our understanding of the objects. The model then is circular.

We can see the creative results of this interplay between ethnology and museum study in the work carried out by the recipients of the museum research fellowships awarded by the Committee on Anthropological Research in Museums. Museum Research Fellow Sandra Dickey Harner, in "Knotless Netting Structures from South America," has demonstrated what can be done by working solely with collections to classify and improve typology. Furthermore, Harner's work has implications for archaeologists, provides a guide for the study of this ancient and widespread technique, and finally underscores the importance of proper training. This study "has demonstrated that anthropological research can yield results available through no other source. Certain of this research, in aspects of technology, can be done by people other than anthropologists. But anthropology is not training its students to do such work, and in the main existing faculties of anthropology are not interested if they are aware of the possibilities awaiting the student in such research" (Wenner-Gren Foundation 1968, pp. 18–19).

In neglecting the material basis that underlies, limits, and to a degree determines social life, anthropology is not fulfilling its mandate to study whole cultures. Unless anthropologists study technological advances and problems, as Phillip Dark and John C. Ewers warn us, the gap will be filled by others untrained in cultural interpretation. With all the studies we have of Pueblo ceremonialism and politics, we are still in the dark about the material culture of the Keresan pueblos, which Martin Murphy, a student of Leslie White, is undertaking in the museum and in the field.

The ability to relate artifacts to other aspects of culture comes from the inevitable emphasis on functionalism that derives from ethnographic training. Adrienne Kaepler's "Reconstruction Ethnography of Society Islands Material Culture," undertaken at the Bishop Museum with CARM support, presupposes such training.

Dated artifacts in museums afford good evidence of culture history. Given the poor state of catalogs of most early museum collections here and abroad, to be able to relate an object to a particular dated expedition or voyage such as Captain Cook's or the voyage of the *Beagle* is often the best evidence available as to period and provenience. The logic of having such collections studied, cataloged, and related to documentary sources seems compelling. CARM has supported the preparation of a catalog of Polynesian artifacts from the Wilkes expedition (1838–1842) by Martha Cooper.

In nonliterate societies artifacts provide models of the past. Frequently memory systems depend on spatial arrangement of objects or designs for recalling long streams of verbal information (Fenton 1950, 1971). Two studies undertaken by museum research fellows are to the point: the first is an examination of Santa Clara Pueblo pottery in the museum and in the field by Betty Le Free; and the second involves scrutiny of Bella Coola ceremonial art in collections and discussing them in the field with informants by Margaret Stott. Perhaps these examples of research undertaken on specific problems will attract more students than general preachments.

Of greater importance to the development of anthropology are the indications of new directions of research that flow from the discovery of improved methods of research on museum collections. Some of these derive from the "new archaeology"; others derive from ethnoscience. The application of attribute analysis to ethnographic specimens is illustrated by Carol Kauffman's research into Haida carving, which utilized museum collections and extended to the observation and interview of carvers on the Northwest Coast. A parallel study in another medium is Margaret H. Friedrich's application of structural models and methods to the analysis of design and style, the effects of social interaction among artists, and the implications of ethnographic analysis for archaeological interpretation. Working on San Jose painted pottery in Mexico and at the Field Museum, Mrs. Friedrich has put her archaeologist colleagues on notice as to the limitation of inferences that can be made from lesser-known materials (Friedrich 1970).

Current Problems in Museum Work

In recent years American students have not clamored for access to the ethnographic collections in museums. This is not true in Europe. There, material culture studies show some vigor and enjoy modest status. Two beautifully illustrated catalogs of ethnographic collections in Germany and Austria greeted the Americanist Congress meeting in Stuttgart in 1968 (Feest 1968; Benndorf and Speyer 1968). And I am told by George Henri Rivière (former director general of International Council of Museums, UNESCO) that, during the student demonstrations in Paris in 1968, one of the demands was for access to the museum collections and some instruction in their study (see also Sturtevant 1969, p. 639). This demand is partly due to the decline in opportunities for fieldwork abroad and partly reflects suggestions emanating from French structuralism as to how the collections can be rearranged for viewing and study at various levels of competence. Indeed, Rivière used many of Lévi-Strauss' ideas in the plan for the new Musée National des Arts et Traditions Populaires. The latter sees the anthropological museum as an opportunity for the extension of the field of research; he advocates that every teaching department of anthropology should have a museum attached to it; and its purpose should be not so much to preserve objects as to help men to understand other men (Lévi-Strauss 1963, pp. 375–76). The plan calls for synchronized exhibits of objects, sound, and light together with pertinent manuscripts illustrating a major cultural activity, backed up by study collections of varying degrees of complexity as the student penetrates his specialty.

The whole problem of access to collections and improving their usefulness for research is a complex question that can be touched on only briefly here by sketching the principal findings of CARM. The first problem is one of inventory. What is there, how much of it, and where is it? The baffled student needs answers to these questions before he can plan and undertake research. In North America alone collections are concentrated in large museums and scattered widely in small repositories, many of them private. There are no true duplicates of ethnographic specimens and they are not interchangeable, for "museum specimens are unique cultural and historical documents" (Sturtevant 1969, p. 640). By a careful estimate, there are a million and a half such specimens in the United States alone; of these, half are in five large museums (there are two hundred thousand specimens in the U.S. National Museum alone). There are perhaps four and a half million specimens in the museums of the world. It would require 140 man years to prepare an "Index Ethnographicum," such as I proposed more than a decade ago (Fenton 1960), at a cost of fifty cents per specimen. Time and inflation run on while the specimens deteriorate at an alarming rate (Ricciardelli 1967a, 1967b).

Several things can and are being done about it. Under the direction of the late Stephan de Borhegyi of CARM, John Hunter prepared an inventory of ethnological collections in museums of the United States and Canada (1967), which has gone through two editions. Second, the pilot study for inventorying ethnological collections, which Ricciardelli and his students carried out from the Stovall Museum in the museums of Oklahoma, with National Science Foundation support and the guidance of CARM, has since been extended to Missouri, New Mexico, and Arizona. Mary Jane Schneider, one of Ricciardelli's student supervisors, has overseen the expansion, which has been greatly facilitated by the preparation of *A Guide to Inventorying Ethnological Collections* (Schneider 1970), an essential dictionary for data processing.

There is no longer any excuse for not making documented collections in the field. Sturtevant has provided students with an excellent *Guide to Field Collecting* (1967), and in recent years CARM has made some modest grants to students going into the field to enable them to collect systematically specimens for their host museum.

The future of material culture studies is linked to the future of museums of man, which are going to have to be liberated from the sleeping giants, the offspring of the Victorian era, called natural history museums, with which anthropology has an unnatural affinity. Most thoughtful museum anthropologists feel that our natural affinity is with history and art, and they point to the success of the Musée de l'Homme and the National Museum of Anthropology in Mexico City. Access to study collections at all levels is essential. Exhibits will be concept oriented and worthy of modern anthropology. As research institutions they will be communities of scholars, staffed by scientists, curators, aids, interns, and students. Responsibilities for the collections will be defined clearly, and curating must be given equal rank with teaching.

A serious problem facing museums today is the integrity of collections. Keeping large blocks of material intact is essential for research purposes. It must not be allowed to deteriorate, it should be restored, and it should be kept for posterity. Museum conservation is no longer in its infancy, it is well developed in art museums, and it has now spread to the Field Museum which has established a laboratory of considerable importance for anthropology.

A more serious question is how to maintain the collections in the face of demands for their return to the descendants of original owners. This is partly a matter of local pride that state and national museums have continually to face and compensate for and partly a misunderstanding of the nature of museums. From civil rights activists we now hear the bogus principle enunciated that no museum should keep objects relating to a living culture. By Red Power advocates it is stated in genocidal terms: "No museum should harbor the artifacts of an ongoing culture when the act of harboring inhibits the very life of that culture." It does not matter if the facts run contrary; the mere fact that the principle is stated is tantamount to truth. It usually has religious overtones as in the recent controversy over the New York wampum collection: to keep it for all of the people including the

Indians or return it to the heirs of its original keepers at Onondaga. In these confrontations history is no longer relevant. Objects which formerly were primarily political in character are now endowed with religious significance, and the mere assertion of religious symbolism is sufficient to weigh the balance of equity without having to show cause why they have become religious lately. We anthropologists are equally at fault and we should not complain too loudly because we find ourselves caught up in the feedback from our own field studies. Our published reports have made evident what was not previously plain to a generation that largely ignored the old people with whom we worked.

Another area of museology on which material culture studies bear is the testing of museum exhibits as teaching tools. The museum public is a community of a kind that should attract the social anthropologist. There has been surprisingly little research of visitor behavior in museums. The best such study of *Anthropology and the Public: The Role of Museums* (1960) is by a Dutch ethnomuseologist, Dr. H. H. Frese, which might well be emulated in another cultural setting: it tells us a great deal about anthropology in museums but even more about museums and Dutch society. Marvin Harris' experiment with filming the behavior of museum visitors at the Metropolitan Museum of Art offers intriguing possibilities. Borhegyi's surveys at the Milwaukee Public Museum should not be overlooked.

Ethnographic collections become of increasing importance as cultures vanish from the world. Since many of these contain specimens that are undocumented, we can learn much from the archaeologists about how to study them. Museums of Europe are full of what I call "Ethnological Chippendale": the specimens are what someone says they are; but where the documentation exists to prove their authenticity, we can extrapolate from them to similar pieces, in the manner of the art historians who can teach us much. The other source of information is from ethnologists working in the field with descendants of the original makers.

So let us get it all together—the ethnographic field study, the museum study collection, and the archaeological excavation. In the field of material culture studies there is much work to be done. With stimulation and training provided by groups such as the Committee on Anthropological Research in Museums, with an ethnology sensitized to the material side of life, and with a revived, vibrant museology of man, this work will go forward.

References Cited

Benndorf, Helga, and Arthur Speyer
1968 *Indianer Nordamerikas, 1760–1860.* Offenbach a. M., Deutschen Leder-museum.

Birket-Smith, Kaj
1965 *The Paths of Culture.* Madison: University of Wisconsin Press.

Boas, F.
1888 *The Central Eskimo.* Sixth Annual Report, Bureau of American Ethnology. Washington DC: Smithsonian Institution.

Boas, F., *et al.*
1938 *General Anthropology.* New York: Heath.

Buck, Peter H. (Te Rangi Hiroa)
1930 *Samoan Material Culture.* Bernice P. Bishop Museum, Bulletin 75. Honolulu.
1950 *Material Culture of Kapinga-Marangi.* Bernice P. Bishop Museum, Bulletin 200. Honolulu.

de Laguna, F., ed.
1960 *Selected Papers from the American Anthropologist, 1888–1920.* Evanston IL and Elmsford NY: Row, Peterson.

Dixon, Roland B.
1902 Basketry Designs of the Indians of Northern California. *Bulletin,* Vol. 17, No. 1. New York: American Museum of Natural History.
1928 *The Building of Cultures.* New York: Scribner's.

Feest, C. F.
1968 *Indianer Nordamerikas.* Wien: Museum für Völkerkunde.

Fenton, William N.

1950 The Roll Call of the Iroquois Chiefs: A Study of a Mnemonic Cane from the Six Nations Reserve. *Smithsonian Miscellaneous Collections* 111 (15): 1–75.

1960 The Museum and Anthropological Research. *Curator* 3:327–55.

1966*a* Field Work, Museum Studies, and Ethnohistorical Research. *Ethnohistory* 13 (1–2):71–85.

1966*b* Review of Birket-Smith, 1965. *American Anthropologist* 68:530.

1968 Report of the Committee on Anthropological Research in Museums. In Ch. Frantz, ed., *Annual Report, 1967.* American Anthropological Association. April, 1968. Pp. 47–49.

1971 The New York State Wampum Collection: The Case for the Preservation of Cultural Treasures. *Proceedings of the American Philosophical Society* 115:437–61.

Forde, C. Daryll

1937 *Habitat, Economy and Society.* New York: Harcourt, Brace.

Foster, George M.

1948 Some Implications of Modern Mexican Mold-Made Pottery. *Southwestern Journal of Anthropology* 4:356–70.

Frantz, Ch., ed.

1968 *Annual Report, 1967.* American Anthropological Association. April, 1968. (Subsequent reports are available for 1969 and 1970.)

Frese, H. H.

1960 *Anthropology and the Public: The Role of Museums.* Medelingen van Het Rijksmuseum voor Volkenkunde, No. 14. Leiden.

Friedrich, Margaret H.

1970 Design, Structure, and Social Interaction: Archaeological Implications of an Ethnographic Analysis. *American Antiquity* 35:332–43.

Gould, Harold A.

1957 The Implications of Technological Change for Folk and Scientific Medicine. *American Anthropologist* 59:507–16.

Greenman, Emerson F.

1945 Material Culture and the Organism. *American Anthropologist* 47:211–29.

Harrison, H. S.
1930 Material Culture. *Encyclopaedia Britannica.*

Hirschberg, Walter, Alfred Janata, W. B. Bauer, and C. Feest
1966 *Technologie und Ergologie in der Völkerkunde.* Mannheim: Bibliographisches Institut.

Hunter, John E.
1967 *Inventory of Ethnological Collections in Museums of the United States and Canada.* 2nd ed. Milwaukee: Committee on Anthropological Research in Museums, American Anthropological Association.

Kluckhohn, Clyde, W. W. Hill, and Lucy Wales Kluckhohn
1971 *Navaho Material Culture.* Cambridge: Belknap Press of Harvard University Press.

Kroeber, A. L.
1900 Symbolism of the Arapaho. *Bulletin*, Vol. 12. New York: American Museum of Natural History. Pp. 265–327.
1902 The Arapaho. *Bulletin*, Vol. 18, Pts. 1–2. New York: American Museum of Natural History.

Lévi-Strauss, Claude
1963 *Structural Anthropology.* New York and London: Basic Books.

Linton, Ralph
1923 *Material Culture of the Marquesas Islands.* Memoirs, Bernice P. Bishop Museum, Vol. 8, No. 5. Honolulu.
1955 *The Tree of Culture.* New York: Knopf.

Lowie, R. H.
1916 Plains Indian Age-Societies. *Anthropological Papers*, Vol. 11, Pt. 13. New York: American Museum of Natural History.
1920 *Primitive Society.* New York: Horace Liveright.
1929 *Culture and Ethnology.* New York: Peter Smith.

Mason, Otis T.
1894 North American Bows, Arrows, and Quivers. *Annual Report, 1893.* Washington DC: Smithsonian Institution. Pp. 631–79.
1902 Aboriginal American Basketry. *Report, 1902.* Washington DC: U.S. National Museum. Pp. 171–548.

1966   *The Origins of Invention.* Cambridge MA: MIT Press. (First published in 1895.)

Morgan, L. H.

1881   *Houses and House-Life of the American Aborigines.* Contributions to North American Ethnology, Vol. 4. U.S. Geographical and Geological Survey of the Rocky Mountain Region. Washington DC: Government Printing Office.

Osgood, Cornelius

1940   *Ingalik Material Culture.* Yale University Publications in Anthropology, No. 22. New Haven.

Parker, Arthur C.

1910   *Iroquois Uses of Maize and Other Food Plants.* New York State Museum, Bulletin 144. Albany: University of the State of New York. (Reprinted in W. N. Fenton, ed., *Parker on the Iroquois.* Syracuse University Press, 1968.)

Quimby, George I.

1968   Material Culture. *Encyclopaedia Britannica.*

Ricciardelli, Alex F.

1967*a* A Census of Ethnological Collections in United States Museums. *Museum News* 46 (1):11–14.

1967*b* A Model for Inventorying Ethnological Collections. *Curator* 10 (4):330–36.

1967*c* A Pilot Study for Inventorying Ethnological Collections. Norman: Stovall Museum of Science and History, University of Oklahoma.

Robbins, Michael

1966   Material Culture and Cognition. *American Anthropologist* 68:745–48.

Sapir, Edward

1916   *Time Perspective in Aboriginal American Culture: A Study in Method.* Memoir 90, Geological Survey of Canada, Anthropological Series, No. 13. Ottawa.

1921   *Language.* New York: Harcourt, Brace.

Sayce, R. U.

1963   *Primitive Arts and Crafts.* New York: Biblo and Tannen. (First published, Cambridge, 1933.)

Schneider, Mary Jane

1970 *A Guide to Inventorying Ethnological Collections.* Columbia: Museum of Anthropology, University of Missouri.

Shepard, Odell, ed.

1927 *The Heart of Thoreau's Journals.* Boston: Houghton Mifflin.

Speck, Frank G.

1914 *The Double-Curve Motif in Northeastern Algonkian Art.* Memoir 42, Geo logical Survey of Canada, Anthropological Series, No. 1. Ottawa.

Spier, Leslie

1921 The Sun Dance of the Plains Indians: Its Development and Diffusion. *Anthropological Papers,* Vol. 16, Pt. 7. New York: American Museum of Natural History.

1928 Havasupai Ethnography. *Anthropological Papers,* Vol. 29, Pt. 2. New York: American Museum of Natural History.

1930 *Klamath Ethnography.* University of California Publications in American Archaeology and Ethnology, Vol. 30. Berkeley.

1933 *Yuman Tribes of the Gila River.* Chicago: University of Chicago Press.

Spier, Robert F. G.

1968 Technology and Material Culture. In James A. Clifton, ed., *Introduction to Cultural Anthropology.* Boston: Houghton Mifflin. Pp. 130–59.

1970 *From the Hand of Man: Primitive and Preindustrial Technologies.* Boston: Houghton Mifflin.

Sturtevant, William C.

1964 Studies in Ethnoscience. In A. K. Romney and R. W. d'Andrade, eds., *Transcultural Studies in Cognition. American Anthropologist,* Special Pub lication 66 (3):99–131.

1967 *Guide to Field Collecting of Ethnographic Specimens.* Information Leaflet 503, Museum of Natural History. Washington DC: Smithsonian Institution. 41 pp.

1969 Does Anthropology Need Museums? *Proceedings of the Biological Society of Washington* 82:619–50. Washington DC

1973 Museums as Anthropological Data Banks. In Alden Redfield, ed., *Anthropology Beyond the University.* Southern Anthropological Society Proceedings, No. 7. Athens: University of Georgia Press.

Waugh, F. W.

1916 *Iroquois Foods and Food Preparation*. Memoir 86, Geological Survey of Canada, Anthropological Series, No. 12. Ottawa.

Weltfish, Gene

1958 The Linguistic Study of Material Culture. *International Journal of American Linguistics* 44 (3):301–11.

1960 The Anthropologist and the Question of the Fifth Dimension. In Stanley Diamond, ed., *Culture in History*. New York: Columbia University Press. Pp. 160–77.

Wenner-Gren Foundation for Anthropological Research

1968 *Report for the Fiscal Year, February 1, 1967–January 31, 1968*. New York: Wenner-Gren Foundation. Pp. 18–19.

1969 *Report for the Fiscal Year, February 1, 1969–January 31, 1970*. New York: Wenner-Gren Foundation.

1971 *Report for the Fiscal Year, February 1, 1970–January 31, 1971*. New York: Wenner-Gren Foundation.

Wissler, Clark

1904 Decorative Art of the Sioux Indians. *Bulletin*, Vol. 18, Pt. 3. New York: American Museum of Natural History.

1910 Material Culture of the Blackfoot Indians. *Anthropological Papers*, Vol. 5, Pt. 1. New York: American Museum of Natural History.

1914 Material Culture of the North American Indians. *American Anthropologist*, n.s. 16: 447–505. Reprinted in 1915 in *Anthropology in North America*. New York: G. E. Stechert. Pp. 76–134. Also in de Laguna 1960, pp. 801–61.

1923 *Man and Culture*. New York: Thomas Y. Crowell.

1934 *North American Indians of the Plains*. Handbook Series, No. 1. Rev. ed. New York: American Museum of Natural History.

The Iroquois in the Grand Tradition of American Letters

The Works of Walter D. Edmonds, Carl Carmer, and Edmund Wilson

A title of this scope might lead the reader to expect some discussion of two great nineteenth century writers: Lewis H. Morgan and Francis Parkman. Indeed Morgan's *League of the Ho-de-no-sau-nee, or Iroquois* (Rochester, 1851) started scientific ethnography in America; and Francis Parkman's classic on *France and England in North America* ran to seven parts, and the remainder into twelve volumes, which represent a kind of literate narrative history that is no longer fashionable among historians. Parkman is not without his biases toward the savages, and he does not lack critics today.[1] However thorough his research, and however much he distorted sources to support his views, as Francis Jennings has charged, he was a great writer and a master of historical style. "Parkman's work is one grand historical novel," as Edmund Wilson once reminded me, and he should be read in that light. Early on Parkman intended to write an Iroquois history, but he abandoned the plan when he found that he could not connect the culture of their living descendants with their historical past. Instead he turned to the then still viable cultures of the Plains as represented in his personal experiences of the *Oregon Trail* (1872) and derived from the buffalo hunters of the northern Plains the inspiration for the Indians that populated his novel. I remain a Morgan and a Parkman enthusiast, their works merit separate treatment, which I have accorded them elsewhere,[2] and they are not my present concern.

A third writer on the Iroquois, Arthur C. Parker (1881–1955) brings us to the period of the three writers whom I shall discuss. Parker was part Seneca, and he identified ideologically with Native Americans. He wrote well enough to attract the attention of Edmund Wilson, the distinguished critic, who planned to include Parker's work in an American *Pleiade*, which one day may come to pass. Since I have already paid tribute to his ethnology in *Parker on the Iroquois* (Syracuse, 1968), he need only be mentioned here.

Rather I shall concentrate on three writers who are not anthropologists or historians per se, but who are essentially men of letters. I have known all of them more or less personally, and two of them—Carmer and Wilson—I introduced among the Senecas. Walter D. Edmonds, historical novelist of upstate New York, I met much later and know the least. Carl Carmer, self-styled "American folklorist and informal historian," sought me out at Tonawanda in the thirties. And Edmund Wilson, essayist and critic and sage of Talcottville, called upon me in 1957 at the New York State Museum. Each of these writers has made a special contribution to the literature on the Iroquois, and each has seen them with peculiar insight drawn from a wide-ranging acquaintance with literatures. From two of them I have learned how another writer can observe and interpret the same phenomena in a different light. The two, Carmer and Wilson, assisted me significantly at critical states of my own career.

II

Walter D. Edmonds (1903–[1998]) and I did not meet until Edmund Wilson brought us together at dinner one summer evening in the "Old Stone House" at Talcottville, Wilson's summer home. The Edmonds winter in Cambridge, Massachusetts but return summers to Remsen, N.Y., where they have a house not far from Boonville, his birthplace. These annual returns enable Edmonds to renew an intimate familiarity with the waterways of upper New York State, the region of his important writing. Edmonds must be one of the few persons from the north country to attend Choate and St. Pauls to prepare for Harvard where he graduated in 1926 with the A.B. and was elected to Phi Beta Kappa. Because of the library resources for a historical writer in greater Boston it is understandable why Edmonds settled in Cambridge. As a distinguished alumnus he has served on the Board of Overseers at Harvard, and the American Academy of Arts and Sciences honored him with membership. The latter is the learned body which John Adams founded and to which the Rev. Samuel Kirkland, missionary to the Oneidas, was elected in 1791 for his Census of the Six Nations. These are the bare facts of a distinguished career that can be gleaned from *Who's Who in America* and *Contemporary Writers*. Beyond these obvious sources, I cannot say that I really know him.

Drums Along the Mohawk appeared in 1936. My wife and I were recently married and living in Akron, New York, a small upstate village in western New York adjacent to the Tonawanda Seneca Indian Reservation where I was posted as Community Worker in the U.S. Indian Service. This residence represented my participation in the New Deal for the Iroquois, now a matter of record.[3] One of the projects that we started was a library for the Tonawanda Senecas in cooperation with the Grosvenor Library of Buffalo. Having emerged from Yale and Westport, Connecticut, where I matured among artists, writers, and book reviewers, I set about tapping sources of current literature. We enlisted Carl Carmer, to scrounge review copies of books from his Greenwich Village neighbors and send them on to us. Our copy of Edmonds' *Drums*, however, came through a book club membership to which my wife, then an English teacher, subscribed. Whenever a shipment arrived certain persons were bound to turn up.

Cephas Hill, the reservation's resident intellectual, was our most frequent caller. Cephas owned the first edition of Morgan's *League*, which had been written out of research at Tonawanda in the previous century. Cephas had also discovered in an attic some correspondence between Morgan and Ely S. Parker concerning the Tonawanda

Longhouse ceremonies, which I afterward published and persuaded Cephas to let the University of Rochester Library have the originals for the Morgan Collection.[4] With Cephas we never ran short of conversation. When he borrowed *Drums*, which my wife and I had both read, I wondered how he would react to it.

Within a few days Cephas returned all excited. "Blue Back," Edmonds' wily Oneida character, reminded him of Barber Black, a Tonawanda sachem chief and a whimsical local personality both among the Senecas and the White people of Genesee county. Apart from his official duties for the Bear Clan in the council, Ba Ba's specialty was weather prediction. Every October he walked the fifteen miles to Batavia to con his friend Larry Griswold, the then editor of the *Batavia Daily News*, out of a few dollars for the long range forecast on the coming winter. Ba Ba's data were such signs as the thickness of the hickory bark, the pile on the "Woolly Bears," and the height of some farmer's woodpile. What still fascinates me is that Edmonds could create an authentic and convincing character of an Iroquois personality, certainly the Trickster of his piece, with whom our Seneca friend could identify.

Even more interesting is that Edmonds makes no pretense of knowing Indians. On re-reading *Drums* some forty years later, when I have come to know the setting much better, I still find "Blue Back" credible. Moreover, I admire Edmonds' certain knowledge of the Mohawk-Oneida country, his familiarity with tracking and related techniques of deer hunting, the cultural geography of the Palatine settlements, his mastery of rural New Yorker English, and his ability to build suspense. In a second reading I found some questions penciled in our copy: what was the source of the report of the Oneida and Onondaga delegation at Fort Stanwix in 1777 that the council fire of the League that had burned from time immemorial at Onondaga was extinguished (p. 143)? And what is the source of their carrying around the sacred fire in a stone pot when a village was removed to a new site (p. 145)? At times Edmonds has his Seneca warriors garbed and equipped straight out of the color plates of Morgan's *Reports to the Regents*,[5] an authentic source in the absence of other information; but once or twice I questioned the wearing of the classic Seneca headdress with single twirling feather during a campaign. The settlers of German Flats certainly had every reason for hating Joseph Brant, and Edmonds conveys their sentiments toward the Loyalist Mohawk war leader unequivocally. But if one reads Brant's post-Revolutionary correspondence with Kirkland, whom he had known since boyhood, and General Israel Chapin, U.S. Agent at Canandaigua, Bryant reveals himself as highly intelligent, human, and politically astute. Brant deserves a critical historical biography to replace that of W. L. Stone (1838).[6]

Edmonds confessed uncertainty about such matters when writing to his classmate Oliver La Farge.[7] He thought that La Farge had revealed more of himself than of Navajo life in *Laughing Boy*, and wrote that he liked *Sparks Fly Upward*, another La Farge novel of Navajo life, "twice as much as *Laughing Boy*." In return, Edmonds fully expected his classmate, "the Harvard Indian authority to lance me for my Indians." Indeed presently he wrote to La Farge again telling how he was "stunned to hear from one in the Indian Service," for I had written to Edmonds that Blue Back was convincing. Moreover, a Menominee woman wrote to him repeatedly from Wisconsin that his "Iroquois were real honest to god . . . Indians." Yet some time later in March of 1938, after G. P. Putnam's Sons, the publishers, had asked him to write a history of the Iroquois, Edmonds confessed to La Farge: "I don't know much about the Iroquois really." He had worked them up from the settler's point of view, and then attempted to view them from the inside by reading the standard ethnographic sources, which he lists. Such a history, he estimated, would require 150,000 words because "the Iroquois are a long story," and he did not feel up to it, not being a genuine Indian authority. He was rather more attracted to the great Indian personalities—Hiawatha, Handsome Lake, Brant, Cornplanter and Red Jacket. In this correspondence he professes a

special view of Brant—that he was vain, vindictive, as well as great—
and he noted that virtually all of the Mohawk massacres occurred
when Brant was present. As for the history, every writer who has
attempted it has learned that it takes too long and is too long.

Edmonds made two other literary attempts involving Indian
themes. *In the Hands of the Senecas* (1947) addressed the Indian
captivity literature, so popular in the nineteenth century, through
the medium of fiction. He learned that twentieth century readers
are not as vitally concerned with these tragic adventures as were
the nineteenth century descendants of the victims. And in writing *The Musket and the Cross* (1968), Edmonds viewed the "Indian
World" through historical documents bearing on the ancient theme
of Parkman—the struggle between France and England for control
of North America. To enrich the reader's understanding of Indian
participation in the events described Edmonds makes good use of
the rich ethnological literature on such topics as the Feast of the
Dead, the Condolence ritual, and the persistent belief in the power of
the Little Water Medicine to sustain life. But with all this, "the work
peters out," as I noted at the close of reading the work ten years ago;
as Edmonds feared, it was too big a canvas and too detailed to reach
any destination. He had undertaken a task which thirty years earlier
he considered impossible. But he then thought that Carl Carmer
might carry it off.

On receiving Jesse Cornplanter's *Legends of the Longhouse* (1938),
for which Carl Carmer wrote the Foreword, Edmonds again wrote
to La Farge, expressing the notion, "perhaps a ridiculous one, that
Carl Carmer could . . . write (the Longhouse book), if he wanted to
be thorough."[8] Edmonds had liked Carmer's New York book, which
had appeared two years earlier, although he frequently found it in-
accurate. He concluded his letter: "The trouble is he is a kind of
atmospheric reporter, tremendously effective in some ways, not so
hot in others." And this about sums up my own experience with this
charming and talented person.

III

Carl Lamson Carmer (1893–1976) was born in Cortland in the very heart of upstate New York, the son of a school superintendent. He attended Hamilton College and graduated with the PhB in 1914, receiving the PhM three years later, after taking an MA in English at Harvard in 1915. World War I interrupted his graduate career, but he once told me that he could not abide the thought of writing a doctoral dissertation on some arcane subject. Hamilton made up for any oversight by awarding him an honorary LhD in 1941.

When I first met him in 1935 he had already abandoned teaching college English and was a full-time writer having done a best-seller on the Deep South. After two summers and a winter of fieldwork among the Allegany Senecas, and having exhausted the available fellowships at Yale, I had heeded Commissioner John Collier's summons to anthropologists to join the U.S. Indian Service and was sent up to New York Agency in February as "Community Worker" to the Tonawanda Band of Senecas. I was to spend the next two and one-half years on this assignment. With the uncertainties attending the Indian New Deal, and not wishing to abandon a career in anthropology, I was resolved to keep my sanity by continuing ethnological fieldwork as time afforded. As the new anthropologist in the region I was presently invited to address the Lewis H. Morgan Chapter of the New York State Archaeological Association in Rochester. In my previous research on the Allegany Reservation I had discovered and worked out the underlying ritual pattern that governs the celebration of the calendric cycle of Longhouse ceremonies at Coldspring Longhouse and my first publication was in press.[9] The pattern concept being my forte, I asked Jesse Cornplanter to come along and illustrate the songs which make up the cycle. Jesse's performance on that occasion made the presentation a signal success. Carl Carmer was in attendance and that was our first meeting.

I would soon learn that creative writing marches to a different drummer than historical ethnology. As a literary artist Carl Carmer was not above altering chronology, shifting scenes, and substituting characters and roles to fit the needs of creative writing. Although Arthur Parker had introduced Carmer to Cornplanter and to me after our Rochester performance, Carmer in writing chose to place our meeting after a camp meeting at Akron, which he came out to attend in early summer and where I was present with Cephas Hill, not Jesse, as Carmer has it in *Listen for a Lonesome Drum* (1936:26). His version makes a better story. What is more he wrote to me before he left home in New York City to expect him there and he sent best regards to "Jess, Cephas . . . and also that most attractive squaw— Olive," an English teacher in nearby Oakfield to whom I was engaged. By this time for a fact he had already visited Akron and had stayed with me. We three and Jesse had gone down to Cattaraugus together to collect the origin myth of the Dark Dance, a ritual of four cantos that is sung in the dark for the Little People who once conferred hunting magic on a Seneca hunter.

Naive as I was about some things, I had learned how to conduct and record an ethnological interview and I was glad to share field-work with a successful writer whose company I enjoyed. Here was a chance to exchange observations on techniques of interviewing. Carmer never made any notes at the time, while I was an inveterate scribbler, filling the right hand pages of notebooks with texts and comments of informants and reserving the left hand pages for corrections and additions. This was a technique that Leslie Spier had taught us in an informal course on field methods at Yale. The next step was to transcribe from these notebooks fairly promptly accounts of ceremonies, folktales, texts, etc.

At the time I was concerned that Carmer would not remember the details and was certain that, without my transcribed notes, he would not get things right. Perhaps out of some compulsion to be helpful, I shared with him typescripts of events and interviews where we both had been present. He evidently made good use of my notes. Some months later when our copy of the book arrived suitably inscribed,

I was both pleased and somewhat shocked to see my words in print but without direct acknowledgement. He mentions my presence at the Dark Dance which we both attended at Jesse Cornplanter's (p. 91), but he does not say that I elicited the origin legend which he prints (p. 96). Likewise, he describes the Maple Thanksgiving ceremony from my notes and his own memory; but not knowing what to expect and not recording observations at the time, he confuses the number of singers carrying rattles and drums to the singers' bench in the longhouse, and singers do not sit on their instruments (p. 107). Only one drum is involved, and the drummer is supported by a chorus of several singers with horn rattles. Moreover, no instruments are used in the Trotting Dance, which is a typical stomp dance of the Eastern Woodlands, in which the leader and supporting singers in the file behind him sing in antiphonal (p. 108).

Calling attention to these lapses in ethnographic observation, which could have been corrected in proofs by submitting them to someone familiar with the ceremonies, as Edmund Wilson did later, in no way deprecates Carmer's ability to recall whole conversations, his genius at capturing a mood, and his considerable skill as a writer. Tonawanda Seneca readers liked what he wrote and recognized the accounts of his Tonawanda visits as authentic. They were then less demanding than academicians.

During two years at Tonawanda I had published three articles, filed a dissertation and defended it, was awarded the PhD, and was seeking an academic connection. When our small family arrived at St. Lawrence University in the autumn of 1937 to begin my first teaching, virtually no one had seen or read my publications. Nevertheless I was something of a celebrity for having appeared as a character in *Listen for a Lonesome Drum* the preceding year. It was soon made clear to us that living with the Indians and mention in a best-seller counted for more with academics and students than election to learned societies or my own publications. So I should not fault Carmer for clearing the path for us.

Years later, and after several other successes, Carmer returned to Indian themes in *Dark Trees to the Wind* (1949). This time he acknowledged printed sources and cited persons consulted. There are two spare quotes from Red Jacket's speeches early in the nineteenth century: on the Crucifixion (p. 104), and his Farewell, before he died in 1832 (p. 181). There is a splendid account of a twentieth century Cayuga patriot (pp. 105–117), Levi General, whom his people knew as *Deskaheh*, the leading title on the roster of Cayuga chiefs in the council of the Iroquois Confederacy. When in 1924 the government of Canada disbanded the Council of Life Chiefs at Six Nations Reserve, which had functioned as local government since 1784, and the Royal Canadian Mounted Police confiscated the wampum belts, Deskaheh carried the cause of Iroquois nationalism to the Council of the League of Nations in Geneva. Denied a hearing before that prestigious body, Deskaheh and his lawyer hired a great hall, they packed the house, and after Deskaheh plead his cause, he received a standing ovation. Europeans reared on the novels of Cooper and the German writer, Karl May, who never visited America, retain to this day a romantic attachment to *les sauvages amériquains*. Finding himself unwelcome on returning to Canada, Deskaheh crossed the Niagara frontier and died in exile among the Iroquois of western New York. Carmer treats this tale of Native American illusion, romantic imagery, and personal tragedy with great sympathy.

Of all the captives who preferred Indian society to returning to Yankeedom, Mary Jemison, "the White Woman of the Genesee," has special appeal to Yorkers. Her story seizes Carmer's imagination. The name that the Senecas gave to Mary Jemison is spelled *De-ge-wa-nus* in the many editions of her life. But appealing as it may be this name cannot be interpreted as "Pretty Girl," for the Senecas still know the name as *degiwä ⁿ-neʔs*, "two women's voices falling." No less an authority than J. N. B. Hewitt so interpreted the name for the 1932 edition (p. 333),[10] and I have recorded it from living Seneca speakers at Allegany.

Seventeenth century French writers found *Le Festin à tout manger*, or the "Eat-all Feast" of English chroniclers, particularly arresting. There was one celebrated occasion in 1655, when the French mission at Onondaga was severely threatened, that the French turned the Indian custom of exaggerated hospitality around and gorged the principal Onondagas. Having fed them to satiety the French slipped away in the night while their invited guests slept off their torpor. Carmer makes quite a yarn of this incident (pp. 195–215).

Perhaps my view of Carmer's writing on Indians is best expressed in a review that I wrote: "*Dark Trees to the Wind* shows a maturity of style and makes masterly use of both oral and written tradition. Neither a proper folklorist nor a true historian, Carmer belongs rather to the *belles lettres*."[11]

IV

By all odds the greatest man of letters to confront the Iroquois literature and observe and interview them in the field was Edmund Wilson (1895–1972). Wilson's career as America's foremost critic and essayist in this century has been fully covered by other writers, so I shall confine my remarks to his Iroquois adventures which I shared in part. During the fifteen years that I knew him until his passing, he lifted up my mind, as the Iroquois would say, from the sloth of administration, convinced me that I should and could write prose free of anthropological jargon, and persuaded me to give up my job or find a research professorship where I could discharge my obligations to scholarship. Our meeting had a profound effect upon my life that I could in no way have anticipated.

Wilson sought me out in late October in 1957. I was then Assistant Commissioner for the New York State Museum and Science Service; it must have been a busy day for there are no entries in my diary for October 28, when in the afternoon my secretary ushered in an unexpected caller, a not infrequent occurrence in the life of a public official. The visitor was not tall but close-coupled and on the pudgy side. He was florid-faced, dressed in a brown Brooks Brothers' suit of comfortable cut, and carried a brown wide-brimmed felt hat. As he sat down in the chair across the desk, he wheezed a bit and then stammered as he commenced to speak. (My first reaction was a mental note: another person who must see the Director and needs to talk but who should be seeing an analyst.) "All the paths lead here," he said. "Everywhere I have been among the Iroquois, I have been told that I must see Fenton." I asked him where he had been, and he told of his visits to St. Regis and Caughnawaga among the Mohawks where he had been introduced by Harry White, a Mohawk schoolman in the village of Port Leyden near his summer home in Talcottville. As I listened, I came to realize that this man is no nut and he may indeed be Edmund Wilson, as he says. The flow of his well-structured sentences and the pertinence of his questions moved me to dig out a bibliography and to suggest that we both watch the ascent of the Pleiades and mark the first full moon after the winter solstice so as to be ready to visit the Senecas at the Indian New Year twenty days later. Wilson left for a plane to Boston, and wrote me next day from Wellfleet that he would be ready.[12]

I thought little about this interview for several months, but as the time approached when one could count twenty days to the fifth night of the next new moon, I sent Wilson a wire. If he were still interested, he should show up in Albany on or about January 22. Again I was preoccupied with other things. On that day the then State Archeologist, Dr. William A. Ritchie, was scheduled to report on the first season's work under a National Science Foundation grant. In the midst of the seminar, Wilson wheezed in hobbling with a cane, and announced: "I am here, but I have the gout. I am ready to start when you are." The taxi driver who followed him put down heavy bags and Wilson sat down to hear the rest of Ritchie's presentation. At the end he asked Richie several pointed questions. Meanwhile, my secretary had ordered up a State car for what I had resolved should be an official visit to the Senecas. It was the first of several such trips in the next year or two that Wilson and I made together, which facilitated much good talk as we drove and enabled me to share fieldwork with him.

After a late start, toward evening as it began to snow, we stopped off at Geneva to have dinner and spend the night at the Hotel Seneca. Edmund wrote to Elena his wife that I talked a blue streak all the way, but much to the point. I wanted Edmund to see Canandaigua, the site of the Pickering Treaty of 1794, in daylight, and possibly view the document in the Ontario County Historical Society, because at the time that treaty was thought to be crucial to the Kinzua Dam controversy which was at its height just then. The Allegany Reservation, where we were going to see the Midwinter Festival, was the affected area and the Coldspring Longhouse settlement was at the center of the lake. I had the feeling that the ceremonies which I had commenced studying in 1933 would never be the same again. Moreover, there were certain positions that I personally favored but as a public official could not take which I hoped that Edmund would be moved to discuss in print.

Our journey that morning took us beyond Batavia, the legendary place of the giant mosquito, and the earthwork enclosure near Oakfield and into Tonawanda Reservation at Basom. Crossing the creek and heading "down below" to the Longhouse district, we met two Seneca matrons about to go shopping for the Longhouse who affirmed that tomorrow was indeed the New Year, the same as at Cattaraugus and Allegany, a coincidence worth noting given the variations in the lunar calendar and how the old people set the date. The Faithkeepers having confirmed my own prediction of the date, there was time to call on Nick Bailey (originally Billy) and his wife Edna and get him to tell Edmund about the people who had built the fort at Oakfield and originally inhabited Tonawanda village. I gloss these details from my diary because the interview afforded me my first opportunity to watch Edmund at work. The old labor journalist listened well and asked a few precise and apt questions on which Nick expanded. Wilson took no notes, although I wrote down the Seneca terms for the three earlier peoples on the Niagara frontier. Next day in Salamanca, Wilson discharged his memory of the interview in a letter to his wife.[13]

I was interested in how he worked, and having observed him in this first interview, asked him. He had established rapport almost immediately. Indeed I had never seen anyone get into the confidence of informants so rapidly, and this was to be repeated in the days that followed. He told me that he habitually kept a journal in which he wrote, as time afforded, first-draft accounts of events and his own impressions as soon as possible after the event or interview, that he had schooled himself to retain whole conversations and to recall situations sometimes several days afterward. He also wrote letters to his wife, to his publisher and to friends of varying length, the first being the more substantive and Elena kept these until his return. These materials he mined later in his writing, as the interview with Nick Bailey in *Apologies* (pp. 186–88). Wilson's method may be suited to the kind of critical journalism of which he was master, and I have employed it in situations where notebook and pencil or tape recorder offends other participants in the situation, but I know of no substitute for taking texts then or afterwards, nor does it have the precision of getting informants who know the culture to recall afterward the significant parts of an event or ceremony that is patterned in their unconscious. One's observations include much accidental behavior that may not be significant, and until the observer learns the pattern that governs such events he may miss much that is important.

Wilson had prepared himself for the field by reading widely in the literature to which I had called his attention. He commented on my ability to operate in the native language, which I control but imperfectly, and kept asking for study materials. Wallace Chafe's *Seneca Morphology and Dictionary* (1967) was then in the formative stages, and his *Handbook of the Seneca Language* (1963) was several years away; but Wilson's demands inspired me to finance the field-work for both undertakings. He kept saying that the want of such materials handicapped him greatly, and Elena, whom I presently met on a visit to Boston, remarked that "*Apologies*" was hurried. This was also the period when Edmund was being harried by the Internal Revenue Service.

From Tonawanda we crossed the flatlands to Gowanda, some 30 miles southwest of Buffalo, where Cattaraugus Creek dissects the Allegheny Plateau. We kept a dinner date with the attorney for the Seneca Nation, picked up pills for Edmund's gout, and stayed over hoping to catch the round of the Bigheads at Newtown next morning. In a late start we first called on Cornelius Seneca, sometime President of the Seneca Nation, that Edmund might hear his views on the Kinzua affair. At noon the Bigheads were making their second round of the houses when we reached the Longhouse at Newtown. The officials greeted us cordially just as the heralds entered by the opposite door, bumping their cornpounders and chanting indistinctly, apparently unsure of their lines. One wore a bear skin, the other an old blanket; both trailed cornhusk anklets but wore no other cornhusk decoration, a somewhat inadequate wardrobe for the role. At least Edmund got to see and hear the Feast of Dreams announced, albeit it was a poor performance.

To the Senecas, going over the hills to Allegany is "to the other side," or to Ohi:yoʔ. That evening we visited Franklin and Mary John at Quaker Bridge, which is now inundated. Mary, matron of the Beaver clan, insisted we stay for supper, which enabled Edmund to share in Seneca hospitality and listen to Franklin foretell the gloomy future of his Nation. Often its President, Franklin, then Allegany's lone working farmer, nevertheless commanded a vigorous style of address, both in Seneca and in English, that recalled the great Cornplanter. I never heard him in better form than in response to Edmund's questions.

There was a blizzard in the night so we stayed in Salamanca next morning until noon. Over a leisurely breakfast Edmund urged upon

me the writing of an Iroquois classic, he volunteered to speak to
his publishers, and we discussed alternate plans for a work which I
have never managed to fulfill. My tutor pronounced: "I have read
your papers and you do not use the anthropological jargon. What
the book needs is a clear style from one steeped in it—an authority."
We estimated that such a writing project would take two years, that a
sabbatical might break the back of it. "Could you get a year off from
your job?" he asked. With two youngsters in college just then, this
prospect seemed impracticable. (I had first to convince the Commissioner of Education to inaugurate a plan of leaves of absence,
chair the planning committee, and then manage six months of leave
with pay as a reward.) The chapters written since 1960 for the great
work have appeared in various journals and their publication recalls
the folkloristic motif of magic flight—hindrances thrown off to the
pursuing monsters—without ever delivering the manuscript.

It would be unproductive to compare my diary entries on the
Midwinter Festival with the account Edmund printed in *Apologies*.
At the time I read the pertinent chapters in typescript and made corrections then when the events were fresh in mind. What impressed
me then as now was Edmund's receptiveness to criticism and his
willingness to re-write even in galley-proof to get it right. He told me
that with him six or seven drafts were not unusual, although I would
have settled for his second or third. This is a lesson for academics:
that even the consummate master of American prose in our century
did not bring it off in a single draft.

Edmund's gout proved something of an asset with the old men
of Coldspring Longhouse. Jake Logan, who had known my father
and who had previously treated me as a neophyte, immediately came
to Edmund's assistance with prescriptions of herbal remedies. Albert Jones, a great singer and speaker, and Ed Coury, though mostly
white, who had understudied with Chauncey Johnny John, my old
informant, joined the consultation. Jake, then 83, recalled the building of the then present longhouse when he was a boy of perhaps 10,

which would date its erection about 1886. "The old longhouse," he said, "stood out near the road; it was built of logs and plank-sided up and down."

Having settled in among the old men at the north stove, we listened as the speeches flowed and the ceremony progressed. Indians have a great capacity for boredom. In the long intervals, however, boys grow restless, although their antics seem not to bother the speakers. They were soon quieted with watching Edmund perform feats of magic: manipulating coins to appear and disappear, a handkerchief mouse that kept appearing from his coat sleeve—all done in low key, which even the older Seneca men and women enjoyed.

Whether it was the gout pills, Jake Logan's advice, or fulfillment of the Seneca aphorism—"perhaps all he needs is a little dance"—within a day or two Edmund improved sufficiently to walk around the singers' bench in Feather Dance, an act which endeared him to the Longhouse leaders, for whom participation is the essence of respect and the key to acceptance.

People who live in the oral tradition are rather sensitive about writing. The Senecas since Red Jacket's day have reason to believe they have been done in by "all that pen and paper business." While they wish to maintain their tradition and have their children learn the lore and ceremonies in the native language, they are reluctant to see it made explicit; they often used to ask me "are we really like that?"; and they suspect that writers of books make money off their religion. In a sense that is true. But, in my experience, they avidly snap up and cherish the monographs of ethnologists going back to L. H. Morgan, and one sees some woefully dogeared copies circulating on the reserves. This ambivalence raises some ethical questions.

What does the ethnologist, who has enjoyed the confidence of traditional people, who has participated in their "doings," and who has striven to learn and get things right, do with his field notes? He has an obligation to himself for having invested his time in a profession, he owes a debt to the academicians who trained him, and his colleagues expect that he will write up his notes and share them. This means publishing. How then should he treat materials that are sensitive? In my experience subjects that were formerly not classified have been added to the list of tabu topics by younger Indians who have recently discovered their cultural roots and resent persons who have applied themselves to learning their culture but are never part of it. Many topics once discussed openly were recorded by folklorists and became part of the literature a century ago. I have particular reference to the origin legend and the ceremonies of the Little Water Medicine Society. Parker published on it in 1909, although the origin legend was known much earlier.

The relevance of this argument to Edmund Wilson and to myself is that when he first applied for admission to attend the all night sing to renew the strength of the Medicine, which I had been attending for years, word came back that he would be admitted if I came too and if he promised not to write anything about it.[14] The following June we went up to Tonawanda together to honor an invitation that was renewed. We arrived in the late afternoon at the home of Chief Corbett Sundown, whose wife Priscilla insisted that we take supper with them because it would be a long night. I remember distinctly Edmund's explaining to Chief Sundown that he was a writer and he planned to write an account of our visit. Perhaps Sundown did not get the point, or was too polite to make an issue of it. Chapter nine of *Apologies* says it all, and it represents our combined observations on that occasion. Although I sat with the singers, I wrote nothing at the time, but I did read and correct Edmund's manuscript. I still regard this chapter as one of the finest pieces in the Iroquois literature and the people are lucky to have it from one who had written hundreds of notices of Broadway performances.

Our parting at daybreak with Chief Sundown was most cordial, just as Wilson ends his book. On reaching home I wrote Chief Sundown thanking him for his hospitality and the privilege of sitting with the singers.

The New Yorker ran much of Wilson's material before the book appeared toward the close of 1959. For me the collaboration was a great learning experience. But it did not end as I had expected. No Seneca objected until a certain self-appointed protector of Tonawanda tradition went up to Tonawanda and confronted Chief Sundown with a copy of the *New Yorker* in hand. The person also called on Nick Bailey and questioned the propriety of his having received us and demonstrated the flute music, an instrument on which he was a virtuoso performer. This is an example of the way that White people sometimes patronize Indians, a process that I had observed at Tonawanda during the New Deal, and it also illustrates how adept Indians are at manipulating White people. In this particular case Carl Carmer had devoted more attention to me than perhaps I deserved, and Wilson had ignored such patrons of the Tonawanda people altogether. The pity of it all is now that the one book which lifted the cause of Iroquois cultural autonomy into the realm of *belles lettres*, a work which generated support for the Seneca case against the U.S. Corps of Army Engineers over Kinzua, a book that was read by President Kennedy and discussed in the White House, should end up on the proscribed list at the Seneca Iroquois National Museum.

V

Of the three literary men whom I have discussed and of their images of the Iroquois, Edmonds created convincing characters of Indians without pretending to know them. Carmer, who was fun to be with and had a real feel for a story, seemed less interested in digging for the truth, and might with a little more effort have created more than a mood. And Wilson perceived the Iroquois world view intuitively and overcame any obstacle to get at the truth. Indeed he frequently proclaimed that he made his own version, one that I came to respect. Men of his ilk walk the earth but seldom and I am glad to have shared the path with him for a few brief years.

Notes

1. Francis Jennings has remained Parkman's most persistent critic. His indictment of Parkman's use of sources is devastating. See Jennings, "A Vanishing Indian: Francis Parkman Versus His Sources" (1963).

2. See Review, *Letters of Francis Parkman*, ed. Wilbur R. Jacobs, *American Anthropologist* 63 (1961): 849–50; Introduction, 1962 edition of Morgan's *League of the Iroquois* (New York: Corinth Books), pp. v–xviii; Review, *Lewis Henry Morgan: the Indian Journals, 1859–62*, ed. Leslie A. White, *Science* 131 (1960): 402; "The Iroquois Confederacy in the Twentieth Century: A Case Study of the Theory of Lewis H. Morgan in "Ancient Society," *Ethnology* 4(3), (1965): 251–65.

3. Laurence Hauptman, *The Iroquois and the New Deal* (Syracuse NY: Syracuse University Press, 1981).

4. "Tonawanda Longhouse Ceremonies: Ninety Years after Lewis Henry Morgan" (1941).

5. See Morgan 1850, 1851.

6. William L. Stone, *Life of Joseph Brant-Thayendanegea . . .* (1838).

7. I am indebted to Professor Laurence Hauptman of New Paltz for finding and excerpting for me the Edmonds–La Farge correspondence in the La Farge Papers at the University of Texas Library, Austin. Quoted by permission.

8. La Farge Papers.

9. William N. Fenton, "An Outline of Seneca Ceremonies at Coldspring Longhouse" (1936).

10. Seaver, *A Narrative of the Life of Mary Jemison: The White Woman of the Genesee* (1932).

11. Fenton, "Review Note: C. Carmer, *Dark Trees to the Wind*" (1950).

12. Wilson to Fenton, October 29, 1957, in Elena Wilson, ed., *Edmund Wilson* (1977):553.

13. Wilson to Elena Wilson, January 24, 1958, in *ibid.*, pp. 553–54.

14. William N. Fenton diary, entry for January 7, 1959.

References

Carmer, Carl

1936 *Listen for a Lonesome Drum: A York State Chronicle.* New York: Farrar and Rinehart.

1949 *Dark Trees to the Wind: A Cycle of York State Years.* New York: William Sloane Associates.

Chafe, Wallace L.

1963   *Handbook of the Seneca Language*. New York State Museum and Science Service, *Bulletin* No. 388: 1–71. Albany.

1967   *Seneca Morphology and Dictionary*. Smithsonian Contributions to Anthropology, No. 4, Washington: Smithsonian Institution

Cornplanter, Jesse J.

1938   *Legends of the Longhouse*. New York and Philadelphia: J. B. Lippincott.

Edmonds, Walter D.

1936   *Drums Along the Mohawk*. Boston: Little, Brown & Co.

1968   *The Musket and the Cross: The Struggle of France and England for North America*. Boston: Little, Brown & Co.

Fenton, William N.

1936   "An Outline of Seneca Ceremonies at Coldspring Longhouse." *Yale University Publications in Anthropology*, 9(13): 1–23.

1941   "Tonawanda Longhouse Ceremonies: Ninety Years after Lewis Henry Morgan." Anthropological Papers, No. 15, Bureau of American Ethnology *Bulletin* 128: 140–166.

1950   "Review Note: C. Carmer, *Dark Trees To the Wind*." *U.S. Quarterly Book List*, 6: 87. Washington: The Library of Congress.

Fenton, William N., ed.

1968   *Parker on the Iroquois*. Syracuse NY: Syracuse University Press.

Jennings, Francis P.

1963   "A Vanishing Indian: Francis Parkman Versus His Sources." *The Pennsylvania Magazine of History and Biography* 87(3): 306–23

Morgan, Lewis Henry

1850   "Report to the Regents of the University, upon the Articles furnished to the Indian Collection." In, *Third Annual Report of the Regents of the University on the Condition of the State Cabinet of Natural History and the Historical and Antiquarian Collection, annexed thereto*. Pp. 1–95; 17 Plates. Albany.

1851   *Report on the State Cabinet of Natural History* . . . V: 67–117. Albany.

1851   *League of the Ho-de-no-sau-nee, or Iroquois*. Rochester: Sage. (Reprinted 1962 with an Introduction by W. N. Fenton, pp. i–xi, New York: Corinth Books.)

Parker, Arthur C.

1909 "Secret Medicine Societies of the Seneca." *American Anthropologist* 11: 161–85.

Parkman, Francis

1865–92 *France and England in North America*. Boston.

Seaver, James E.

1932 *A Narrative of the Life of Mary Jemison, The White Woman of the Genesee*. Revised by Charles Delamater Vail. New York: The American Scenic & Historic Preservation Society.

Stone, William L.

1838 *Life of Joseph Brant—Thayendanegea, Including the Border Wars of the American Revolution*. 2 vols. New York: George Dearborn & Co.

Wilson, Edmund

1960 *Apologies to the Iroquois: With a Study of the Mohawks in High Steel by Joseph Mitchell*. New York: Farrar, Straus & Cudahy.

Wilson, Elena, ed.

1977 *Edmund Wilson: Letters on Literature and Politics, 1912–1972*. New York: Farrar, Straus and Giroux.

Return of Eleven Wampum Belts to the Six Nations Iroquois Confederacy on Grand River, Canada

Abstract

A case study in the repatriation of a museum collection illustrates the ethnohistorical research prerequisite to a decision to return the objects to the heirs of the original owners. It also treats several of the legal and ethical issues entering the decision. The ceremony of return highlights the Iroquois sense of appropriate behavior on such an occasion and the mutual satisfaction of both parties to the transaction. The writer was both a participant and an observer.

Recent demands from native groups for the repatriation of objects long held in museums evoke the need to establish when and by what means objects come to museums. Further considerations are the museum's investment in preserving them and determining under what conditions a particular collection may be deaccessioned and repatriated. The eleven wampum belts that individual Iroquois sold to T. R. Roddy, a dealer, in 1899, that George G. Heye purchased through another dealer in 1910, and that the Trustees of the Museum of the American Indian returned to the Six Nations Confederacy on the Grand River in Canada in 1988 represent a precedent in satisfying such a demand. As an ethnologist who has observed Iroquois ceremonies for fifty years, I describe the ceremony of repatriation. I trust that this account demonstrates how ethnology illuminates historical inquiry. I mention three belts and strings of wampum that tradition engraved in living memory. The tortuous history of the claim follows, then a discussion of wampum in the context of Grand River politics, in circumstances that living traditionalists chose to ignore, and the wasting of belts in native care. Actual custodianship varied from native theory. When the chiefs sought to recover the belts on the death of the keeper, they encountered shifts in values from national to private property. How the belts were "persuaded to leave" the reserve and how museologists contended for possession or return of them raise ethical questions. I recount the failed efforts of two anthropologists and a public official to recover the belts from Heye, and how the chiefs frustrated officialdom. How the trustees of the Museum of the American Indian–Heye Foundation met with the chiefs, the actual transfer, and my role in it end the article. The formal conclusion speaks to policy on repatriation.

The Repatriation Ceremony

The Museum of the American Indian–Heye Foundation (MAI-HF) returned eleven wampum belts to the traditional chiefs of the Iroquois Confederacy on the Grand River that the museum had held since its founding in 1916. In an elaborate ceremony held on May 8, 1988, on the grounds of the Onondaga longhouse, anthropologists and officers of the museum fulfilled a 1914 pledge of Edward Sapir and Frank G. Speck to recover the belts that were sold to a dealer by unauthorized persons at the turn of the century. Roland W. Force, president and director of the museum, James G. E. Smith, curator, and Mary Anne Force carried the belts from New York. As chairman of the Collections Committee of the Trustees, I drove up from Albany with Denis P. Foley, a former graduate student. In making the presentation, I recalled that in 1935 Sapir, my mentor at Yale, had suggested to me that I inquire at Grand River how the belts were "persuaded to leave" the reserve. No one thought then that the belts could ever be retrieved. That they were is a tribute to native persistence and cooperation among the chiefs of the Confederacy, their lawyer, Paul Williams, and trustees of the museum.

For weeks the chiefs and faithkeepers of the Onondaga and Seneca longhouses on the Grand River met in council two nights a week to prepare for the great event. They thought of every contingency and appointed persons to various tasks: groundskeepers, security, public relations, cooks. After considerable discussion, the chiefs and clan mothers decided to dress in traditional costume for the occasion—an indication of its solemnity, since they normally reserve dress for burials and regularly put on feathers for religious festivals. Not even performances of the Condolence Council to raise up new chiefs, in my experience, rate such attention.

The ceremony was a model of organization. In a great tent erected behind the longhouse, the chiefs of the Confederacy and the clan mothers, including representatives from the New York reserves, seated themselves in the traditional arrangement: the Onondaga chiefs at the head of the fire, Mohawk and Seneca chiefs to one side, and the younger brother Oneida and Cayuga chiefs opposite them, leaving one side of the fire open to the visiting delegation. A crowd of upwards of five hundred persons surrounded the tent. The faces were predominantly Iroquois, but I recognized colleagues: Annemarie Shimony of Wellesley, Iroquoian linguist Roy Wright of Cornell, anthropologist David Damas and historian Charles Johnston of nearby McMaster University. The grounds swarmed with photographers, both native and outlander. Tim Johnson of the *Turtle Quarterly* rated special privileges as council-appointed photographer. Michael K. Foster of the Canada Ethnology Service, Canadian Museum of Civilization, directed a TV crew. Senior writer Harvey Arden and photographer Steve Wall represented the National Geographic Society. I chatted briefly with Sam Cronk, Iroquoian musicologist of Queen's University, and his wife, and enjoyed meeting Ivan Kocsis, native Hungarian artist and illustrator who has devoted his talent to Iroquois subjects since coming to Canada. The weather was perfect, the atmosphere friendly, and everyone sensed it was a historic occasion.

Roland Force carefully unwrapped individual wampum belts that were laid out in the square before us on a white cloth by director Tom Hill and curator Sally Buck of the Woodland Institute of Brantford, where the belts now are housed. Together, the two native museum officials, both in traditional costume, carefully checked the inventory prepared by registrar Lee Callandar of MAI.

The Six Nations chiefs had appointed Kevin Deer of Caughnawaga as their speaker. At their prompting, he invited the chiefs and then the clan mothers to inspect and authenticate the belts. This was an awesome moment for persons who had waited a lifetime to welcome the belts home. The chiefs, followed by the clan mothers, filed by and shook our hands. One or two greeted me by my adopted Seneca name. Fifty years had passed since my residence at Tonawanda.

The MAI-HF trustees had wondered whether the elected councillors, the legitimate government of Six Nations Reserve under the Indian Act of 1924, would object to the return of the wampums to the hereditary chiefs. In an unexpected gesture, chief councillor William Montour ended our concern by returning to the hereditary chiefs seven strings of wampum, five white and two purple, that make up the "mace" of the old government, which the speaker once employed when kindling the fire and covering it at the opening and close of council business. He had recently discovered the hank of wampum, long thought lost, in the council safe. This gesture of national unity almost overshadowed the main event.

No Iroquois event of spiritual import goes forward without a tobacco-burning ceremony. Shagohendehtha ("he is leading them") Reg Henry, Cayuga linguist and teacher of Iroquoian languages to his people, performed this rite at a fire just north of the tent. (I am unaware that anyone recorded the text.) Likewise, *Ganonhonyonk*, the opening thanksgiving address, invariably precedes all public events. Cayuga chief Jake Thomas, holder of the title Dayothowehkonh ("cold on both sides"), which occurs eighth on the Cayuga roster of League chiefs, and the reigning ritual holder at Six Nations when not teaching at Trent University, picked up the burden of the main ceremony. Bob Jamieson, whose Cayuga name, oho:dra ("basswood"), is not a chiefly title, interpreted. The effort to communicate the meaning of the native texts to Western ears reminded me of the role of the interpreter in Iroquois treaty transactions and how much of the rich Iroquoian languages escaped through the mesh.

Chief Thomas then proceeded to "read" the Friendship Belt and after that the famous Two Row Belt, employing his own reproductions of the originals that lay outstretched before him, too fragile to handle. During these lengthy presentations, an aside by the interpreter inadvertently cleared for a moment a mystery and confirmed a hunch as to the identity of the persons through whose hands the belts had passed when leaving Grand River at the turn of the century. As a working hypothesis, I had assumed that Clara Jamieson was the wife of Cayuga chief James Jamieson, and that the Jamiesons had financed the sale to Roddy. Now it appeared that Clara was an earlier wife and that Chief Jamieson had remarried before rearing Bob Jamieson, the interpreter.

Bob Jamieson apologized for getting ahead of the speaker, saying that he had been raised by old people, namely, James and Beatrice Jamieson, from whom his knowledge of council affairs descended. J. N. B. Hewitt had worked with Chief John Skanawati Buck in 1888 when he recorded information on eight wampum belts (Buck, cited in Hewitt 1892: 146–48); and on one of his field trips to Grand River he had photographed Chief Jamieson with the so-called Brant Belt draped over one shoulder, using it as an illustration years later (Hewitt 1933: Fig. 84). Clara Jamieson, daughter of Buck, who was keeper of the wampum, and sister of Joshua Buck, was a third party to the wampum sale from whom T. R. Roddy later claimed to have bought the belts through the Jamiesons. She then had a photograph of herself taken on this occasion as a little girl sitting with the chiefs at a wampum reading performed by her father. Bob Jamieson, with whom Roland Force spoke briefly after the ceremony, stated that the woman who raised him was named Beatrice, evidently a later wife of Chief Jamieson. Roddy last revisited James and Clara Jamieson in 1910; the subsequent seventy-eight years would readily accommodate Bob Jamieson's life span.

Chief James Jamieson (Cayuga) was a relatively prosperous farmer at Grand River and founder of the Six Nations Agricultural Society. He evidently acted on behalf of his wife Clara and her brother Joshua in the sale. He possessed at least one of the belts that Roddy claimed to have purchased from him. In Hewitt's photograph, Jamieson posed with the Path Belt, which terminates at both ends in squares, representing peoples. This is the Brant Belt of 1750, an impossible attribution, for Brant was then eight years old (Beauchamp 1901: 424, Plate 16, Fig. 186). For some reason Hewitt waited until years later to publish the photograph. This disposes of the issue of where and from whom Roddy obtained the eleven belts.

For the ceremony our hosts had prepared a handout that sketched the chronology of the eleven Roddy belts according to research done at MAI and by the attorney for the chiefs. It now seems appropriate to flesh out the chronology with data drawn from a memorandum that I prepared in 1985 for the trustees of MAI-HF on behalf of the Collections Committee (Fenton 1985).

History of the Eleven Belts

The belts in question bear MAI catalog numbers 3/1899 through 3/1909. None of the belts is now tied to a specific historical event, and they most probably date from the second half of the eighteenth century, although their symbolism is much older. They have been so long separated from the verbal streams once woven into them to recall transactions and agreements later that the attributions that accompanied them to the museum now serve only to identify them. Roddy was not a trained ethnologist, he made no systematic inquiries, and Joshua Buck did not hand down his father's knowledge. Three of the belts greatly impressed the present Six Nations chiefs because they sustain their political traditions. Jake Thomas, who has long concerned himself with such matters, had already reproduced two of the belts, which he proceeded to interpret using the facsimiles, because the originals were too fragile to handle. The first was the Friendship Belt, depicting two human figures, one Indian and the other white, connected by a path on a white background, which reaffirms an early bond of alliance, notably the chain concept. The second was the Two Row Belt, two parallel lines that never converge on a white background, representing the enduring separation of Iroquois from European law and custom. A third, the Brant Belt, served to identify Chief Jamieson. On it three adjacent rows of white wampum form a path connecting two squares, symbolizing an alliance. Still other belts feature sets of linked diamonds equal in number to the parties participating in a transaction. These latter belts interested the chiefs, who were seeing them for the first time.

George G. Heye, founder of the museum, acquired the belts in 1910 through the Indian Trading Company of New York City in a negotiated purchase for $2,000. Conveyed in the Heye Foundation Trust of 1916, they formed an integral part of its Northeast Woodland collection for seventy-five years. The fact that the Indian Trading Company was acting as agent for T. R. Roddy of Chicago and Black River Falls, Wisconsin, who procured the belts at Six Nations Reserve on the Grand River in 1899, may or may not have been known to Heye at the time of his purchase, as recent claimants have alleged. There is no evidence that they were stolen; they were simply sold by persons whose title has been questioned. Canadian authorities in 1914 failed to recover the belts for the Six Nations when the chiefs in council bypassed a request for evidence as to how the belts were persuaded to leave the reserve, although they asserted that the belts were national and not individual property and named councillors who could identify them. The matter was dropped. Such is the background of the recent claim.

On March 17, 1977, the Union of Ontario Indians, through its attorney, Paul Williams of Toronto, requested that the museum list and describe wampum belts in the MAI-HF collection, indicate source of acquisition, and supply supporting ethnographic information, as the belts might bear on particular treaties between Indian nations and European powers. The then vice chairman of the board replied that MAI had neither the staff nor the time to undertake such research. Meanwhile, I had volunteered to identify the inquiring organization and to bring up to date previous research on wampum belts of the Six Nations.

Unable to reach Williams during a visit to Toronto, I learned from other sources in Canada that the union was a semiprovincial organization greater in name than in substance, that its composition was predominantly Ojibwa, that it then had no formal connection with the Six Nations elected band council, and that Williams's interests as a lawyer centered on the council of the traditional hereditary chiefs, who aspire to reclaim governance of the reserve. This sensitive subject involved the government of Canada, and we were advised to move cautiously.

I reported my findings to Curt Muser, then chairman of the board of MAI, in a letter dated July 14, 1977. A carbon copy of that report was on file in a folder marked "Wampum" at the Newberry Library, Chicago, where I was then associated with the Documentary History of the Iroquois Project. There it lay when a group of searchers from the union visited the library. In the absence that day of project directors, the searchers had free access to the files and made off with documents from the Newberry wampum file, including the carbon copy of my report. It was subsequently returned on the demand of the library president, but it nevertheless bears the penciled end-of-page marks of a copyist. It was afterward quoted in an anonymous brief on the belts in question that reached the museum in April 1981.

Ethics were shaky all around, and my research inadvertently fueled the claim.

In May 1985 Paul Williams approached the museum, this time as attorney for the Six Nations Confederacy chiefs, and asked for a meeting with the trustees to discuss the eleven belts. Enclosed were copies of correspondence, mainly from PAC, which in his view and that of his clients indicated the source, proved that the belts were stolen property, and showed that Heye must have known it when he denied his connection with Roddy at the same time that he was dealing with him. In sum, he questioned the museum's title.

A letter addressed to the secretary of the Six Nations Iroquois Confederacy at Grand River brought confirmation that the chiefs had indeed instructed Paul Williams to assist them in recovering the eleven wampum belts in question (if there had been any question about Williams's being attorney for the council, the letter of inquiry confirmed his appointment). The museum could not expect Canadian authorities to sanction Williams's status as lawyer for the hereditary chiefs, inasmuch as they do not recognize that body's legal status.

The claimants and the Collections Committee of MAI-HF employed some of the same sources, mainly the "Wampum File" at PAC, although considerable background information surfaced during the committee's investigation that filled gaps in the chronology of events, shed light on the museum world of the day, and documented Roddy's efforts to resell the belts.

Wampum Politics at Grand River

What the loss of the belts meant to the Six Nations people may be appreciated by recounting the history of wampum politics at Grand River. After the American War of Independence, the survivors of the Six Nations raked up their council fire at Buffalo Creek and divided the treasury of wampums. One belt relating to the founding of the Confederacy they cut in two so that each might retain half (Krehbiel, cited in Beauchamp 1901: 416). The Loyalist chiefs took their half of the belts and in 1784 moved to the Grand River, where they rekindled the fire of the League in Canada (Johnston 1964; Norton 1970). The other half of the belts remained at Buffalo Creek until after the sale of the reservation, when in 1847 they were carried back to Onondaga and the council fire was rekindled at its ancient site (Clark 1849, 1: 124–25; Beauchamp 1901: 410). These belts were destined to end up in Albany (Fenton 1971).

In reconstituting the League in Canada, the council lacked an Oneida roster of chiefs. Only part of the Onondaga chiefly families had come to Canada, while virtually all of the Cayuga population resettled at Grand River. Virtually the entire Seneca nation remained in New York. The consequence of these splits was that throughout the nineteenth century, the titles of the fifty founders of the League that are recited in the eulogy or roll call during a condolence council often lacked incumbents (Weaver 1973a: Tables 12, 20, 21). Mohawks and Cayugas predominated, Onondagas presided at councils and held the wampums, but large elements of the reserve population felt left out.

Beginning at midcentury, agitation for reform produced an attempt in 1861 to abolish the hereditary system. It was greeted promptly by a countermove on the part of the hereditary chiefs. Between 1875 and 1890, reform movements intensified, on the part of both the disenfranchised elements of the population and the warrior party who demanded a voice in government (ibid.: 118ff., 155ff.).

The council of chiefs was soon preoccupied with contemporary problems. They were confronted with property disputes that involved an appeal to British common law (Noon 1949). As the Confederacy became a mechanism for local government, the problems facing it shifted from intertribal affairs to relations with the Dominion of Canada, from treaty making to applying social sanctions on individual behavior, conserving timber and other natural resources, settling boundary disputes, adjudicating cases of inheritance, building roads, providing schools, and regulating finances. The use of wampum for opening and closing council lapsed, and custom law retreated to the age-old ceremony for mourning and installing chiefs. There were concerned persons among the traditionalists.

A nativist revival arose in response to the movement for an elective council. Its principal architect, Seth Newhouse (1842–1921), a Mohawk-speaking Onondaga and a traditionalist although raised a Christian, set out to rectify lapses in council protocol by codifying custom law and traditions. By 1885, with ink he made from native barks and berries, he had drafted in an unmistakable hand the first version of his "Constitution." It was twice rejected by the chiefs in council because it accorded too much prominence to the Mohawk in history and provoked disagreements over the structure of the Confederacy (Fenton 1949; Weaver 1984).

Instead, the council appointed its own committee on traditions and ritual and charged it with drafting an official version of the origin of the Confederacy and its structure. Chief John A. Gibson, having differed with Newhouse, was the principal resource. Meanwhile, the Warrior Party had demanded a revival of the lapsed custom of opening and closing councils with wampum.[1] Nevertheless, the resolve to return to the traditional ways of the Confederacy soon gave way to the press of urgent business (council minutes of June 22 and 29, 1885, cited in Weaver 1973a: 164–65; Weaver 1973b: 200).

Such was the climate of affairs during the closing decades of the nineteenth century, when the belts began to disappear. The sources all indicate a steady deterioration of wampum belts in native care both in New York and in Canada and a corresponding move by concerned scholars to have extant belts preserved in museums. Beauchamp (1901), Carrington (1892), Converse (see Clarke 1931), and Hale (1963 [1883]) manifest such concerns, which paralleled growing indifference at Onondaga NY and at Six Nations on the Grand River as to their care and use in council. At each reported viewing their number had declined and their condition had deteriorated. Who then was responsible for their care?

There are always discrepancies between native theory and native practice. Practical considerations intervene. Tradition assigned the role of wampum keeper to Hononwiehdi, the seventh title on the Onondaga roster of league chiefs. But note that John Skanawati Buck, though he held the fourteenth title on the Onondaga roster, acted as wampum keeper at Grand River for fifty years. His brother George held the proper title part of this time, but after 1883 it passed to David Skye. The wampum nevertheless remained in Buck's care for another ten years. Evidently, leadership roles and responsibilities fell to the able and dedicated.

In 1893 Buck died. His heirs failed to return Confederacy belts to the Council of Chiefs and treated all of the wampum in the estate as personal property (the Buck family owned wampum besides the eleven belts in question). The chiefs failed to prosecute their claim with vigor.

Buck's heirs included two known sons, John Jr. and Joshua, and a daughter, Clara, wife of Cayuga chief James Jamieson. Inasmuch as their mother was by descent an Onondaga-Tutelo, neither of the sons was elevated to a chiefly title, although they were both learned traditionalists and served J. N. B. Hewitt (1859–1937) as informants. Joshua found a market for wampum belts among collectors for museums and was still offering Tutelo wampum for sale as late as 1913 (Waugh 1913). Joshua knew collectors, notably David Boyle (1842–1911) of Toronto and Harriet M. Converse (1836–1903), who visited his father up until his death seeking to acquire the belts.

In the spring of 1893 a delegation of the council intervened but failed to recover what it regarded as "national belts" (the council nevertheless paid the delegation for its effort [Weaver 1973b]). The Buck heirs had already begun selling.

The chiefs were more successful the following year. In the fall of 1894, several national belts that Joshua Buck had sold to David Boyle were recovered. The council, following a long discussion over further losses, decided to take no action "against one of the chiefs" but ordered him to "go and redeem them and have them returned to the Council on the first Tuesday of the next month" (ibid.; Waugh 1913). The chiefs sought to cover their losses, acknowledging their failure as trustees, by not reporting these discussions, either to official agency records at Brantford or to Ottawa. Instead, in February 1895, they deposited the four belts remaining in their possession in the safe of the general store in Ohsweken, the seat of their government (Chadwick 1897: 76–77).

Four years later, William M. Beauchamp (1830–1925) attended council and obtained permission to photograph six extant belts. He commented that after John Skanawati Buck's death most of the fine Canadian Iroquois belts had quickly disappeared (Beauchamp 1901: 426, Plate 14). That same year the chiefs refused to lend these belts for an exhibition in Toronto.

How the Eleven Belts Were Persuaded to Leave the Reserve
In 1899, T. R. Roddy, Chicago dealer and showman, purchased eleven belts from Joshua Buck and the Jamiesons. Within the year, Harriet M. Converse, New York journalist, folklorist, and collector for museums, knew of the sale. In a letter dated February 1900, she wrote to Indian superintendent E. D. Cameron at Brantford that Roddy had acquired eleven of the twenty-two belts that John Skanawati Buck had shown her in 1892, and that Roddy had offered one belt to the Buffalo Historical Society for $2,000 (see Beauchamp 1900: 189). (Converse's outrage should be measured against the fact that she had herself purchased one belt from Buck, presumably in 1892 when he showed her his entire collection, and had her eye on the rest [Clarke 1931].) Cameron informed his superiors in Ottawa, who authorized him to warn Roddy that no title had passed and not to dispose of the belts.

Roddy had virtually no market for the belts after New York state archaeologist Arthur C. Parker (1881–1955), who would later become literary heir to Converse, advised the principal museums of America not to purchase them. Indeed, Roddy had the eleven belts in Chicago in 1899 when he offered Beauchamp illustrations and interpretations for his forthcoming bulletin (Beauchamp 1901: 106).

No party in this controversy enjoyed a monopoly on virtue. Parker, having shut down Roddy's market, ten years later wrote to Seth Newhouse, whose "Constitution" was being prepared for publication by the New York State Museum, offering good offices to restore the belts or seek council validation of Roddy's title to them. Parker (1899–1909) then wrote to Roddy, asking him to quote his "lowest price." Nothing came of this.

Roddy had other irons in the fire. From January 1904 until November 1906, he relied on George A. Dorsey of the Field Museum of Natural History to act as broker for the belts, offering them first to the Field Museum for $2,000, and, when this failed, to write to Clark Wissler of the American Museum of Natural History. Dorsey apparently thought it impolitic to approach Wissler. Roddy next sought Dorsey's help in arranging shipment of the belts to New York City for examination by an unnamed party, whom Roddy said was not a museum but a private person, at an opening price of $3,000. If the New York buyer was Heye, Dorsey was willing to undertake the shipment. Roddy did not know then whether the buyer was Heye or not. Now desperate for funds, he borrowed $500 from Dorsey, who arranged the shipment with the Adams Express Company, which was to hold the belts in its offices for thirty days during the examination. The Indian Exhibits Company then wrote to Roddy that it could sell the belts in case his other deal collapsed. Roddy agreed with his agent, M. F. Savage, that it was "embarrassing to take a person of wealth to an Ex ofs [Express office] to look at a C.O.D." Whether Heye saw the belts at this time remains uncertain. The belts were returned to Dorsey and Roddy repaid the loan (see Roddy 1904–6).

Between August 1908 and November 1909, the belts were on deposit at the State Historical Society of Wisconsin Museum while its director, Charles E. Brown, sought to raise $3,000 toward their purchase.

Unable to find an "angel" among the society's membership, Brown returned the belts to Roddy. With their accession in mind, Brown had catalogued the belts while they were in Madison (see Roddy 1908–10). This record may be helpful to the Six Nations chiefs.

Back on the reserve, the work of the Committee of Chiefs on traditions and ceremonies stimulated one member, William Sandy, to write the governor general of Canada in 1909 to request his good offices in securing the return of the eleven missing belts (PAC 1900–51). Meanwhile, the secretary of the council, Josiah Hill, circulated a photograph of the eleven belts among parties interested in the recovery effort (ibid.; Sapir 1910–25; Speck 1903–50). (Years later, while I was a graduate student at Yale, Sapir would hand me a photograph of the wampum belts as I was about to depart for the field and charge me with the task of finding out how the Six Nations wampum belts had been persuaded to leave the reservation.) Finally, in 1910, after a decade of unsuccessful efforts to place the belts in museums in Chicago, New York, and Madison, Roddy took up the negotiated offer of the Indian Exhibits Company and sold the belts for $2,000. George G. Heye was the purchaser.

A Failed Effort at Recovery

Heye, as a trustee, exhibited the eleven belts at the University Museum in Philadelphia, where Frank G. Speck saw them. He compared them with the photograph of missing Six Nations belts circulated by Josiah Hill and wrote to his former colleague, Edward Sapir, then head of the Anthropological Survey of Canada in Ottawa, forwarding the photograph as proof that the eleven belts on display were the same as those formerly kept by John Skanawati Buck and published in William Beauchamp's (1901) monograph on wampum (see also PAC 1900–51; Sapir 1910–25).

Hoping to strike a blow for the Six Nations, among whom the survey was conducting research, Sapir wrote and then called on Duncan

Cameron Scott, deputy superintendent general of Indian affairs in Ottawa, whom he knew from their participation in the same literary circle. Sapir's letter affirmed that the eleven belts on exhibit in Philadelphia were the same as those documented in the photograph and published by Beauchamp, and that he was prepared to make an affidavit as to their identity, citing Speck's letter. He cautioned Scott that it would be absolutely necessary for the Six Nations Council to prove that the belts were tribal, not personal property, and that they were stolen from the tribe as a whole. Subsequent events proved this a naive assumption (ibid.).

Scott wrote a series of letters to Heye, who at first evaded the issue and demanded proof that the eleven belts he had purchased were from Canada. The exchange of letters between the two men steadily grew less cordial. (Some of them were published in statements supporting the recent claim.) Heye maintained that he had bought the belts in good faith, that he did not think they came from Canada, and that he was not inclined to return them. Scott then sent a photograph, whereupon Heye acknowledged that they were the same belts he had purchased but demanded evidence that they were stolen (PAC 1900–51; Heye 1914).

As early as 1910, the year in which Heye acquired the belts, Roddy was being pushed to demonstrate his title. Roddy went out to Grand River, revisited the Jamiesons, with whom he regularly stopped, and was reassured that his title was "absolute." From Niagara Falls Roddy wrote nearly identical letters (he evidently collected hotel stationery) on February 12 to Charles E. Brown and to the Indian Exhibits Company. To Brown he reported, "I investigated title to my wampum belts which I found to be absolute. I am having copy made of a Picture owned by Clara Jamieson of [the] Onondaga Council whose father owned the belts 50 years & of whom I purchased. [This reference must be to John Skanawati Buck.] This [picture] shows belts in use by council, showing identity of belts. Clara Jamieson's father & two uncles & 3 or four other chiefs. This was taken 25 years ago [1885]" (letter from Roddy to Brown, February 12, 1910).[2] The letter to the Indian Exhibits Company reads in part, "I found no one who claimed ownership to my Belts. They have been in the Jamieson family at least 50 years, and they were the property of James Jamieson from whom I purchased them." On the picture Roddy comments, "Clara was a little girl about 10 years old when the picture was taken. She is seated in the foreground."

Returning to Heye's demanding of Scott evidence that the belts were stolen, Scott set the Indian Department bureaucracy in motion. In 1915 he directed the superintendent at Brantford to obtain from the Six Nations chiefs definite proof in the form of an affidavit that the belts were national and not individual property and could not be disposed of save by national consent. The chiefs in council ducked the issue. They failed to provide Scott with proof that he could take to the attorney general of Canada. They failed to identify the person or persons who had disposed of the belts, but they asserted that the belts were national property, and they named six chiefs who could identify them. The council minutes state that John Skanawati Buck, as firekeeper, was custodian for the nation, but the belts were disposed of by a person not presently known.

Here the matter dropped. Scott learned to his dismay that the chiefs appeared uninterested in pursuing the matter; the necessary affidavits were not forthcoming, and Scott was left without evidence with which to press Heye. In Sapir's words, "Nothing happened, largely, I think, because some of the Indians were not interested in finding out how the belts had been persuaded to leave the Reservation" (Sapir 1935). Superintendent Smith, however, learned informally that a member of Buck's immediate family (Joshua, as I was told by Hilton Hill, who for many years served as chief clerk of the agency and interpreter for the council) was reputed to have sold the belts to Roddy. Scott was annoyed and, finding himself in an untenable position, quit. Speck and Sapir were frustrated. The chiefs were obviously covering up their own lapse as trustees of a national treasure and at the same time protecting one or two of their own people. The bureaucracy had failed. The eleven belts reposed in the Museum of the American Indian for more than seventy years, remembered by a few traditionalists and unknown to the majority of residents at Six Nations. This was the situation in 1977, when Paul Williams's inquiry stood matters on their head.

Return of the Belts

Within a year after the Confederacy chiefs appointed Williams negotiator in the matter of the wampum in 1985, the trustees of MAI-HF charged its Collections Committee with briefing the board. Accordingly, its chairman researched the background of the claim for the board (Fenton 1985). By mutual agreement the Collections Committee and then the board of trustees met with the chiefs and their attorney in New York City, heard their plea, and reserved judgment. It was a cordial and instructive meeting. The then chairman of the board, Barber B. Conable, Jr., presided, and the chiefs and their attorney acquitted themselves with great dignity. The negotiations continued. At a later meeting of the board, the trustees reached the decision to return the Roddy wampum belts to the chiefs at a mutually convenient date and place. A contract was negotiated and drawn. (The signed agreement between the two parties in no way affects further claims.)

The return of the wampum was finally accomplished with due ceremony at the Onondaga longhouse on the Grand River on May 8, 1988. When asked to respond, I spoke as chairman of the Collections Committee of the Trustees and addressed the council, employing the customary greetings to the chiefs, warriors, and women and closing with the usual formality in the Seneca language. The chiefs responded by presenting to the museum gifts from individual artists and craft workers of the reserve, including paintings, carvings, miniature figures, and a lacrosse stick, together with a roster of donors.

These mementos of goodwill were accessioned in due course by the museum and are now on exhibit.

Anthropology had made good on an ancient promise.

Conclusion

Requests for repatriating objects in museum collections confront trustees with unique cases that they must consider on their own merits as they observe the requirements for deaccession set forth in museum policies on collections. MAI has published such a policy. Trustees have the responsibility for maintaining a public trust, and museum collections are by law in the public domain. They should be acquired honorably and curated in the public interest. MAI's Collections Committee of the Trustees researched the background of the claim and presented its findings to the board, and the board met and heard the chiefs. Then they considered the matter. There were legal grounds sufficient for retaining the belts, but the board decided that the circumstances of accession were ethically shaky, and that there was more goodwill to be gained by returning the belts to their original owners than by resisting the claim. I trust that the ceremony and the spirit of the occasion justified the board's decision.

Notes

1. Peter Wraxall, *An Abridgement of the Indian Affairs . . . Transacted in the Colony of New York, from . . . 1678–. . . 1751.* Edited with an introduction by Charles Howard McIlwain (Harvard Historical Studies, vii. XXI; Cambridge, Mass., 1915.)

2. A. E. Jones, *Ancient Huronia*, (1909), pp. 464, 466.

References

Beauchamp, William M.

1900 Papers, Vol. 8. New York State Library, Albany.

1901 Wampum and Shell Articles Used by the New York Indians. New York State Museum Bulletin 41: 321–480.

Carrington, Henry B.

1892 Report on the Condition of the Six Nations of New York. *In* Extra Census Bulletin: Indians. Thomas Donaldson, ed. Pp. 19–83. Washington: Bureau of the Census.

Chadwick, Edward M.

1897 The People of the Longhouse. Toronto: Church of England Publishing.

Clark, John V. H.

1849 Onondaga or Reminiscences of Earlier and Later Times, Vol. 1. Syracuse: Stoddard and Babcock.

Clarke, Noah T.

1931 The Wampum Belt Collection of the New York State Museum. New York State Museum Bulletin 288: 85–122.

Fenton, William N.

1949 Seth Newhouse's Traditional History and Constitution of the Iroquois Con federacy. Proceedings of the American Philosophical Society 93(2): 141–58.

1971 The New York State Wampum Collection: The Case for the Integrity of Cultural Treasures. Proceedings of the American Philosophical Society 115(6): 437–61.

Fenton, William N., chair

1985 Letter from Collections Committee to trustees of Museum of the American Indian–Heye Foundation. Museum of the American Indian–Heye Foundation, New York.

Hale, Horatio E.

1963 [1883] The Iroquois Book of Rites. Toronto: University of Toronto Press.

Hewitt, John N. B.

1892 egend of the Founding of the Iroquois League. American Anthropologist 5: 131–48.

1927 Ethnological Studies among the Iroquois Indians [portrait of Joshua Buck]. Explorations and Field Work of the Smithsonian Institution in 1926: 237–47.

1933 Field-work among the Iroquois Indians of New York and Canada. Explorations and Field-Work of the Smithsonian Institution in 1932: 81–84.

Heye, George G.
1914   Correspondence with Duncan C. Scott, Heye Papers. Museum of the American Indian–Heye Foundation, New York.

Johnston, Charles M.
1964   The Valley of the Six Nations. Toronto: Champlain Society.

Noon, John A.
1949   Law and Government of the Grand River Iroquois: Viking Fund Publications in Anthropology, No. 12, New York.

Norton, John
1970   The Journal of Major John Norton 1816. Carl F. Klinck and James Talman, eds. Toronto: Champlain Society.

Parker, Arthur C.
1899–1909   Correspondence, Arthur C. Parker Papers. New York State Library, Albany.

Public Archives of Canada (PAC)
1900–51   Wampum File. Record Group 10, Red Series, Vol. 3018. Ottawa.

Roddy, T. R.
1904–6   Correspondence with George A. Dorsey, Dorsey Papers. Field Museum of Natural History, Chicago.
1908–10   Correspondence with Charles E. Brown. State Historical Society of Wisconsin, Madison.

Sapir, Edward
1910–25   Correspondence. Canadian Museum of Civilization, Ottawa.
1935   Letter to William N. Fenton, September 21. Department of Anthropology, Yale University, New Haven CT.

Speck, Frank G.
1903–50   Papers. New Guide to the Collections in the Library of the American Philosophical Society, No. 1174. Philadelphia.

Trigger, Bruce G., ed.
1978   Handbook of North American Indians. Vol. 15, Northeast. Washington: Smithsonian Institution.

Waugh, Frederick W.
1913   Letter to Edward Sapir, May 11, Edward Sapir Correspondence. Canadian Museum of Civilization, Ottawa.

Weaver, Sally M.

1973a Politics of the Iroquois: An Analysis of Political Change. Unpublished manuscript.

1973b The Wampum Case. *In* The History of Politics on the Six Nations Reserve. From Records and Council Minutes, Brantford, Ont. Indian Office. Pp. 62–79. Unpublished manuscript.

1984 Seth Newhouse and the Grand River Confederacy at Mid-Nineteenth Century. *In* Extending the Rafters. M. K. Foster, Jack Campisi, and Marianne Mithun, eds. Albany: State University of New York Press.

Williams, Paul

1977 Letter to Museum of the American Indian, March 17, Wampum File. Museum of the American Indian–Heye Foundation, New York.

He-Lost-a-Bet (Howanʔneyao) of the Seneca Hawk Clan

The Iroquois have a long history of adoption. Indeed, adoption was public policy of the Iroquois Confederacy from earliest times. During the seventeenth and eighteenth centuries, the Confederacy took in whole populations to replace losses from epidemics and warfare. Invariably colonial officials with whom they dealt acquired Indian personal names, often puns on their English or French surnames, for everyone in Iroquois society must have a name and occupy a niche in the social system so as to move socially and deal politically. Clan affiliation of those early names remains obscure; but in later times we know that the Seneca Hawk clan awarded a name to L. H. Morgan at mid-nineteenth century, and they honored New York governor Nelson Rockefeller a century later. After me, they gave a name to anthropologist George S. Snyderman, and not to be outdone, the Seneca Turtle clan conferred Gaheʔdago:wa: (Great Porcupine) on Frank G. Speck, whom we all greatly admired. So I was not alone, although the account of my adoption may be unique.

The Fentons of Conewango valley in western New York and the family of Amos Snow of the Seneca Nation kept up an association going back to the 1860s. The Fenton farm on Flat Iron Road lay halfway between the Cattaraugus and Allegany Reservations of the Seneca Nation, and Seneca families "going to the other side," as they said, camped on the hemlock ridge at the back of the farm. One bitter winter morning, my father's father at chore time reported to his widowed mother that smoke was rising from the hemlock ridge beyond the swamp. His mother suggested that he go see how the Indians were faring. He took an ax and went afoot, intending to split up some firewood that he had felled. He found an Indian family encamped in a lean-to that they had constructed of hemlock bows: a man, an old woman, and a young girl with a newborn baby. They were shivering. When he returned to the house for dinner, he reported what he had seen to his mother. She insisted that he hitch the team to the pung, fill the bed with straw, throw in a buffalo robe, and go fetch the family to the warm farmhouse. By suppertime she had installed the Indian family in the hired girl's room off the kitchen.

The Seneca family stayed for a week until the weather moderated and permitted travel. When they departed, the old lady thanked my great-grandmother for shelter, sustenance, and hospitality, saying it was the first time they were invited to sleep and eat in a white home. It was an Indian custom, she added, to bind a friendship with a present, whereupon she unfolded an old burden strap, an obvious heirloom, that was decorated with dyed deer hair and porcupine quill embroidery worked in a geometric pattern, and edged with seed beads, which she handed to my great-grandmother, Fanny Carr, widow of Captain William Fenton, the seafarer.

The Seneca hunter was Amos Snow, a stout, jovial fellow who became a lifelong friend of my grandfather: companions on squirrel- and pigeon-shooting expeditions, trotting horse fanciers, good for shared labor on the farm. On occasion Amos would show up with his young family and stay for a meal. At some point he entrusted to my grandfather two old wooden False Faces that he produced from under the wagon seat. My grandfather kept them in a round wooden cheese box (Fenton 1987:248). Later, Amos left a string of purple wampum that commemorated some event long since forgotten. These items, however they came to us, formed the nucleus of an ethnological collection that was kept in a special attic room known as the "Indian collection," where I was privileged to climb steep stairs on a rainy summer afternoon. When visitors, sometimes Indians, came to the farm, I was allowed to tag along and listen. I recall Warren King Moorehead from Andover Academy, on the way to or from the Ohio mounds; Arthur C. Parker, the New York State archaeologist, himself of Seneca descent; and M. R. Harrington of the American Museum of Natural History. Their comments aroused my curiosity.

Amos Snow's son Jonas lived at Allegany Reservation and worked on the Erie Railroad with the "regular gang." Jonas and my father shared an interest in the arts, one carved masks and made snapping turtle rattles; the other was a painter. After my family acquired a Buick in 1916, going to the reservation to visit the Snows and their neighbors became favorite summer outings. We could depend on Jonas's wife to have huckleberries, which she picked along the Erie tracks and shared with us. Sometimes I played with the Johnny John boys— Arthur and Richard, by their English names—while Father sketched along the Allegheny River. Chauncey Johnny John, their grandfather, amused my father with tales of other collectors, including George Heye of the "Indian Museum" in New York City. I witnessed my first green corn dance in 1924 when the then unintelligible speeches in Seneca and the singing puzzled me. I still remember watching Johnny Armstrong perform in the drum dance.

Years later, as a graduate student at Yale, when approaching my first fieldwork in ethnology, and deciding where to go, I recalled the Snow connection and the Coldspring longhouse community, and I mentioned this to Edward Sapir, who said he had money to support my research. (Sapir had directed a program of Iroquois research on the Six Nations Reserve while chief of the Anthropological Survey of Canada, 1910–25). He encouraged me to take up the Allegany connection while advising me to find a field of concentration early so that I should have a subject for a dissertation, and not just to collect field notes. He suggested ceremonialism, with asides in material culture. He urged me to make a census so as to get acquainted and to afford data on social organization.

I had attended Sapir's seminar on phonetics where we practiced on various languages, but the Seneca language would be new to me. To get me started, he loaned me a copy of *Phonetic Transcription of American Indian Languages*, of which he was joint author. These hints would prove a boon to a novice fieldworker, but I soon sensed that the Seneca themselves would control my learning and that their interest would govern its progress.

Snow Street was a short cut connecting Highway 17 from Steamburg east to the road coming north from Quaker Bridge that passes the Coldspring longhouse, forming a triangle within which most of the community activity took place. That first summer I set up a tent in Jonas Snow's dooryard where I became an adjunct to his household. From this vantage point I kept a journal, which is a miscellany of family life, medicines, rattlesnakes, turtles, drunks, feuds, friends, ball games, singing society sessions, mutual aid activities, and social dances at the longhouse. It was all quite confusing at first.

My progress was affected more by accident than by the good advice of my professors or the strategy I had worked out for my fieldwork. Members of the Snow family helped me sort out the bits and pieces that came to me all at once, but they had concerns of their own that left little time for my queries. Whenever they could, they included me in their activities.

Formal work with an informant on herbal medicines yielded systematic data, and by way of getting acquainted I recorded family genealogies, noting personal names belonging to the several clans that later enabled me to identify participation in ceremonies.[1] But it was not these structured efforts at ethnology that were most rewarding. It was the after-hours informal activities that I shared with members of my "family" that brought me in touch with the culture and enabled me to experience Seneca society as a going concern.

Evenings, the Snow boys—Windsor and Linus (Kala) (afterward a casualty at Saint-Lô during World War II)—led me on the paths that cut through the brush to the ball ground where we fielded grounders or practiced lacrosse. Or perhaps we poled over the river in a john boat (a flat-bottomed skiff with square ends) to Crick's Run, or at night we went "torching" (spearing fish with a light), or we swam in the gravel pit where I taught Seneca lads to swim the six-beat crawl. Coming home we stopped at a house where we heard singing.

The singers sat facing each other on two rows of chairs or benches. The lead singer held a water drum and beater, with which he lined out the song, while the others kept time beating horn rattles in the palm of one hand while bumping their heels with the drum beat. Then they repeated the song together, drum and rattle vibrato, while maintaining the slower tempo with their heels. The song belongs to the repertoire of *en:ska:nye:ʔ*, "Women's shuffle dance," I was told. The singers formed a mutual aid society that performed charitable work in the Coldspring community. The hostess passed me a brimming bowl of hulled corn soup, saying, "His face is white, but maybe he likes soup. Perhaps later he may learn to sing."

Presently, Albert Jones of the Snipe clan, then married to Jonas Snow's sister of the Hawk clan, having gathered the horn rattles from the singers and put them with the drum in a hand basket, paused at the door to say to me, "We are glad that you came. You are welcome to sit with us. We will let you know where we next meet." I had found the Senecas a charitable people.

At midnight Jonas Snow, Linus, and I walked home along Snow Street. I remarked on the brilliant night sky, which prompted Jonas to designate several constellations by their Seneca names—the "Dancing Boys" (Pleiades), which I would later learn regulated the Seneca calendar; the Loon; and the North Star in Ursa Major.

Singing societies are found in other longhouse communities, and learning to sing that summer at Coldspring would afford a passport later at Tonawanda and at Six Nations, for the water drum and horn rattle are to the Iroquois what the violin and tambourine are to the gypsies.

Sessions for rehearsing songs are social occasions that afford the

setting for conversations. People soon asked me what clan I was going to join. They assumed it would be the Hawk clan, that of Jonas
Snow, his sisters Alice Jones and clan matron Emma Turkey, and
their children, particularly my interpreter, Emma's daughter Clara
Redeye. The question came from two members of the Snipe clan who
were married to Hawk women. Hawk clan was the logical choice,
although I sensed that the Snipes would accept me. Only later would
I learn that a clan functionally includes a fringe of spouses—men
who had married in.

The Hawk clan regarded my beat-up station wagon as a means
of transportation. Of a Sunday my family decided to visit their relatives at Cattaraugus and attend the lacrosse match at Pine Woods.
Our company included Jonas's then current drinking companion,
otherwise the village villain, which called for stops at the back of
taverns to visit bootleggers in East Randolph and at Lawtons by Cattaraugus, after which our progress included calls on Jonas's maternal
kin. Between pauses, my vehicle served as a taxi between drinks
and the ball ground, as Jonas picked up friends and relatives, while
introducing me to the elite of Seneca informants.

On a visit one touches base with one's clansmen. We stopped at
a log house, the home of Jonas's mother's sister. The old log house
was spotless and surrounded by well-kept grounds and a weedless
garden. The old lady, victim of several strokes and bedridden, nevertheless appeared glad to see me. When Jonas explained my family
connection, her face brightened. I thought she said she was the one
born in the shanty on the hemlock ridge, but I later learned that I
was mistaken. But she surely knew of the incident. Before we sat
down to dinner, our hostess insisted that I read to her from the Bible,
which made me think that she was a Christian. But the gesture was
a courtesy to me, for she was later to be buried from the longhouse.
Whatever this reunion of the Hawk clan lineage of Jonas's mother's
mother might mean to Jonas's immediate family, to me it represented
a symbolic reinforcement of the link between the Fenton family and

the Senecas. I was beginning to find it difficult to separate my role as anthropologist from my role in my adoptive family. The Sunday visit to Newtown on Cattaraugus served as prelude to a summer's fieldwork.

My involvement in the affairs and concerns of the Hawk clan intensified during the next two months. As the Green Corn Festival approached in late August, the sisters of Jonas Snow discussed giving me an Indian name. Formal adoption in the Hawk clan would establish my place in the community. But for some reason they did not get around to naming me at Green Corn, which postponed my formal adoption until I returned for the Midwinter Festival. The third day of Green Corn and the eighth day of the Midwinter Festival, or Indian New Year, are the two times when names are announced or changed for adults.

The death in September of Jonas's mother's sister, the old lady whom we had visited in early summer, put everything else aside. The bereaved relatives naturally turned to me for transportation to the funeral. This was my first opportunity as an anthropologist to observe a longhouse funeral, and it was surely under unique circumstances. As we drove the forty miles from Coldspring to Newtown that evening, I became aware that the people riding with me regarded me as next of kin. And that is how I was treated when we arrived. I sat with the mourners half of the night, and after midnight I went aloft to sleep. They assigned me a mattress near the wall. I can still visualize "my family" bedding down around me. Once I awakened to hear women dismissing drunks. Toward dawn I awoke to see not three feet away the beautiful face of the young woman who, throughout the long illness, had cared for her grandmother and conducted the wake, and who was now snatching a few moments of sleep before the funeral, secure in the taboos of exogamy, in the common bed of the Hawk clan (Fenton 1972:108–112).

An earlier extension of Hawk clan outreach occurred in July of that summer. One evening while writing up my journal on Snow Street,

I could hear someone singing Seneca songs north of the Erie tracks. I asked the Snow family, "Who is that singing?" I was told, "That's Johnson Jimerson practicing his songs. He wants to learn." Johnson was then a lad of 15, some ten years my junior, and it was soon apparent that his eagerness to master and perform the ceremonial songs of the longhouse amused older, accomplished singers almost as much as my stumbling effort to acquire the Seneca language.

At the suggestion of George Herzog, then at Yale, I had brought an Edison wax cylinder (the then available recording devices) and found Coldspring singers willing to sing their repertoire of social dance songs into the metal horn. Johnson frequently attended these sessions. In a sense he and I were both beginners, although he spoke Seneca as a first language. But the old people did not accept Johnson as a singer; instead of encouraging him, they ridiculed his efforts, and ridicule is a powerful sanction in Seneca society. Somehow Johnson and I became friends. Perhaps it was evenings at the ball ground, going to the river, or swimming at the gravel pit—activities that required little verbal communication.

My journal entry for July 3, 1933, reads:

> Johnson Jimerson has been singing his songs after supper on the hill at Fatty's. [Sam Fatty, his maternal grandfather, specialized in making bent willow wood chairs, and his daughter Esther Fatty, Johnson's maternal grandmother of the Hawk clan, was one of four "head ones" in the longhouse, representing her moiety of clans. With this household Johnson should have been well connected.] Presently Johnson came down to Snow's. He seemed anxious to know whether I had heard him. He said that he wanted to record great feather dance [one of four sacred rites of the longhouse cycle]. He told me, and Jonas Snow agreed, that great feather dance has 36 songs, of which 16 are regularly sung as the first part; then comes old-time women's dance, after which 20 more songs follow. It would take 18 cylinders to record the cycle.

Unfortunately, we never got around to it, for I was hoping to persuade one of the reigning singers to record the cycle before I ran out of cylinders.

On a return visit to Sam Fatty's place, I found the old man working at his drawshave bench. He told me that Johnson was the son of a deceased daughter, but no one knew who his father was. Here was the fulfillment of the classic theme of "Thrownaway" in Seneca folklore: the fatherless boy, living on the margins, ridiculed by his elders but avid to learn, the outcast who would grow up to become a leading ritualist among his people.

And this is what happened. Years later, Johnson found a girl at Cattaraugus, but World War II intervened before he returned and raised a family. Having mastered everything of consequence in the Coldspring round of ceremonies, including the formal speeches and announcements, Johnson rose to become speaker of the Newtown longhouse. We had not seen each other in years.

At the moon of midwinter 1968, I returned to witness the ceremonies at the new Coldspring longhouse where it had been relocated during the Kinzua Dam flooding. The sixth night of the festival, or "Husk Face night," always brings visitors from Cattaraugus, Tonawanda, and sometimes Six Nations. I spotted Johnson in the crowd. The winner that night by acclaim of the impromptu dancing contest among the False Face beggars proved to be Johnson's son, whom the proud father brought over to meet me. I was fascinated to witness the learning that a father had transmitted to his son. Johnson had indeed, to use his words, "raised him right." Thrownaway of our youth at Coldspring had become a *hodi:ont*, or "Faith-keeper," in the Newtown longhouse and leader of the singing society where he now lived. We did not meet again, and it really sent me back to Snow Street to read of Johnson's passing in 1984.

It would be amiss to expect that other lineages of the Hawk clan would accept me that first summer at Coldspring. Esther Fatty, a powerful voice in longhouse matters, expressed her doubts to Jonas

Snow and to his sisters about my presence, and old John Jimerson opposed my activities as an ethnologist on the floor of the longhouse. His remarks, however, prompted John "Twenty Canoes" Jacobs of the Bear clan, a respected elder with whom I had been working, to remind his age-mates that at least I listened while other young people ignored them, and it was clear that "this young man thinks what we do is worthwhile."

It was late in August before John Jimerson began to take me seriously and allowed me to climb High Bank for tutorials from his rocking chair. At best he was a difficult but learned informant. His youngest son, Avery, then a lad approaching 20, lived with his father. Avery liked to draw, and during one of my High Bank visits, he presented me with a pencil sketch of a Seneca masked dancer, which showed a considerable talent that he later converted to carving. Within a few years Avery would become the master carver of his generation (Fenton 1987:160, 257).

From opposition John had moved to a guarded rapport. When after Green Corn he decided to attend the renewal at Newtown of the "Little Water Medicine," the quintessential sacred rite in the Seneca cycle, he suspended doubts about me because I had a car. It was the first time for me of many such all-night sessions when I would hear the complete repertoire of songs, again at Coldspring and later at Tonawanda.

It was far easier to work within the lineage of Jonas Snow's elder sister, Emma Turkey. With her daughter, Clara Redeye, serving as interpreter, Clara's spouse, Sherman Redeye (Snipe clan), acting as intermediator, and his father, Henry Redeye (Bear clan), as primary source, we undertook systematic work on the ceremonies that first year. Henry, then speaker of the Coldspring longhouse, also preached the "Good Message" of Handsome Lake, and he had long since mastered the old forms. Sherman could fill in for his father any time. This would be my team the following year when they invited me to live with them.

Before returning home that fall, Henry clued me in on how to fix the date of the Indian new year. Watch for the "Dancing Boys" (Pleiades) during the fall until they are on the zenith at dusk during the full moon of "Short Days" (at the winter solstice), count twenty days, and the "Great ceremonial mark" (*gaiwanonskwa ʔgo:wa:h*) should fall on the fifth day of the following new moon. This would be the second day of the Midwinter Festival, because the first, or preliminary, day is for naming children born since the Green Corn Festival. (Actually Henry depended on "Dr. Miles's calendar" to ascertain the phases of the moon.)

Following similar devices, in mid-January I took the Erie sleeper to Salamanca, New York, where Albert Jones met me and drove me in his vintage Model-T Ford sedan over icy roads to Henry Redeye's place near Quaker Bridge. My kindred were there to greet me and install me overhead above the kitchen. (The family slept downstairs.)

Mornings Henry and I walked upriver to Coldspring, where he conducted the ceremonies, while Sherman and Clara stayed behind. Returning at noon, I shared my observations with Sherman, who explained what I should have seen and heard, for he knew what was significant and distinguished it from incidental behavior. Soon I began to sense the pattern of events, and within a week I knew what to expect.

My formal adoption into the Hawk clan took place on January 26, 1934, at Coldspring longhouse of the Seneca Nation. Naming of adults occurs on the eighth day of the Midwinter Festival during the celebration of Adon:weh (personal chant), which is the third of the Four Sacred Ceremonies prescribed by the prophet Handsome Lake. The other three were the great feather dance, the drum dance, and the great bowl games, each of which also has its day as at Green Corn (Fenton: typed field notes 1934).

Before a person is adopted, he must first be accepted by a clan, which is the basic unit of Seneca society. After being advanced by a particular maternal family within the clan and accepted by their clan relatives, one is taken into the larger group or community, which comprises the segments of eight clans. A public ceremony at the longhouse sanctions adoption. Ultimately, other Seneca communities recognize such actions.

The adoptee has a certain amount of choice. I recall that during the previous summer Albert Jones (Snipe clan), then spouse of my Hawk clan sponsor's sister, advised me: "You must decide what clan you want to join." He was prepared to put me up in the Snipe clan, and Sherman Redeye was ready to second it. Although I was never told, I surmise that Clara Redeye advanced my candidacy with her mother, the Hawk clan matron, who in turn spoke to her younger brother, Jonas Snow, my host of the first summer, and persuaded him to sponsor me as a Hawk. The matter had been agreed upon at a family feast in my honor that was held the previous summer when my name was supposed to be awarded at the Green Corn Festival.

A Seneca man is privileged to grant a personal name that belongs to his clan set, a name that he himself has abandoned and is therefore free to offer an outsider whom the clan wishes to adopt and whom he agrees to sponsor. Jonas Snow (Hononwiyaʔgon, "He parts the riffles") of the Hawk clan, my host in 1933, formerly held the name Howanʔneyao, "He loses a game, or a wager." This name was now free, and he wished to give it to me. Jonas was at the longhouse on the eighth morning prepared to release it.

An adoptee may have additional sponsors, known as "friends," who need not be of the clan of the primary sponsor and adoptee. Albert Jones (Snipe clan), husband of Jonas Snow's sister Alice, would be my friend. He had helped me get started in my research that first summer.

Having secured permission of the two male longhouse officers— Levi Snow (Heron) and Reuben White (Bear)—who represent opposite moieties, Jonas and Albert approached the speaker, Henry Redeye (Bear), to announce that Hononwiyaʔgon (Jonas Snow) was giving me his boyhood name. Albert (Hanoje:nenʔs) as conductor

directed Jonas and me to sit together on the north end of the singers'
bench, facing west toward the headmen. (The same setting is observed
when raising *honondiont*, officers in the longhouse.)

The formal speech of adoption is called simply "Giving a name"
(*howonseno:aʔ*). Phrasing depends on the speaker. Later Sherman and
Clara Redeye recaptured the text for me, which follows in English:

> As it has happened in the past, names have been given to white
> men. That is the reason that the Hawk clan decided to award a
> name belonging to that clan, namely, the Hawk clan, whom we
> call *Hodiswenʔga:yoʔ*, "the striped kind." The name that they have
> given, which shall be his name, is *howanʔneyao*. That is what you
> shall call him, the person whom you see here present, for he has
> come from the other side of New York. Here you see him where
> we are gathered [in this meeting]. He also thinks that it [what we
> do] amounts to something, for so he says. That is all.

Following the nominations speech, my two sponsors, the former
holder of the name and my friend, stood me up and alternately
performed Adon:wenʔ in my honor, marching me in measured ca-
dence the length of the longhouse toward the women's side and back,
while chanting their personal songs, Jonas first and then Albert, in a
powerful voice. One or two other men repeated the gesture. Shortly
thereafter, Sherman Redeye taught me to sing a personal song of my
own taken from the Snipe clan repertoire: "Snipe woke me / Yeah,
the Great Snipe woke me." There followed a public greeting, which
amounted to a sanction by the community.

After the nomination is confirmed, a longhouse officer, usually
a friend of the candidate, asks the adoptee and his sponsor to rise
and accept pledges of friendship from the people. First, the women
of the clan file by and shake hands with their new clansman. The
men of the clan follow. The women say anything they wish, such
as, "Nia:wenh ske:non" [Thanks, are you well?] The institute may
reply, "Do:gens" [Indeed]. [This is the ordinary greeting between

friends.] Another person may inquire whether the initiate knows his name and ask him to repeat it, then tell him, "That shall be your name until the old people change it, or you assume office, or you die." All of this, and perhaps more, was said to me, as Clara Redeye afterward told me.

Next it is up to the "Head Ones" of the longhouse (two women and two men of opposite moieties), followed by lesser officers, to congratulate their new tribesman. In each rank the women take precedence over the men.

After these persons of exalted names, anyone may greet the adoptee. Sometimes a friend may approach him and in a joking way say: "You are a bad Indian, but if you are as bad as I am, everyone knows that you will be a pretty bad Indian." Then in a serious vein the joker may ask the recipient to address his new relatives, pledging his loyalty to them and his devotion in times of hardship. He must remember that whenever there are ceremonies at the longhouse that he should contribute. But it is not required that the recipient acknowledge the honor with a speech.

The above remarks are couched in the words of my hosts, Clara and Sherman Redeye. Indeed Clara was daughter of my clan mother, Jonas Snow's elder sister, formally Ganegojentha? but fondly known as Gojin. My notes say nothing further.

In following years I would learn more of the obligations of clanship, its benefits, and demands. The name given me followed or preceded me wherever I went among the Iroquois people. My name remained years later even when I stayed away. In the words of a recent correspondent, "My mom gave you that name in a ceremony many years ago. You can never be un-adopted!"

Tonawanda is the central hearth of the Handsome Lake religion. In going there the first time with the Coldspring Guardians of the Good Message, for whom I provided transportation, I met their peers from other longhouses during their annual September convention. I did not then have a name. Nor did I anticipate that I would serve for two and a half years there as community worker for the U.S. Indian Service. When I returned two winters later, my Indian name had preceded me. Tonawanda Hawk clan residents regarded me in a special way as one of theirs, and they were quick to imply my obligations. Older people daily addressed me in Seneca and expected me to reply, and as with children they coached me on what to say. Certainly I afforded them endless amusement. I sat with the Salt Creek Singers, a mutual aid society, who met at Jesse Cornplanter's and Elsina Billy's house. Indeed criticism soon mounted from more progressive elements of the population that I spent too much time among the longhouse people "down below."

My term as community worker eventually ran out, I had filed a dissertation at Yale, and anthropologists were no longer fashionable in the Indian Service. I turned to teaching, which I then thought was the way to professionalism in anthropology. I did not dare to dream of a career in research. Unbeknownst to me, Jesse Cornplanter, an inveterate letter writer, had touted my capabilities to J. N. B. Hewitt, the Tuscarora-Iroquoian specialist at the Bureau of American Ethnology, and Hewitt had shared the letter with M. W. Stirling, director, whom I met on the Plains several summers previously. Stirling was impressed because, he later told me, Indians usually complained about anthropologists.

Jesse Cornplanter (1889–1957) had been my first contact and principal collaborator at Tonawanda. He grew up on Cattaraugus Reservation during the height of the Handsome Lake religion, of which his father, Edward, was the leading preacher. Jesse knew collectors from museums, and he had developed a reputation as a boyhood illustrator of traditional Seneca activities. He was aware of his culture, and working with ethnologists was not new to him. Jesse had come to live at Tonawanda with Elsina Billy, whose house stood behind the longhouse where the Coldspring Keepers of the Faith introduced me in 1933. It mattered not that Jesse was a Snipe and Elsina a Beaver; Jesse, the resident intellectual, became my tutor on Seneca culture (Fenton 1978).

The summer of 1938 found me back at Allegany with a party of students working on ethnobotany. My Hawk clan relatives and their spouses came to our assistance as informants and interpreters. Hewitt had died, leaving a pile of unpublished manuscripts on Iroquoian topics and creating a vacancy at the Bureau of American Ethnology. As summer's end, while preparing to return to teaching at St. Lawrence University, I received a wire from Stirling inviting me to accept Hewitt's post. How soon could I report?

Saint Lawrence had promoted me to assistant professor, and I felt obliged to return for at least the first semester while the college found a replacement. After Christmas, my small family remained in Salamanca, while I finished the fall term in time for the Midwinter Festival down river at Coldspring. My wife, Olive, who by then was expecting our second child, and I commuted daily to attend the doings at Coldspring, where Olive, bundled in a raccoon coat, aroused solicitous inquiries and advice from Hawk clan matrons. We were present on the eighth day of the festival (January 31, 1939) to hear an animated discussion about adopting white people.

A Seneca tribesman had brought to the longhouse a white man whom he wished to have adopted. John "Twenty Canoes" Jacobs (Bear clan) was present to act as agent for the candidate when the way was open for giving names. However, because of the discussion that ensued, no action was taken. I was told that, at a meeting of the longhouse officers on the fifth day, sentiment had prevailed against further adoptions just then.

The speaker of the longhouse, Henry Redeye, said that he opposed giving names belonging to clans to white people. In recent cases white adoptees had claimed hunting and fishing rights on the reservation by virtue of adoption as "Indians." The longhouse officers did not wish to confer the privilege on white men. Charles Butler, who interpreted for me that morning, said he disagreed that such conveyance of status was legally possible. He had attended the meeting on the fifth day when the majority of officers opposed adoptions.

I inferred from Henry's statement that some Senecas regarded adoption, when done wholeheartedly, as conferring complete status as a member of the Seneca Nation. Still other elder Senecas opposed adoption on principle, inasmuch as they expected persons adopted to behave as Indians, which would imply rights to hunt and fish, privileges which they did not wish to convey. Other Senecas who regarded adoption as honorary did not expect full participation from those whom they honored, and they would confine the honor to an exclusive few persons who were genuinely interested.

That morning Chauncey Johnny John, ranking elder of the Turtle clan, arose from his seat facing the speaker and the "head ones" to comment on the speaker's remarks. He was not opposed to adopting white people as much as he opposed the way certain Indians exploited persons whom they adopted for their own personal gain. For instance, he pointed to me with the stem of his pipe, saying:

> That white man over there we adopted. He comes back here frequently. Just the other day he gave the longhouse money. He gave it here before the crowd in the longhouse. He handed the money to the head ones (the women) right here before all of us. I suppose that if he gave it to the officers outside, they would put it in their pockets and not bring it here to the longhouse. That is the way we Indians are. When we get hold of a little money, we put it in our pockets.
>
> And then there is *haowanʔgo:wa:* ("Big boat") [attorney Charles E. Congdon of Salamanca] whom we adopted. He always gives to the headmen.

There was some latent jealousy of the Wolf clan matron who had sponsored Congdon. She and her son lived adjacent to the longhouse. They had been censured by implication for the disappearance the previous night of firewood brought to the longhouse for heating and cooking. Others in the community resented the gains that this family made in the form of clothing and the odd dollar from this adopted person. The way that this matron and her son strained to fulfill all the perquisites of office, which few people acknowledged they were entitled to, aroused further enmity among their peers. Seneca society encourages participation, but overzealous achievement arouses resentment.

Chauncey continued his commentary: "Last summer near Corning, New York, I met a white man whom we had adopted. He has been sending money and groceries here to a certain family intended for the longhouse festivals, so he says. But we all know that it [his donations] has not been brought here. That family has kept it for themselves."

Here Chauncey paused to knock the ashes out of his pipe on the heel of his left hand, which he then brushed against his trouser leg before solemnly putting the pipe into his coat pocket. He turned slowly and walked toward the men's (north) door of the longhouse, where he paused and said, "I know who that family is, but I will let that white man come here and himself tell who the family is." Chauncey went out the door, not waiting for a rebuttal. However, he returned later for the feast.

A sense of what adoption into a Seneca clan means expanded in the 1940s when the Beaver clan gave names to my wife and children. Grandma Nephew of Quaker Bridge then presided over the Beaver clan, and on the urging of her daughters, she assigned free names taken from the roster of names released by deceased holders, or names of persons who assumed new names on passing from childhood to adulthood. We had rented a house that summer from two elder daughters of the Nephew lineage, and next door the lively children of Franklin and Mary John afforded playmates for our children. Olive and Mary John developed a real bond, and Mary and her younger sister advanced Olive with their mother, who made the arrangements with the longhouse officers to have the names announced on the third day of the Green Corn Festival. Soon, the Nephew lineage held their annual Beaver clan picnic at Franklin and Mary John's, a sumptuous feast that included the Fentons. Although affiliated with the Hawk clan in the other moiety, I soon became aware, as I talked with other men present, that functionally a Seneca clan includes a fringe of spouses—men who have married into that clan. As one of them remarked to me in jest, "We all have in common the misfortune to be married to Beaver clan women."

Wherever I went among the Six Nations,[2] people asked me, "What is your Indian name? And what is your clan? Your people are yonder," pointing with chin and lips to a particular house. That identified me and afforded a body of fictive kindred, and it decided with which moiety I should sit in the longhouse.

After a long absence, in 1988 I went up to the Six Nations Reserve in Ontario to represent the trustees of the Museum of American Indian–Heye Foundation in returning some wampum belts that were long in contention. It fell to me to make the presentation. Afterward, as the women filed by to shake the hands of the museum delegation, one matron from Tonawanda quietly greeted me, as of years ago, "Nia:wenh ske:non Howanɂneyao," as if I had never gone away (Fenton 1988, 1989).

Following the presentation, a young woman approached me to say that she was the daughter of Theresa Snow, who was the teenage daughter of Jonas and Josephine Snow when I first slept in a tent on Snow Street. Theresa, having followed a husband to Canada, became the matron of her family; she sat quietly nearby where we chatted briefly of days at Allegany.

Notes

1. The Seneca clan system comprises eight clans, divided equally into two moieties or "sides," seated on opposite sides of a symbolic fire. They are:

BEAR		DEER
Wolf	X	Snipe
Beaver	FIRE	Heron
Turtle		Hawk

A Seneca clan is an exogamous kin group that reckons descent, inheritance, and succession matrilineally. A clan holds a "bag" of personal names that it awards at birth, changes at puberty, and confers on elevation to an exalted status. Adoption is strictly a clan function, rarely national. The moieties are primarily ceremonial units, performing reciprocal services for each other. They support each other in medicine society rights, they contest in games, they separate the community at midwinter and late summer when they contest in the bowl game, and they separate and condole each other's dead. Marriage between moieties is optional, if somewhat preferred, although marriage between clans of the same side is common practice.

2. Mohawks, Oneidas, Onondagas, Cayugas, Senecas, and Tuscaroras constitute the Six Nations Confederacy.

References

Fenton, William N. 1933–40. Seneca field notebooks. American Philosophical Library, Philadelphia.

———. 1936. *An Outline of Seneca Ceremonies at Coldspring Longhouse*. Yale University Publications in Anthropology 9.

———. 1972. Return to the Longhouse. In *Crossing Cultural Barriers: The Anthropological Experience*, ed. Solon T. Kimball and James B. Watson, 102–118. San Francisco: Chandler.

———. 1978. "Aboriginally Yours": Jesse J. Cornplanter, Ha-yonh-wonh-ish, the Snipe, Seneca, 1889–1957. In *American Indian Intellectuals*, ed. Margot Liberty, 177–195. Proceedings of the American Ethnological Society, 1976. St. Paul: West.

———. 1987. *The False Faces of the Iroquois*. Norman: University of Oklahoma Press.

———. 1988. Keeping the Promise: Return of the Wampums to the Six Nations Iroquois Confederacy, Grand River. *Anthropology Newsletter*, October, pp. 3, 25. Washington DC: American Anthropological Association.

———. 1989. Return of Eleven Wampum Belts to the Six Nations Iroquois Confederacy on Grand River, Canada. *Ethnohistory* 36(4): 392–410.

Swanton, John R. 1938. John Napoleon Brinton Hewitt. *American Anthropologist* 40:286–290.

Book Reviews

Review of *The Wars of the Iroquois: A Study in Intertribal Trade Relations* by George T. Hunt

As long ago as 1915 McIlwain pointed out[1] that the trade in furs was a much more important factor in the continuous alliance of the League of the Iroquois with the whites on the Hudson than the revenge of Champlain's ill advised assistance to the Huron and Algonkin in 1609. McIlwain's work covers mainly the English period of Wraxall's Abridgement while Hunt's deals with the earlier period: from Cartier's second voyage (1535) to Denonville's defeat of the Seneca (1687). However, he also shows that competition for trade was the great operating cause of the Iroquois wars.

Hunt considers the Iroquois problem part of a continental struggle between stone age peoples and a civilization which had perfected the mechanism of exploitation (p. 3). Allowing that the existing intertribal relations determined the first organization of Indian-white relations, he goes on to show how the fur trade influenced all subsequent intertribal relations. He has also focused attention on the far reaching effects of this trade on aboriginal culture. Previous writers on the Iroquois have largely missed the significance of this cultural revolution. Nevertheless, I question how deeply this revolution penetrated tribal society. Iroquois fought their kinsmen for beaver to trade for European goods and their women gave up pottery making, but female maize horticulture continued to support them in large villages until 1779 and they continue to maintain a matrilineal clan system despite all efforts to obliterate it. Certain fundamental patterns of Iroquois society have survived four hundred years of white contact and the remarkable fact in Iroquois culture history is not the changes which have taken place but the resiliency of certain of their institutions which have enabled the Iroquois to retain their culture identity after a century of reservation life and labor at white men's occupations. We need a study of these culture changes and survivals which will parallel the economic and political history which Hunt proposes.

Hunt reduces Iroquois war motives to fundamental economic realities. Tribes that occupied two strategic waterways which traversed the northeastern fur area fought these wars to control the trade. The Huron and Algonkin, who controlled the St. Lawrence–Ottawa route, became allies of the French. The Iroquois longhouse, standing astride the Hudson and Mohawk route, gravitated to the Dutch and English. It was against French interest to permit the Huron to make peace with the Iroquois lest Canada lose the trade of the Upper Great Lakes to Albany. Ultimately this policy precipitated the Huron dispersion. Hunt ably demonstrates the factors operating in this situation. He also shows that the extent of the Iroquois conquests have been greatly exaggerated and he even questions how important the Iroquois were to North American History!

Hunt finds the stock explanations of Iroquois success unconvincing. Morgan's great prestige has given wide currency to his theory that Iroquois expansion rested on a superior political organization conceived by superior intellects. Hunt proves that Morgan's much vaunted League failed to function. Nevertheless, I do not think that historical evidence of lack of unanimity among the tribes of the League is as important as the psychological fact of belief in the efficacy of the League. This prevented open intra-tribal warfare and contributed to the morale of member tribes when acting independently in the name of the League. The fiction of "universal peace," which the Iroquois stretched to include subjugated neighbors, was similar to the Nazi concept of the racial state. Members of society behaved as if they believed in it.

Aware that previous theories have the weakness of monistic explanations, Hunt (pp. 10–12) seeks to find some general condition of Indian life at the period by which Iroquois military success may be explained. He hits upon their strong military position which enabled them to take advantage of the expanding fur trade which was providing the economic basis for the new culture. His continual return to the thesis of the "universality of the economic basis in intertribal relations" (pp. 65, 115) becomes an all-or-none position. It leads him to neglect other factors which an ethnologist would consider. The prestige achieved through individual military success, and the flexible social organization which enabled Iroquois society to ingest aliens, both as individuals and as populations, were probably as important as economic factors in enabling the Iroquois to remain almost constantly at war. Surely the Iroquois of modern times do not show any genius for truck and barter, but their political astuteness and individual arrogance have not diminished.

Hunt outlines the ethnographic setting and trade routes of the Huron trading empire, illustrating his discussion with a graphic map (p. 53ff). His chapters on the Huron and their neighbors, the Upper Canada and Michigan tribes and the Wisconsin tribes, contain useful statements of tribal location, political alignment and movements during the historic period, although on minor points such as the identity of the Mascouten there may be question. His analysis of the Huron trading empire raises larger issues of fundamental cultural type and borrowing between Huron-Iroquois and Algonkins. The birch canoe industry and canoe trade routes rest on fundamental elements of an Algonkin type of northern hunting and fishing culture and were probably borrowed by the Hurons before the coming of the whites. Maize horticulture by Huron women, supplemented by hunting, supported relatively large populations in compact villages which were moved to new sites at approximately ten year intervals. In the trade that emerged from the exchange of corn, tobacco and hemp, probably not domesticated (p. 56), for fish, skins and Algonkin artifacts, non-economic factors at first probably were more important than the profit motive. When these exchanges developed into the later fur trade the resulting modifications in Huron culture were mainly in the sphere of men's activities. The female horticulturalists remained at home like the Seneca women of 1687, whose farms supported the nation. Hunt has not adequately supported his statements that Huron production of foodstuffs declined measurably (pp. 59, 63), although his inference that by 1649 they had become so dependent on Neutral and Petun farms that they lacked reserves to withstand conquest is an important contribution. Also, I think that the basic economy of the Hurons and Neutrals was enough alike for Huron proportions to be used in calculating Neutral population (p. 50). I would interpret Huron kin, clan, and government as being older than the trade and as having affected its organization. Incidentally, the so-called Huron clans of the Relations were probably bands; the Arendaronons were the Rock people, not the Bear (p. 62).[2]

Hunt tries to devaluate Iroquois political organization by showing that before 1640 the 12,000 Iroquois were either peaceably disposed or unsuccessful against the Huron, with whom French interference prevented peace. He contends that exaggerated estimates of the League's power have derived from retrospective observations of Lafitau in the early eighteenth century and of Morgan in the nineteenth (p. 67). It must be admitted, however, that Lafitau had as a source Garnier, who had worked for years among the Seneca, and that he remains the most satisfactory of the early writers on the Iroquois. I do not agree that these men failed to consider the "mutability of political institutions, particularly aboriginal ones" (p. 67). What both they and Hunt have failed to recognize is the stability of the pattern of aboriginal institutions and the violation in practice of native political theory. Hunt himself (pp. 77–78) cites unmistakable evidence of the existence prior to 1645 of the Requickening Address of "fourteen matters," which is as vital to all League political ritual as parliamentary rule is to democratic assembly. The political mechanisms of the League were ancient and have remained its most conservative aspects. In this connection I doubt that the custom of compounding murder with presents grew out of the trade (p. 62). Rather the presents were added to punctuate speeches of condolence that followed the time worn requickening pattern.

In conclusion, Hunt is at the nub of Iroquois history when he points out that Iroquois diplomacy was sound, but social control was weak (p. 155). He concludes that intense nationalism and success were inevitable results of economic need and a strong military position, and not due to generic lust for blood or superior organization. He overlooks the fact that Iroquois institutions of adoption were what gave unity to a polyglot people, and the reviewer questions seriously that an Indian society with a hunting band type of organization, for example, could have been as redoubtable. I cannot agree that the Iroquois were entirely the victims of circumstance. Hunt's great contribution is a sober judgment on the failure of the League to function, a sane delimitation of Iroquois fictitious empire to coincide with a restricted dominion, and an able demonstration that the European trade was the major circumstance of northeastern intertribal relations, and that Iroquois history was a phenomenon of that contact.

Notes

1. Peter Wraxall, *An Abridgement of the Indian Affairs . . . Transacted in the Colony of New York from . . . 1678– . . . 1751*. Edited with an introduction by Charles Howard McIlwain (Harvard Historical Studies, vii. XXI; Cambridge MA, 1915).

2. A. E. Jones, *Ancient Huronia* (1909), pp. 464, 466.

Review of *Indian Affairs in Colonial New York: The Seventeenth Century* by Allen W. Trelease

This is the most important book to appear in 20 years on the history of contacts between American Indians and the colonial powers, and it is the only study by a historian of the coastal Algonquians and the Iroquois in relation to the Dutch and later English colonies that uses both documentary sources, published books, and articles—the usual apparatus of historiography—in conjunction with the recent ethnological literature. Historians would ascribe it to the genre of McIlwain's Introduction to Wraxall's *Abridgement of Indian Affairs* (1915); to the class of Hunt's *Wars of the Iroquois* (1940); or possibly to the style of Leach's recent book on *New England in King Philip's War* (1958); but it is like none of these. It is a piece of ethnohistorical research and writing of the best sort. It suggests that a new type of graduate student is emerging from the history departments of universities long famous for colonial studies. Anthropological classics have gained a new acceptance among historians.

It is a welcome book for another reason. With the virtual disappearance from circulation of certain 19th century classics on the Algonquian and Iroquoian tribes, such as E. M. Ruttenber's *Indian Tribes of Hudson's River* (Albany, 1872), Horatio Hale's *Iroquois Book of Rites* (1883), and even such 20th century monographs as Hunt and the reviewer's article in the Swanton volume (Smithsonian Msc. Coll., vol. 100, 1940), which, like the sources on which they are based, are available to students only in libraries, it is comforting to have a reliable history of the culture contacts of both peoples.

Indian affairs during the 17th century in New York fall roughly into two main divisions involving two European powers—the Dutch to 1664, and the English—in contact with two Indian ethnic entities— the Algonquians, who were pretty much "expendable" because their "economic value as consumers of . . . trading goods failed to outweigh their destructive capacity," and the Iroquois, who proved "valuable" Indians because they "controlled the peltry supply." This is an interesting concept because it was to the advantage of the Dutch to appease inland tribes who were strong and to enhance their strength. By the time the English controlled New York, the coastal Algonquian bands had already declined in importance, and, as the struggle for the West began, the Iroquois Confederacy and central Algonquians or "Far Indians" were courted as allies. It is here that Trelease makes his contribution in seeing that the early economic importance of the Iroquois, which is the core of Hunt's thesis, became subordinated to their political and military value as buffers, and even as mercenaries, between the English colonies, unable to field an army, and the numerically inferior French. And this policy had disastrous effects on the Iroquois themselves, depleting their man power; but they reacted by establishing a position of neutrality between the two European powers at the opening of the 18th century. This is the historical origin of Iroquois independence which enabled them to survive until the American Revolution and it is behind their intense feeling of nationalism today. (See Edmund Wilson, *Apologies to the Iroquois*, 1960.)

Opening with a general chapter on the Indians of New Netherland at the time of discovery, to which I shall return, the affairs of the Algonquians around Manhattan, such as Governor Kieft's War, the early importance of the Mahican around Fort Orange in the fur trade, then the subjugation and the submergence of these people, occupy the first half of the book; and what might be called the Mohawk and Fort Orange, or the Five Nations–Albany axis, comprise the climax chapters. The first half represents the greatest contribution to learning because the ethnography and acculturation of the Hudson Valley, Jersey, and Long Island has so long needed systematic treatment; but in the discussion of the Iroquois and the English, where the sources are richer, there is nicer balance of ethnological theory and historical fact.

The reviewer and Anthony Wallace had read the opening chapter in manuscript. It is most gratifying to find historical depth for my own findings on the Iroquois, and those of Wallace on the Delaware, that the village band rather than the tribe is the basis of social and political organization, and then to see that the author has read and credited the pertinent references. This ability to accept discovery sets the structure on a firm footing, as is evidenced in relation to confirming Mooney's findings on population and in furthering an understanding of the nature of aboriginal land holding and its bearing on the nature of the economy in the aboriginal east, with its mixture of agriculture and hunting and fishing, its annual round of seasonal activities, the causes of village removal, and the effect of these things on social and political organization.

Trelease makes the most reasonable estimate yet on the probable reason for the historic rise of the League of the Iroquois, a phenomenon which has suffered in appraisal from too much enthusiasm and monistic thinking. He discusses a series of contributing factors and, without minimizing the element of morale which made the *Ongwe onwe*, "men preeminently," in their own light, and without overestimating the role of the League in Iroquois development, he hits on three reasons: (1) unity (they were better organized than their neighbors); (2) access to guns and ammunition (the trade in furs and firearms favored the Albany-Onondaga axis); and (3) their location (astride the summit of three drainage systems). Reasonable approaches to complicated issues are refreshing.

In the game of three-cornered politics, the policies of the French and the Dutch (and English) present fewer difficulties than the problem of Iroquois motivation. Almost without records, save their own wampum belts, and remembered in historical documents only through interpreters, the filters of three languages, and the pens of half educated clerks, it is small wonder that the sources communicate as much as they do today. And Trelease perceives that a primitive society need not have had the same motives as advanced European societies. Indeed "Indian civilization . . . was a composite of more ingredients than the search for wealth." Abandoning Hunt's economic determinism, he prefers Snyderman's analysis of motives behind Iroquois warfare and success. The economic was only one of a myriad of causes. The theory advanced by McIlwain in 1915 and elaborated by Hunt in 1940—the idea that the Iroquois struggled to be middlemen in the fur trade—has since become the standard interpretation. "The theory has never been proved," resting as it does on the statements of several Frenchmen at later dates, "and it is not sustained in the Dutch and English records," which speak of early hunting, along with robbery, as the significant source of peltry, and the Iroquois are not alleged to be middlemen until 1700 (p. 120). It is, moreover, absurd to argue that peaceful trade relations would emerge from warfare, but more reasonable to guess that in their western wars "they were reaching out for new hunting lands at the expense of their neighbors." "It would be foolish to deny that the Iroquois ever acted or aspired to act as middlemen, but that this was the central feature of their warfare and diplomacy is equally unlikely" (p. 120).

The paradox of the Iroquois position at the end of the 17th century, which was first discerned by Lahontan about 1700, has never been set forth as clearly: It "lay in the fact that although the Iroquois constituted the greatest economic and military threat to Canada they were also the only factor keeping Albany from opening direct relations with the Ottawa and thus crippling the Canadian fur trade" (p. 246). But Trelease, in crediting Iroquois prowess, is by no means naive about the limitations of social control in Iroquois polity. In their quest for neutrality the Iroquois were "far from pursuing a complicated game of balancing the English and the French against each other, as the latter often suspected, the sachems' policy at this time was still relatively simple. The difficulty was that they lacked either the decision or the power to follow it consistently" (p. 342).

The task of writing a cultural history of the Iroquois has been advanced considerably.

Review of *Conservatism among the Iroquois at the Six Nations Reserve* by Annemarie Anrod Shimony

If Iroquois studies are indeed a classical field of inquiry in American ethnology, the interest in them today and their apparent vigor derives principally from the quality of personnel that has been attracted by the interesting problems they pose and is only partly owing to the historic fact that Morgan first commenced ethnological inquiries among the Seneca. A surprising number of Iroquoianists has come out of Yale University. Of the professional and amateur scholars who attend the annual Conference on Iroquois Research, the writer of the report under review stands in the forefront of those who have made solid contributions to ethnology. The Iroquois themselves are shrewd judges of men; I venture to guess that Shimony ranks high on the contemporary roll call of ethnologists with whom they have collaborated. Few have enjoyed better rapport with the old people of the Longhouse; no one has pushed these advantages as far for the advance of systematic ethnology; and none has contributed a taller monograph. In the light of these superlatives, let us see just how this is so.

In the generation since the *Memorandum on the Study of Acculturation* (Redfield, Linton, Herskovits, AA 38:149, 1936), studies of culture change have been legion, and but few studies have approached the reasons or sought to explain cultural stability. Shimony set out . . . "to understand the means by which so much of Iroquois culture is preserved at Six Nations in spite of intense acculturative pressure" (p. 3).

She found the answer in a principle of organization that is at work in the institution of the Longhouse which has been able to take on the functions of failing social units, thereby maintaining an internal coherence in the culture. A parallel principle is analogic reasoning that enables the Iroquois to rationalize these shifts of functions. A third is the concept of cultural focus, which for the Iroquois person intensifies a preoccupation with illness and "luck," and is sometimes manifest by "an almost paranoid undercurrent of suspicion" (p. 261), lest one's "luck" or health be "threatened by someone or something" (p. 262), and it is that anxiety that draws him to the fire of the Longhouse and holds him there because only in the Longhouse repose the rituals for this fulfillment of his desires and the satisfaction of his psychic needs.

Shimony undertakes to demonstrate these principles in two paradigms: (1) the *structure* of the orthodox community and (2) the *content* of the orthodox culture. Here she maintains that the outline of the latter represents a hypothesis of interconnection and enumerates the forces that perpetuate it (p. 17).

The Six Nations on the Grand River are 7,000 persons, of whom 1,300 to 1,400 are active Longhouse adherents. This population has more than tripled since 1784, the year of settlement, and it has nearly doubled within this reviewer's memory. Factionalism is a strong feature of present-day social groupings, although locality and neighborhood once defined loyalties and interests that with better communication have fused in the larger community. Colorful place names of neighborhoods, roads, and crossings—Sixty-nine Corners, Tom Longboats (the marathon champion), Smoothtown, Beaver Line, and Sour Springs—commemorate persons, events, and districts that had real meaning until quite recently. I am prepared to argue that something quite radical in this regard has altered the Iroquois view of their geography, toponymy, and sense of tribal separatism since Hale and Hewitt's day (1880's), and between my own and Shimony's observations. Today, tribal distinctions have merged. "There are practically two distinct cultures at Six Nations," . . . "conservative or nonconservative," . . . "and the distinction between them is clear cut and obvious" (p. 15). Of related significance is the manifestation in individuals of a continuum of "Indianness," from quite orthodox Iroquois to completely Canadian. But here too is a paradox—which is generic to the acculturation process—a polarity of change and stability—since "there is now no aboriginal Iroquois culture, nor is there an Indian on the Reserve who does not have some tinge of 'Iroquoianism'" (p. 15). The determination of where a person fits in this spectrum is a delicate task, at which Shimony reveals some discernment, which is matched by an ability to describe the structure and content of the culture in the broadest or most minute terms, and yet convey an image of an ongoing and yet stable culture which can be replicated by other Iroquoianists. Whatever it takes to be an ethnologist, Shimony has it. Without getting mired in the morass of previous historical and ethnographic writing, she, nevertheless, uses the best of it critically to achieve "a partial understanding of the composition and viability of the conservative culture today" (p. 16) and then relies on her own observations to reach such an understanding. This rising above the data has the advantage of an original view which sometimes loses sight of past achievement and overlooks old bench marks.

Four chapters treat of the structure, in which Iroquoianists would agree with the view that the shift of functions to the Longhouse as an institution of old duties of tribe, clan, and lineage represents a recent modification, that indeed they have lost or exchanged many of the functions attributed to them, and, in all probability, the view is correct that distinctions between them were never as sharp as the anthropological literature asserts. The documentation of patrilineal or bilateral kindreds as parts of the social system is a most important revision of the older matrilineal bias. How the Longhouse in turn reinforces clan and moiety by keeping alive roles for them in the ceremonies is not a new discovery. That the Longhouse has emerged as the central institution of the conservative culture was the first premise of studies of the calendric cycle of ceremonies begun by Speck and the reviewer. But no one has gone over the old ground as systematically, or tested the inherent logic in assumptions, or pushed analogies as far as Shimony, who makes a shambles of Goldenweiser's distinction between clan and maternal family, undercuts the basis of Speck's locality and tribal identity for old Longhouse ceremonial cycles, and pushes my exploration of the composition and organization of the League Council and the interrelation of its members to the limits of the data and comes up with some astonishing results. Native system (or was it ethnologists reaching for clarity?) vanishes under her scrutiny.

The composition, organization, and leadership of the Longhouse comprise two chapters to which I shall enter one dissent on the concept of the body of officials, while underscoring the role of the peace chiefs in the Longhouse, which has sheltered them.

Dr. Shimony has repeatedly urged me to get on to the enjoyment of Part II of her thesis, "The Content of the Orthodox Culture," which she herself regards as much the best, and this endorsement suggests that she feels more at home in the minutiae of daily life, in values, in the life cycle, and above all, in medicine and witchcraft, at which she clearly excels, than in structure and historical reconstruction which depend so much upon the data of others. Indeed, she communicates the reality of Iroquois views on legitimacy with such vividness that her relation approaches the tone and vindictiveness of Iroquois matrons (p. 24).

Before I am prepared to accept the definition of agadonihénõʔ as including "all bilateral relatives related to ego through an initial ascending agnatic link" (and not just the father's maternal kinsmen); and the kheyáʔdawēh (offspring), as including "all the bilateral relatives through an initial uterine link in the ascending or same generation" (p. 31), I would like to see these rules exemplified and charted. Moreover, Goldenweiser's data exist in manuscript (at New

York State Museum) and should be consulted, as well as his cited summary reports, before dismissing his distinctions.

On the matter of Longhouse autonomy, I accepted as a working hypothesis the validity of the concept of locality and attendant diversity, as viewed from Allegany, Cattaraugus, and Tonawanda, because it has sharp boundaries among the three local ceremonial cycles and between them as Seneca communities in New York and Cayuga and Onondaga in Canada; whether or not these local differences bespeak ancient tribal distinctions, it is now clear that they do not now hold for the entire Seneca tribe, if they once did (p. 45). But I see no useful purpose in sacking the well understood "faithkeepers" as the term for the honondiont or body of Longhouse officials and adverting to "deacons" (p. 33 passim, 71) which is more appropriate to the "Stone Ridge Baptist Church" and only a shade more acceptable than "vestry" or "wardens." Why not simply "officers," or use the Iroquois term? And while we are throwing ashes, the Sir William Johnson Papers are scattered broadly, but are concentrated mainly at the New York State Library and the Colonial Record Office, not the British Museum! (p. 71).

This is not the place to review or dispute but to applaud details of Longhouse organization (pp. 56–68). Shimony is quite right in stressing the imperative of reciprocity as having sovereignty over structure (i.e., clan and moiety) to which too much controversy has attended (pp. 68–69).

Participation is the index to commitment by Longhouse membership, and it in turn is reinforced by "the idea of mutual obligations and reciprocity" (p. 45). Here one of the theses developed is that "the incorporation of many aspects of culture into one institution, [presenting] the individual with a package arrangement of all or nothing, [contributes to] conserving much of the culture under stress" (p. 46).

Reservation English preserves and reinterprets one archaic usage in the phrase "to pass a dance" (pp. 71, 178, 274). "Pass" here has a causative connotation of obligation to carry a rite through its stages, or means the active fulfillment by an individual of his ceremonial obligations, which if not Biblical in the sense of "to pass the sabbath," at least has Elizabethan parallels. By derivation comes the local usage "pass dance" for any periodic observance which must be fulfilled or celebrated annually. The Senecas say "to put up" or sponsor one's ceremony. Further examples of Iroquoian linguistic virtuosity qualify how one fulfills and distinguishes a celebration with a feast for which one hangs a kettle, the symbol of hospitality, from "passing" the ceremony "dry pole" or "bare pole" (p. 179).

The effect that "ethnological feed back" would come to exert on the retention of Iroquois ceremonial culture was scarcely anticipated by field workers a generation ago. Yet nothing is so gratifying as to have one's monograph become the standard reference of performing ritualists (p. 88). In this process ethnology assumes a political dimension, that, were it foreseen in its full effects in engendering counter-revolution, might have lessened the cordiality and assistance that we visiting ethnographers have received from Canadian authorities. Shimony has laid the groundwork for a brilliant exposition of this process. I am particularly delighted by the full documentation of the Roll Call of the Chiefs, the relationships between them, how the offices are filled and by whom, and the operation of the kinship system in political contexts. My only cavil is with the Seneca system (p. 116), which is barely functional at Six Nations, but functions as I described it at Tonawanda, where it is at home.

In forbearing the temptation to quibble, I also pass up the desire to quote passages that fairly sing (the metaphor of "Longhouse" as "university," p. 130). We need more such monographs: a study of medicine using ethnobotanical evidence; of material culture and games utilizing museum collections historically and treating such activities comparatively. There is actually a set of counters for the moccasin game in the nearby Royal Ontario Museum which would have established a base line for treating the moccasin game which is actually older at Six Nations than the discussion of its features implies (pp. 238–39).

Two editorial strictures: (1) The usefulness of the comprehensive bibliography would have been enhanced by checking against author cards; and (2) the monograph would have benefited by further revision to eliminate repetition; and there are a few passages that are bound to give offense at Six Nations where ethnological writing has avid readers who can be as critical and devastating as the PhD committee. Where once one might have looked for raven tresses in the smoke hole of some Cayuga Longhouse, one now may see the scalps of previous anthropologists fluttering from the Wellesley flag pole.

Huronia: An Essay in Proper Ethnohistory

Review of The Children of Aataentsic: A History of the Huron People to 1660 *by Bruce G. Trigger*

Thirteen years ago several of us journeyed in the dead of winter to Orillia, Ontario, to mark the 350th anniversary of Champlain's sojourn at Cahiagué. Out of this Huron Symposium, held in subzero weather such as frequently greeted the *Ononharoia* (the Huron Midwinter Festival), have emerged some important contributions to Iroquoian studies. The most substantial of these are three book-length studies from the pen of Bruce G. Trigger of McGill University, now Canada's preeminent ethnohistorian. His first book, *Cartier's Hochelaga and the Dawson Site* (1972), with J. F. Pendergast, covered the St. Lawrence Valley during the 16th century; the second work, *The Huron: Farmers of the North* (1969a), is a functional interpretation of traditional Huron culture; and both of these represent trial formulations of the third work, under review.

Trigger's investigations of northeastern ethnohistorical problems, now some 20 titles, belong to the genre of Iroquoian studies that were generated by my contribution to the Swanton Volume (1940a), and the present work disposes of, once and for all, our dependence on the theories of economic determinism advanced that year by George T. Hunt in *The Wars of the Iroquois*, which I reviewed critically in this journal (Fenton 1940b). Trigger also acknowledges his debt to Elisabeth Tooker, whose *Ethnography of the Huron Indians* (1964) systematized the cultural material in the *Jesuit Relations*. Most recently, another Canadian scholar, Conrad E. Heidenreich, has examined *Huronia* as a geographer-historian (1971).

So what was once an obscure problem in the ethnohistory of the Northeast—how 20,000 aborigines near Georgian Bay on Lake Huron came into being, subsisted, regulated their affairs, were missionized by the Jesuits, and were defeated and dispersed by the Iroquois at the mid-17th century—has now been illuminated by the aforementioned studies and put into focus by the brilliant interpretation of Trigger.

Aiming "to write a history of the Huron, not of New France, or the French-Indian relations of the seventeenth century," required a different theoretical orientation from the usual histories of New France, which Trigger sets forth in the Introduction. Just as historians deal in the particulars of individual actors, so Trigger includes specific information where available about Huron personages whom historians would ignore. Similarly those Frenchmen, be they explorers, soldiers, *coureurs de bois*, missionaries, or governors, are discussed in connection with their dealings with Hurons, and with common interests arising from these contacts, while he avoids revising the history of the Jesuit Order or other founders of New France. Trigger has confined his attention to the reinterpretation of printed sources, which are voluminous, without undertaking further archival research; and he is at home in both French and English literature, which monolingual writers frequently avoid to their peril. Often enough the translations of French works are his own. In keeping with his anthropological training, he introduces new terminology, not always felicitous: "headman" for the ambiguous term "chief" (which to this reviewer are synonymous), and "clan segment" for the standard "sib" or "matrilineage." Indeed the latter is consonant with the Iroquoian term which has this meaning and might be preferable.

Writing from an Indian point of view has been one of the persistent aims of ethnohistorians, in which they usually miss the mark. Since how Trigger accomplishes this goes to the heart of the problem of ethnohistory, let us see how he does it. First he examines how historians have viewed Canadian Indians. Two Toronto professors,

T. F. McIlwraith and Harold Innis, anthropologist and economist, first realized that "the Indian and his culture were fundamental to the growth of Canadian institutions," and that the "Indian point of view was a necessary part of understanding Canadian history." These parallel statements in 1930, which Innis developed in his work on the fur trade, formed the basis of the "Laurentian hypothesis," which did for Canadian history what Turner's frontier hypothesis did for that of the United States. This theory went far to explain the course of European settlements, how the French learned from native Indians to make and use the means of survival and transportation in the bush in summer and winter, and how younger Frenchmen came to prefer Indian society to their own (Trigger, Vol. 1, pp. 2–3).

A second important difference in Indian and white relations between Canada and the United States is that the French were content to trade and missionize and did not covet exclusive possession of Indian land. In the symbiotic relationship between Indian trapper and European trader, Trigger remarks that "not once was there a case of serious or prolonged conflict" within Canada. Here he is reminding Canadians of a difference that is not mirrored in the media originating in the United States. But, as he notes, there have been several landmark studies by Canadian scholars, following on the "Laurentian" lead, which seek to explain the fate of the Indians north of the border. The notable contributions are by McIlwraith's student A. G. Bailey (1969); by Léo-Paul Desrosiers, the Montreal librarian, whose *Iroquoisie* (1947) treats Iroquois-French political relations until 1646; and by George F. Stanley, "The Indian Background of Canadian History" (1952). But they left the methodological problems to Trigger.

The biography, which is the preferred form of Canadian writers on famous Europeans, leaves Indians out of consideration for want of literary remains, or treats them as part of the flora and fauna. Even the "life and times" of such celebrities as Pontiac, Tecumseh, and Brant fail to explain what motivated them. Worse are the relapses to previous European stereotypes on the part of historians who fail to internalize new research. Confronting subjects for whom there are no written records demands new techniques and new methods.

Here the comparative view of the anthropologist and recognizing fundamental differences between small-scale and complex societies are helpful. The historian lacks the personal judgment for evaluating the former. He looks in vain for institutions and fails to perceive the network and its projections based on kinship. Small wonder that past historians have concluded that Indian history is not feasible. This melancholy conclusion appeals to two other assumptions, equally fallacious.

There is the romantic fallacy that Indian cultures changed little before the coming of the whites. Until recently it was shared equally by historians and anthropologists. Many of us have been guilty of seeking a cultural stability based on a pre-Columbian culture that was more or less static. Archaeological research, both in Canada and in New York State, has dispelled this illusion and demonstrated remarkable cultural evolution of Iroquoian peoples from a preagricultural hunting and gathering economy to sedentary village life based on corn, beans, and squash horticulture long before Europeans made the first landfall. Indeed the long history of the Iroquoian peoples demonstrates an ability to adapt to the environment, to accommodate change, and to maintain some patterns over long periods of time.

Most welcome is Trigger's argument against the views of the economic historians, notably McIlwain (1915) and Hunt (1940), who maintained that a knowledge of pre-Columbian culture change is irrelevant to an understanding of later events, once the Indian acquired and became dependent on European goods and ideas. This reviewer has never felt comfortable with the image of the Iroquois as "middlemen" in the fur trade as the sole motivation for their behavior, which is inconsistent with the character structure of their living descendants. Trigger's attack on Hunt's thesis, which persists throughout the two volumes into his conclusions, and seeks additional explanations of their behavior, sustains the fallacy of monistic explanations, which I pointed out long ago (Fenton 1940b). Indeed, other factors arising out of existing conditions in native life, such as established patterns of trade, warfare, and diplomacy, governed these contacts.

Further factors in the inability of culture-bound historians and biographers to cope with the role played by Indians in history are transfer of moral judgments from one culture to the other, judging Indians by how they serve the interests of the group under study, and allowing religious biases in our own culture to affect interpretation of Indian behavior. These kinds of stereotype thinking resolve into a simplistic dichotomy of "good" and "bad" Indians, "bloodthirsty savage" vs. "noble savage," each of which has its own history, and which continue to prevail in new guises. For a time anthropologists entertained an illusion of "aboriginal culture" which they sought to recover. There is a romantic element in all of us.

Trigger is probably right in suggesting that the view of the Indian past that native American prophets and writers now advance prefers the "noble savage" stereotype, stressing features attractive to whites and suppressing behavior traits that are repugnant. Indeed such practices as polygamy, scalping, torture of prisoners, and abandoning the elderly, which are easily documented, cause embarrassment and shame to present-day Indians who deny that such practices ever existed or project them on Europeans. Whenever natives or scholars of another culture allow such stereotypes to interfere with the description of aboriginal life, the possibility of an Indian history vanishes.

Trigger's documentation of racial biases in the interpretation of Canadian history may depress but will not surprise anthropologists late in this century; it only serves to emphasize the task still confronting education in America.

The approach known as ethnohistory and its relation to anthropology on the one hand and to history on the other has been forged in just the kind of real problems that Trigger discusses so ably in his Introduction. Each of these has been unique. In the Huron case no living ethnologists since Marius Barbeau could work with Huron descendants who in 1915 spoke their language and retained much of the oral literature. But for the 17th century there is historical documentation aplenty recorded by Europeans, particularly the Jesuit missionaries to Huronia who learned the language, recorded lexicons, and devised grammars, besides describing much observed behavior, particularly ritual performances, which they partly understood. And in the last 50 years in Ontario, archaeological fieldwork, laboratory research, and publication of site reports and problem-oriented investigations have achieved a remarkable sophistication. Yet, as Trigger points out, there is "a gap in our knowledge of the Indian between the prehistoric period, studied by the archaeologist, and the recent period studied by the ethnologist" (p. 11). Trigger maintains that if we are ever to understand how Indian life changed in the interim, only historically oriented research will bridge the gap. Until quite recently neither the prehistorian nor the ethnologist was inclined to forsake the field for the library, nor were they trained to use documentary materials critically. This he sees as the role of ethnohistory. Indeed this is a species of history, which recognizes the special methodology required to study the history of small societies. The anthropologist brings to this study two special qualities—access to a wealth of data of a comparative or cross-cultural nature on other ways of life and training in a discipline—which supplement traditional historiography. These tools enable him to put Indian life in a new perspective and to illuminate much behavior that is otherwise meaningless.

Trigger then confronts a paradox that struck me when I first went into the field in the 1930s. How can ethnological observations and information collected in this century from societies that are going concerns be used for interpreting 17th- and 18th-century sources on the ancestors of these living Indian peoples? How did the Senecas of my day relate to the "people of the hills" described in the *Jesuit Relations*? One learns what he is trained to see, and anthropology dates only from the mid-19th century. Nor was I a Jesuit. The culture had undergone enormous changes, and yet there are persistent patterns and themes that could only come down from the past, and indeed are present in the early literature. The most frustrating aspect of such research is that certain major institutions are only mentioned and seldom described in the early sources. Had they waited for anthropology to be born? Were they innovations?

Trigger has less confidence in this approach than I have, although he cites Tooker's recent work on ceremonialism as an example of how the problems can be met and of the uncertainties at early periods (Tooker 1970). As he says, Iroquois culture has changed rapidly in historic times, and archaeological studies document similar changes prehistorically.

The more ethnohistorians work with European sources the more is it apparent that much of what we formerly regarded as Indian culture is a culture of the contact situation. The most notable exponent of this view is T. J. Brasser, trained at Leiden University, now at the National Museum of Man, Ottawa. His recent study of the emergence of splint basketry in the 18th century and its rapid spread among Woodland peoples suggests that this folk art came to the New World with Dutch and Swedish settlers (Brasser 1975). A similar case has been made for the explosion of wampum out of indigenous resources and its spread over established trade routes once steel drills and grindstones were introduced and facilitated quantity production in New Netherlands (Fenton 1971b). In an earlier study, Brasser (1971) holds that several ceremonial complexes—the Delaware Big House, the Ojibwa Midéwiwin, and the Sun Dance on the Plains—which anthropologists previously treated as aboriginal, have similar histories.

In the Huron case, in contrast with the Iroquois, so little survived the debacle of the mid-17th century that the temptation to project is less, and the problem is to get inside the period through the documents. One way to get around this dilemma is comparison with Iroquoian groups whose culture and societies did survive, and for whom our knowledge begins where the Huron data leave off. Trigger cautions on using this method and questions that Huron prior to 1650 can be treated indiscriminately as an earlier stage of Five Nations Iroquois culture. There are known recorded differences, although the patterns are much the same. He cites the calendric rituals that have been known since L. H. Morgan (1851) for Iroquois, and are certainly not as old as the shamanistic societies, and the dream rites from which they derive—a point which he credits to Tooker (1960) and Chafe (1964); but when and how the Iroquois acquired agricultural festivals depends on wider cultural affiliations that I pointed out in 1940 (Fenton 1940a:164–175) before the *in situ* hypothesis changed our view of Iroquois origins.

Historical ethnography, which implies the use of comparisons and a knowledge of widespread cultural patterns, is a basic ingredient of Trigger's ethnohistory. He does not quite buy the view that ethnohistory proper is the history of a nonliterate people. There is more to it. One should also know something of the processes involved in the history of culture contacts elsewhere. But he sees danger in selecting theories to fit specific situations and the distortion of fragmentary evidence to fit a theory.

Yet anthropology does not provide all of the tools and concepts for interpreting tribal life from documentary sources. The ethnohistorian must control the techniques of historiography. He must learn to evaluate the authenticity of sources, to interpret the document beyond what it says, to assess the personal bias of the observer, and to learn something of the writer's culture and history. Since people see things in terms of what they know and what they are, one must compare the various sources on Iroquois religion and contrast what they say with modern ethnographic sources. One can thus see through the biases to what is reliable.

Self-interest is another tool in Trigger's kit. In the analysis of the Mohawk-Mahican war (1971b), he likened his perception of rival interests—French, Dutch, and Iroquois—to surveyors' triangulation, which enabled him to reach reasonable conclusions about the views of Indian participants, even without independent Indian witnesses. In the present work he extends this method to the analysis of French *coureurs de bois*, missionaries, administrators, and the Indians themselves to reach Indian views of the French.

Scholars and Native Americans have made much of the oral tradition of late. Unlike the Winnebago, the tendency among Iroquoians is to periodize their history in the names of prophets who set a moral tone and produced "cultural revolutions" (Parker 1916:480, Fenton 1971a); memory of first contacts with Europeans, including the Jesuit missions, is wiped from the tape. There is no cultural memory of archaeological sites. Names of the founders of the League are preserved in ritual chants and projected into the Deganawi:dah epic of its beginnings; but these same titles are most difficult to verify in historical sources beyond the middle of the 18th century. While the Hurons lacked a myth of the founding of their confederacy, they retained knowledge of political events during 200 years preceding the Jesuits. Like the Iroquois, their Wyandot descendants recalled little of 17th-century events. These facts leave Trigger skeptical of the use of oral tradition for historical purposes, unless confirmed by other sources.

He has more respect for auxiliary disciplines such as historical linguistics and archaeology. Lexical studies may be the best means of checking theories concerning the relative age of cultural phenomena, and recent work on comparative Iroquoian by Chafe and Mithun, Lounsbury's students, holds promise for interpreting prehistory.

Anyone who has ever tried to identify historic sites from contemporary records is bound to respect the models of scholarship in Canadian archaeology, notably by Kidd (1949), Ridley (1947), and Trigger (1969b). Other reconstructions in Huronia are less faithful.

The present work belies Trigger's statement that the ethnohistorical approach in America has produced few major studies of Indian tribes. He joins the few he cites: Spicer (1962), Hickerson (1962, 1970), and Wallace (1970). But unlike the works cited, which subordinate historical analysis to generalizations about cultural processes, Trigger seeks to fill a void by pursuing as an end in itself the explanation of a specific historical situation. I see his aim as pure history.

He states his methods and assumptions in achieving this end. First, available data and a willingness on the part of the ethnohistorian to heed them control how specific a study of culture contact can be. Previous studies have looked at how whole peoples react to one another in the name of Indian and white relations. Trigger penetrates to individual behaviors which may share common interests in both societies. This approach proves particularly revealing in the analysis of motivation in the fur trade, in warfare, in alliances, and in the missions. Here he makes an important contribution to understanding factionalism, both in a structural sense and in the genesis of factions. Even in societies like the Iroquois and Huron, where factionalism appears to be at home in the culture, the contact situation exacerbates it. His case study of the role of the Jesuit mission program in dividing Huron society into nominal Christians and traditionalists is particularly revealing of the process as well as the structure of factions.

In opposition to structural studies, he examines biography. The life-history method, which examines in detail individual participation in cultural situations, has its votaries among anthropologists since the 1930s. Such detailed studies are unavailable for earlier periods. The familiar "life and times" genre of the early 19th-century local historians lacks cultural insights. Those of us who struggled to overcome the paucity of extant materials in preparing Indian biographies for the *Dictionary of Canadian Biography* learned how difficult this art form can be and how elusive the essential ésprit of the person and his period (see my *Kondiaronk* in Vol. 2, pp. 320–323, 1969).

Trigger (1971a) has further documented the weakness of the biographical approach for Indians in his revisionist judgment of Champlain's Indian policy. Champlain's dealings with Indians turn out to have been far from heroic; he did not really make the effort to understand their culture, and he failed to grasp what the Jesuits later learned—that to change their ways one must work from within. The pity is that the *coureurs de bois* who understood the language and were at home in the culture left no written records. The same might be said of their biographers who failed to understand the Indians with whom their heroes had dealings.

Trigger, however, has discovered sufficient information about individual Indians in specific situations to enable him to interpret their responses to these situations and to link these individuals with others of their ethnic entities and with the French traders and priests in a meaningful way. The bearing of this course midway between structure and biography is "behavior of groups of individuals united by certain common interests" in real historical situations. His concept of the "valid interest group" derives from the theory of George C. Homans (1962) and, in part, the writings of Jean-Paul Sartre (1963).

The application of this theory to ethnohistory is original, and is best expressed in Trigger's words: "The technique of studying social interaction in terms of interest groups provides ethnohistorians with a method of approaching as near as the data will allow to the investigation of historical events in terms of their real agents, individual human beings. In particular, it encourages a far more detailed examination of events and processes than does the study of contact as an interaction between two totally different cultural systems" (p. 24).

Thus, in Canada, as he notes, "Indians and Europeans rarely constituted two homogeneous interest groups." There was competition on both sides for the attention of the other; party and faction, occupation, status, and role linked certain Indians with certain Europeans in alliances across ethnic lines. This approach seeks a certain universality of human behavior cross-culturally.

Given this method, there is still the problem of bias in the sources written by Europeans. Most historians have not succeeded in crossing the boundary of their own culture. Even the ethnohistorian, who may have some insight into Indian culture, discovers that these sources tell him more about Indian and white relations of specific groups than about intertribal relations. Because of this, Trigger perceives that historians automatically "overemphasize the importance of Indian-white relations . . ." (p. 25). At that, it is difficult for the ethnohistorian, using all of the data, to avoid rewriting colonial history. Instead one must pay more attention to the rare data on traditional concepts of Indian diplomacy and preexisting patterns of intertribal relations which continued to influence Indian behavior after European settlement.

In writing his Huron history, Trigger says that he carefully adhered to several procedures. First, as regards historical figures, he concentrated on their roles as members of an interest group. Second, in presenting the motivations of members of each interest group, he strove for clarity and impartiality. He tried to keep the focus on the total situation. He avoided the passions and problems of a particular group.

He feels impelled to take this approach because he apparently does not accept the findings of Hallowell (1946) and Wallace (1952) concerning the psychological characteristics of eastern Indians, although his reason is the want of documentation. Hoping to achieve parity, he eliminates such considerations for Europeans as well. (Is the documentation any better?) A second point is more difficult. Most of his data concern transactions between the Huron and various groups of French. So he hopes by concentrating analysis on intergroup relationships, "rather than on the inner dynamics of the groups themselves," to achieve a better understanding of the Indians (p. 26). He eschews sympathy toward the Indians as inadequate when respect depends on a clear understanding of motives. He urges ethnohistorical writers to strive to make the behavior of Indian groups understandable. While this is a valedictory to Canadian scholars, it applies generally. Such a view of Indians must be balanced by "dispassionate understanding of the motives of European groups." Here he has in mind the Jesuits whose activities tend to polarize opinions.

Eleven chapters of ethnographic, archaeological, and historical explanation and conclusions follow the preceding statement of methods and assumptions and comprise the bulk of the two volumes. The work is illustrated with 51 plates, including reproductions of period drawings and maps and diagrams. Besides there are 37 maps, mostly original, showing schematically intertribal relations at various periods, distributions of villages, trade, and campaigns, which assist the reader in following the author's arguments and draw together information nowhere else available. There are chapter notes for each volume. The extensive and accurate bibliography includes elusive Canadian items in French and English. Moreover, the two volumes are adequately indexed as to topics in Huron culture; authors; persons, both Indian and European; and historical places and events. When it comes to such useful scholarly apparatus, many authors tire or take short cuts.

The discussion of the Huron and their neighbors stands above the sources and rests on Tooker's monograph and Trigger's previous synchronic study (1969a). Indeed the writing of the entire work attains a third level of discourse, one stage above the usual paraphrastic writing, and two stages above the sources. Few ethnohistorians reach this level of discourse, and there are precious few quotes in the entire work. Readers who cherish the flavor of the originals will miss the writing of the period.

I am gratified that Trigger is conservative in estimating Huron population, accepting the lowest figure of 18,000 and favoring the method of Heidenreich over Dobyns and his followers (1966). In this test case, settlement pattern studies and contemporary estimates do not warrant exaggerated figures.

Functional aspects of social groupings are well treated. I should have made more of the ritual sanctions sustaining friendships (p. 45), their origin in dreams, and their fulfillment to sustain luck and avoid illness. Since I once collected case histories of childbirth, I wonder whether the sources specify a kneeling position for parturition (p. 47)?

Trigger's exemplary reconstruction of Huron government (pp.

54–62) presents intriguing analogs in its confederate council with that of the Five Nations Iroquois culture pattern (pp. 90–104), and are contrasted in the following chapter on the "Birth of the Huron" (pp. 156–163). The time frame for the formation of these institutions is set by a complete command of the prehistory of Ontario and New York. Archaeological evidence indicates that conditions were right for the formation of such confederacies during the century following 1450. Trigger correctly perceives these alliances as loose associations for curbing intertribal aggression, and, I might add, for composing blood feuds. Indeed this is the purpose of the whole ritual known as the Iroquois Condolence Council. He finds no evidence that the members of a confederacy were bound to mutual aid in wars, although the Deganawi:dah code specifies this, and these alliances did restrain intertribal warfare and provided a sense of corporate identity for all the members. I cannot agree that we know little about the formation of such confederacies. And I cannot regard 1450 as any more than the beginning of a long process, which the aforesaid myth reaffirms, toward confederation. The precise date 1451, though nicely conformable to an eclipse visible throughout Iroquoia that summer, is derived from two minor variants, neither of which can now be verified, and this episode is not mentioned in any of the three major versions (Fenton 1971a:133, 1975). Trigger observes that even if the Iroquois Confederacy were strengthened to cope with European intrusion during the fur trade, this happened easily. Moreover, its staying power argues for its age. For these and other reasons, he considers it doctrinaire not to heed the Huron claim to the Jesuits that their confederacy began circa AD 1440 (p. 163).

Trigger makes it clear in chapter four, entitled "Alien Shadows," that the concentration of the four groups of Huron near Georgian Bay happened after the arrival of European trade goods in Ontario. He sees both of these events as being related to the early fur trade; but, as he demonstrates, the later Huron trade routes were built on a native commerce in protohistoric times. Moreover, the union of two of the Huron groups preceded the confederacy of four. So both economically and politically, later institutions and events rested on prehistoric foundations (p. 175).

The arrival of Europeans in eastern Canada and the exploration of the St. Lawrence valley, 1534–1609, created shock waves that touched the Hurons north of Lake Ontario and the Iroquois to the south. Trigger treated this period in a previous book on Hochelaga (Pendergast and Trigger 1972). How Algonkian cultures fared during this conflict was explored by Bailey (1969). This period witnessed the disappearance of Laurentian Iroquoians caught between the hammer of European expansion and the anvil of militant Iroquois.

It is in explaining events during the late 16th century and in analyzing the factors going into the French-Algonkin, and later, the French-Huron alliances, that Trigger finds his method of mutual interest more satisfactory than previous efforts to explain these events (pp. 228 ff., and ch. 5). Champlain's campaigns against the Iroquois fall into place. Likewise, the complicated struggle among French, Algonkin, Huron, and Mohawk to control the Ottawa corridor of the fur trade succumbs to the interest thesis more satisfactorily than to the monistic mercantile theory of Hunt (1940). Indeed Trigger's refutation of Hunt's thesis, which is carried through into his conclusions, shows the famous work to have been a distinguished mistake.

The period from 1616–29 spans the "Quiet Years" of Huron history (ch. 6). Commencing with the French-Huron alliance, it covers productive years of the fur trade, until the expulsion of the French from Quebec. Temporarily there was peace with the Mohawk; Sagard and the Recollects followed Champlain to the Huron country; and traders, typified by Étienne Brûlé, became established in Huron villages. These traders had marvelous opportunities to observe Huron ways, they learned the language, but few were literate, and only Boucher (1664), afterward mayor of Three Rivers, left a memoir. The Huron suspected Brûlé of attempting to set up a trade alliance with the Iroquois and had him murdered for political reasons (p. 396).

With a steady eye on social change for each period, Trigger refutes Richard's (1967) finding of a shift from matrilocal to patrilocal residence patterns (p. 419). The French misunderstood Huron kinship, and none of the Jesuits before Lafitau (1724) was prepared to understand a lineage or clan system. Trigger finds it impossible to accept an argument that matrilocal residence patterns were breaking down before 1650 (p. 420).

The concepts of cultural climax and focus find their expression in the famous Feast of the Dead, described in the *Relations* by Brébeuf and illustrated by Lafitau. It survives in the Iroquois Condolence Council, which on these grounds would argue for the lateness of the League. They have the common purpose of promoting continuity of society and solidarity (p. 427).

At this period the Huron view of the French and their ways affords nice insights into their character.

Of the more difficult periods of Huron history, the years 1628–34, the "Interregnum and the Alliance" (ch. 7), is particularly complex. Previously I have found it difficult to find a pattern in the petty raids by Mohawks on the St. Lawrence. Trigger looks behind their affairs in New Netherlands and suggests why they defeated the Algonkin and finds no need for external intrigues when self-interest explains what happened. Every group of Indians wanted to trade with more than one European outlet, but none was prepared to give its enemies, or potential foes, equal access to partners in an alliance (p. 498).

The epidemic diseases which the Jesuits and French traders inadvertently carried to the Huron country yielded a "Deadly Harvest" (ch. 8). They swept away 50% of the population in six years and reached peoples beyond European contact. This tragedy called for shifts in Jesuit policy in response to Indian perception of their mission. At times neither side communicated. Huron hostility inevitably followed from their perception of cause and effect. The French awarded guns to converts. But the Jesuits failed to grasp that Hurons were prepared to accept new cults without becoming French. They still viewed Christianity as a ritual alliance. They linked Baptism to success in the trade. Between 1634–40 they had become dependent on French goods. Having lost half of their manpower, they could no longer defend villages now too large for the population. Old people had died without passing on ceremonies, affairs of state and the trade were disrupted, and persons who knew how to deal with the Jesuits were gone. Whole skills had vanished at every age grade. And the Iroquois enemies had suffered a similar decline.

The year 1640 marked a watershed in the fur trade that has variously been interpreted. Surviving entities in northeastern North America were competing for the same diminishing supply of beaver skins which they now must have to purchase trade goods. This gathering storm that produced the Beaver Wars engendered shifts and conflicts which Trigger handles skillfully. He finds the Iroquois surrounded by horticultural competitors rather than suppliers of furs. Hunts to the contrary, there were still beaver in Iroquoia, but to the north pelts were better. The Mohawk were bound that enemies who had access to the furs should not conclude an alliance with the Dutch to market them. Trade and peace were one and the same. Consequently the Mohawk became fur pirates when they obtained guns in quantity from English and Dutch sources and gained a military advantage over groups to the north (p. 629). New strategies called for smaller war parties, and new tactics evolved. To replace diminished manpower, they adopted erstwhile enemy captives who became "Iroquois by affection" (p. 640).

Mohawk efforts to break the Algonkin-Huron-French alliance, or immobilize the French by diplomacy, were tempered by the fact that the Mohawk were of two minds. The presence of two factions among the Mohawk—one for peace with the French, the other for war—had important implications for the structure of their council in the League. The peace party was composed of the Turtle and Wolf clans and towns, the Bear opposed them. This tripartite division into moieties coincides with the seating arrangement that tradition and ritual procedure project to the formation of the League (Fenton and Hewitt 1945:306). Trigger's synthesis of Mohawk factionalism (p. 645) illuminates an important cultural problem beyond his evaluation of their foreign policy, which had other than economic motives.

Negotiations for the Peace of 1645 witnessed the first recorded performance of the condolence ritual with wampum belts by an Iroquois performer (p. 648 and Thwaites 1896–1901 (27):251–265). Again I call attention to a point that supplements Trigger's argument, namely that these truces served to retain relatives or tribesmen, and that the ritual kinship thus acquired ceremonially allowed the Mohawk hunting privileges in Algonkin hunting territories (pp. 632–633). Here again he denies Hunt and leans on Desrosiers.

Affairs took a new direction following the peace of 1645. While the Mohawk concentrated hunting and raiding in Algonkin territory for furs, the Upper Iroquois moved against the traders in the Huron country. For in fact there was no League-wide attack on the Huron before 1647, which leads Trigger to conclude that the Iroquois were not following a long-term policy, but a number of short-term ones (p. 664).

Of greater significance for the destruction of the Huron country than the striking power of Iroquois war parties was the inability of the Hurons to organize resistance because of the "Storm Within" (ch. 10). No writer previously has examined the career of the Jesuit mission and appreciated just how Christianity divided the Hurons into Christian vs. traditionalist factions which rendered them powerless to fend off aggression. Trigger's analysis of the social impact of Christianity is one of the ablest case studies of factionalism in the literature. He finds it difficult to believe that the Jesuits could fail to understand the implications of their policies. This statement is bound to fuel dissension in Canada today.

As Huron cooperation declined into mutual distrust, the less missionized Iroquois appear to have grown in efficiency, cooperation, and power. However, of the Three Brothers, Onondaga jealousy of the arrogant Mohawk was never far beneath the surface, and the Seneca, secure in manpower, could follow their own interest. The integrity of the Iroquois League was more symbolic than real. In contrast, the Huron confederacy was doomed by factionalism, bad luck, and poor advice (ch. 11). Francis Parkman first told this story, but Trigger's theory of self-interest explains better how war parties of the Iroquois nations could unite and prevail. Sometimes the reader wonders how Trigger can discern policy where it is not stated (p. 726). And in another case, where he has good evidence, it goes against his first hunch (p. 744).

After the breakup of the Huron confederacy in 1649, only one of its named tribes survived as an entity. Fragments of other social units flew to the four winds. They formed one village among the Seneca, and other League tribes incorporated segments of Huron families. One group that fled up the Lakes later had survivors known as Wyandots living near Detroit. Of the bands that went to the St. Lawrence, only Jeune Lorette near Quebec preserves any sense of former identity, and no one there spoke *sauvage* when I called in 1939. The others succumbed to French perfidy when faced with Iroquois aggression in the years that followed the dispersal of the Neutral and Erie. Trigger recounts their "Betrayal and Salvation" (ch. 12). He also imposes some sensible limitations for assessing Huron contributions to later Iroquois culture (p. 836).

I shall summarize this long review of a major work in Canadian-American culture history by abstracting the author's conclusions (ch. 13). (1) Prehistory dispels the notion that the northern Iroquoians were in a state of cultural equilibrium. (2) Change proceeded rapidly in every aspect of their culture, and they were if anything not conservative. (3) On contact, changes were adapted to existing institutions: the confederacies show great political skill and grew out of previously existing structures at the tribal level and required no new principles. (4) In contrast with the Iroquois, the Huron enjoyed developed trading relations with Algonkian hunting and fishing bands north of them which were expanded in later times. (5) Hunt to the contrary, the fur trade has no single, overriding logic. Each group responded in terms of its geographic setting and its local culture. (6) A sense of natural right to cultural superiority ran strong in the French, but they had no power at first to push the Indians around. Unlike the Dutch and English, they had little interest in acquiring their land. The alliance with the Huron conformed to traditional native patterns. (7) Crossing cultural boundaries involved both learning other ways (the *coureur de bois*) and acquiring basic language skills (the Jesuits). (8) Huron headmen who had trading partners governed the trade and made new alliances. (9) As men got more involved in warfare, trade, and hunting far afield, matrilineal tendencies in the society were reinforced and followed a trajectory established in prehistoric times. Trigger finds no evidence that any fundamental restructuring of Iroquoian society took place (p. 845). (10) After 1634 affairs in New France and in Huronia were dominated by the Jesuits who, though involved in "coercive contact," lacked sufficient understanding of Huron ways to predict the dire outcome of their activities. (11) Huron society polarized for and against the French and the Jesuits. (12) Hurons first regarded Christianity as another available ritual cult without realizing that it involved a whole way of life. (13) "Jesuit desire to destroy Huron religion outstripped their search to understand it" (p. 849). (14) Factionalism so divided Christians who received guns from frustrated traditionalists who had opposed the Jesuits that the society was unable to rally to its own defense, having lost its will to resist. (15) The Jesuits unwittingly guaranteed the destruction of the Hurons by the Iroquois. (16) The consequences of people's actions often escape them. As creators and destroyers we are all the children of Sky Woman!

References Cited

Bailey, Alfred G.
1969   The Conflict of European and Eastern Algonkian Cultures, 1504–1700: A Study in Canadian Civilization. Toronto: University of Toronto Press. (First pub. by New Brunswick Museum, Monograph Series, 3, 1937.)

Boucher, Pierre
1664 Histoire véritable et naturelle des moeurs et productions du pays de la Nouvelle-France, vulgairement dite le Canada. Paris: F. Lambert. (The most recent photographic reprint is by the Société historique de Boucherville, 1964.)

Brasser, T. J. C.
1970 Group Identification along a Moving Frontier. Verhandlungen des XXXVIII Internationalen Amerikanistenkongresses, Stuttgart-München, 1968. Vol. 2, pp. 261–265. Munich: Klaus Renner.
1975 A Basketful of Indian Culture Change. National Museum of Man, Mercury Series, No. 22 Ottawa.

Chafe, Wallace L.
1964 Linguistic Evidence for the Relative Age of Iroquois Religious Practices. Southwestern Journal of Anthropology 20:278–285.

Desrosiers, Léo-Paul
1947 Iroquoisie, 1534–1646. Montreal: Institut d'Histoire de l'Amérique française.

Dobyns, H. F.
1966 Estimating Aboriginal American Population: An Appraisal of Techniques with a New Hemispheric Estimate. Current Anthropology 7:395–449.

Fenton, William N.
1940a Problems Arising from the Historic Northeastern Position of the Iroquois. Smithsonian Miscellaneous Collections, Vol. 100. Pp. 159–252.
1940b Review of The Wars of the Iroquois, by George T. Hunt. American Anthropologist 42:662–664.
1971a The Iroquois in History. In North American Indians in Historical Perspective. Eleanor B. Leacock and Nancy O. Lurie, eds. Pp. 129–168. New York: Random House.
1971b The New York State Wampum Collection: The Case for the Integrity of Cultural Treasures. Proceedings of the American Philosophical Society, Vol. 115(6):437–461.
1975 The Lore of the Longhouse: Myth, Ritual and Red Power. Anthropological Quarterly 48:131–146.

Fenton, William N., and Hewitt, John N. B.
1945 Some Mnemonic Pictographs Relating to the Iroquois Condolence Council. Journal of the Washington Academy of Sciences 35(10):301–315, figs. 1–6.

Hallowell, A. Irving
1946 Culture and Experience. Philadelphia: University of Pennsylvania Press.

Heidenreich, Conrad E.
1971 Huronia: A History and Geography of the Huron Indians, 1600–1650. Toronto: McClelland and Stewart.

Hickerson, Harold
1962 The Southwestern Chippewa: An Ethnohistorical Study. American An thropological Association, Memoir 92.
1970 The Chippewa and Their Neighbors: A Study in Ethnohistory. New York: Holt, Rienhart and Winston.

Homans, George C.
1962 Sentiments and Activities: Essays in Social Science. Glencoe: Free Press.

Hunt, George T.
1940 The Wars of the Iroquois: A Study in Intertribal Trade Relations. Madison: University of Wisconsin Press.

Innis, H. A.
1956 The Fur Trade in Canada. Toronto: University of Toronto Press. (First pub. by Yale University Press, 1930.)

Kidd, Kenneth E.
1949 The Excavation of Ste. Marie I. Toronto: University of Toronto Press.

Lafitau, Joseph François
1724 Moeurs des sauvage amériquains, comparées aux moeurs des premiers temps. 2 vols. Paris: Saugrain l'aîné.

McIlwain, C. H.
1915 Peter Wraxall, An Abridgment of the Indian Affairs . . . Transacted in the Colony of New York, from the Year 1678 to the Year 1751. Harvard Historical Studies, Vol. 21.

Morgan, Lewis H.
1851 League of the Ho-dé-no-sau-nee, or Iroquois. Rochester: Sage.

Parker, Arthur C.
1916 The Origin of the Iroquois as Suggested by Their Archaeology. American Anthropologist 18:479–507.

Pendergast, James F. and Bruce G. Trigger
1972 Cartier's Hochelaga and the Dawson Site. Montreal: McGill-Queen's University Press.

Richards, Cara
1967 Huron and Iroquois Residence Patterns 1600–1650. *In* Iroquois Culture, History, and Prehistory. Elisabeth Tooker, ed. Pp. 51–56. Albany: The University of the State of New York.

Ridley, Frank
1947 A Search for Ossossané and Its Environs. Ontario History 39:7–14.

Sartre, Jean-Paul
1963 Search for a Method. New York: Knopf.

Spicer, Edward H.
1962 Cycles of Conquest: The Impact of Spain, Mexico, and the United States on the Indians of the Southwest, 1533–1960. Tucson: University of Arizona Press.

Stanley, George F. C.
1952 The Indian Background of Canadian History. Annual Report of the Canadian Historical Association, 1952. Pp. 14–21.

Thwaites, Reuben G., ed.
1896–1901 The Jesuit Relations and Allied Documents. 73 vols. Cleveland: Burrows.

Tooker, Elisabeth
1960 Three Aspects of Northern Iroquoian Culture Change. Pennsylvania Archaeologist 30: 65–71.
1964 An Ethnography of the Huron Indians, 1615–1649. Bureau of American Ethnology, Bulletin 190.
1970 The Iroquois Ceremonial of Midwinter. Syracuse: Syracuse University Press.

Trigger, Bruce G.
1969a The Huron: Farmers of the North. New York: Holt, Rinehart and Winston.
1969b Criteria for Identifying the Locations of Historic Indian Sites: A Case Study from Montreal. Ethnohistory 16:303–316.

1971a Champlain Judged by His Indian Policy: A Different View of Early Canadian History. Anthropologica 13(n.s.):85–114.

1971b The Mohawk-Mahican War (1624–28): The Establishment of a Pattern. Canadian Historical Review 52:276–286.

Wallace, Anthony F. C.

1952 The Modal Personality Structure of the Tuscarora Indian as Revealed by the Rorschach Test. Bureau of American Ethnology, Bulletin 150.

1970 The Death and Rebirth of the Seneca. New York: Knopf.

Review of *The Ordeal of the Longhouse: The Peoples of the Iroquois League in the Era of European Colonization* by Daniel K. Richter

Not since Trigger's *The Children of Aataentsic: A History of the Huron People to 1660* (1976) has a work appeared of this magnitude and cultural depth on the history of an Iroquoian people. Indeed, in its unique way, Richter's work satisfies a long-felt need for a political history of the *Hodinonhsyoni*, the People of the Longhouse, or Iroquois of the Basque and French, and Five (later Six) Nations of the English. What sets Richter's scholarship apart is his approach, command of sources, and depth of analysis.

His comments on methodology (281–84) read like traditional historiography, as one might expect from his training; however, he has gone beyond that to understudy with the archaeologists of Rochester on Seneca prehistory, and he invokes the pertinent ethnological literature on Iroquois social organization and ceremonialism. No recent dissertation has escaped his notice. He has shared preliminary chapters with fellow Iroquoianists at the annual Conference on Iroquois Research, and profited by the informal give-and-take that characterizes those gatherings. Several of his unique contributions have appeared in print.

The introduction states Richter's preferences, forecasts his approach, and outlines the main ideas and processes that are developed in eleven chapters. He opts for *Haudenosaunee*, L. H. Morgan's rendering of the Seneca term for the League, which is a phonetic abomination, although it is the politically correct spelling favored by contemporary traditionalists. Historians currently insist on adding English plural "s" to tribal names, contrary to the accepted standard of collective singular forms set by the first *Handbook of American Indians* (Bureau of American Ethnology Bulletin 30, 1910), and followed in the current *Handbook*, except where a number of persons is specified. I find the plural forms for tribal entities particularly offensive on maps, in contrast with Tanner's *Atlas of Great Lakes Indian History* (1986), which adheres to the Smithsonian precedent.

Richter strives for a new view of both Iroquois and colonial history by regarding events and processes as much as possible from within Iroquois culture. He identifies four stages of their adaptation, or acculturation: (1) depopulation, (2) slide into dependence, (3) ensnarement by French and English, and (4) incursions into their land and sovereignty. To endure these ordeals, the Iroquois relied on six advantages. Geographically, they (1) straddled major trade routes, (2) enjoyed an inland position that absorbed shock of contact, and (3) served as a buffer between competing European powers; culturally, they (4) created a balanced horticultural-hunting village economy, (5) used an adoption policy to replenish losses, and (6) constructed a League for Peace affording security within, and turning aggression outward, which proved flexible. Of the six, all but two—geography (their buffer position) and the League tradition—faded by 1730.

Richter distinguishes the Iroquois *League*, with its fifty hereditary titles sanctioned by tradition and ritual, from the *Confederacy*, its operating agency of effective village headmen, which emerged in the 1690s for dealing with European powers. Both entities have continued to the present as parallel forces for stability and change, the one as a symbolic entity with sacred overtones, the other as the reality of mundane affairs. Building on earlier work on locality and factionalism—"the village and its headman," a persistent theme in Iroquois culture—Richter identifies three factions (Anglophile, Francophile, and neutralist) that sought alliances beyond their villages, and opposed, combined, and dominated in a myriad of ways during two centuries. The principles of participation, reciprocity, balance, and consensus kept the political system from flying apart.

The Iroquois periodize their history in terms of three charter myths—"The World on the Turtle's Back" (cosmology), "Concerning the League," and the "Good Message of Handsome Lake." (The latter postdates the present work.) Richter's opening chapters treat admirably the basic patterns of Iroquois spiritual thought, social system, and polity. His account of warfare is the best in the literature, and his elaboration of the "Mourning war" concept stands as a corrective to George Hunt (*The Wars of the Iroquois*, 1940). The discussion of council protocol is equally good; he perceives the role of the *rotiyanehr* correctly, but the term "Headman" after Trigger obscures a distinction between ascribed and achieved statuses.

How an interior League for Peace evolved into an external League for War during the Beaver Wars of the seventeenth century merits an explanation beyond simple economic determinism. Richter finds it in expansion of the mourning war compulsion to replace deceased relatives that followed severe depopulation from epidemics after 1633. The quest for northern furs was vital, but the demand for captives and whole populations motivated Iroquois behavior. The power of Iroquois society to ingest alien ethnic entities and enculturate them with values of "Peace, Righteousness, and Power," which together comprise the "Great Law" of the Peacemaker, has not escaped previous scholars. Richter explains that for those caught up in the captivity cycle, home no longer existed. Participation was the key to survival.

During the Dutch reign, the Iroquois dominated the acculturation process by transforming trade goods into customary patterns by old techniques while becoming dependent on the trade. Richter handles economic issues admirably. Factionalism began over the French Jesuit missions and climaxed in the outmigration to the St. Lawrence, for which Richter finds multiple explanations, some economic. Back in Iroquoia, Anglo-oriented leaders emerged to join hands with the

English in the Covenant Chain, the Anglo faction sometimes merging with conservatives, as trade boomed on the Hudson. The French were only partly to blame for the southern wars, which Richter contends resulted from diplomacy of the 1670s, instigated by adopted Susquehanna captives. A different kind of "Beaver War" dominated the final decade of the seventeenth century, for which Richter finds five factors: foreign empires controlled events; colonial politics shaped its course; Iroquois fought their émigré kindred; external diplomacy and military alignments forced village leaders to transform the Five Nations into a confederacy of village headmen; and tripartite factionalism fragmented society.

It was the greatest political crisis since the founding of the League. But having relegated the League to a ceremonial role, Richter employs the term for the homefolks versus their émigré kindred (196–97). As an ethnologist I view the Peace of 1700–1701 with eyes focused on ceremonial protocol. But I applaud his use of "diplomatic balance" for understanding modern Indian politics, a concept first noted by Peter Wraxall at mid-eighteenth century that had its roots in Iroquois culture. The London visit of three Anglophiles and a Mahican to the court of Queen Anne is relegated largely to a note, which as in other instances deserves expansion in the text. One reads this book in two segments—the narrative and the notes on sources; there is an excellent note on missionary behavior (370 n. 38).

After 1710, a policy of neutrality governed diplomacy as balance surmounted factionalism and the influence of French and English agents faded. Neutralists, often traditionalists, swept clean the "Great White Mat of the Law." Despite thriving localism, factionalism, and emerging leaders, Richter holds that consensus on basic issues was achieved by balancing peace and war, maintaining autonomy and spiritual power in diplomacy, and channeling aggression outward, as in the Catawba war. It was a losing game, for after 1720 Europeans called the shots.

Richter takes the Iroquois into the eighteenth century when peace prevailed and they struggled to keep the balance and maintain core values. The transformation of residential patterns into dispersed housing did not obliterate matrilineages, once synonymous with a household; matrons could still name upwards of a hundred people, and even three times that many in this century on the Six Nations Reserve in Canada, where they removed in 1784 and occupied scattered farmsteads. Having described their ordeal up to the mid-eighteenth century, Richter wisely stops before the sources expand exponentially. He has produced an elegant book, beautifully illustrated, and documented with notes and bibliography. May he have the courage to continue.

Obituaries

Simeon Gibson

Iroquois Informant, 1889–1943

Simeon Gibson, warrior of the Cayuga tribe and life-long member of the Onondaga longhouse on Six Nations' Reserve, Canada, left his home on the evening of December 10, crossed the Grand River in a small boat to purchase groceries at Middleport, as was his custom, and it may be presumed that he was drowned during the return trip in the storm that swept the country that evening. His boat was found but his body probably lies below the river's ice. In Simeon Gibson's passing, the Six Nations has lost a genial member and American Ethnology a unique character. For a half century almost every ethnologist who went to the Six Nations retained Simeon Gibson in some capacity. He used to tell me that he couldn't remember a time when there was not some ethnologist visiting the Gibson family.

Simeon Gibson was born August 1, 1889, the son of the Seneca Chief John A. Gibson, who was unquestionably the greatest mind of his generation among the Six Nations.[1] From his eighth year Simeon remembered guiding his blind father over the river to dictate the Deganawi:dah legend to J. N. B. Hewitt, and he translated texts for Hewitt during his last field trip to the Grand River in 1936. Simeon recalled with pleasure traveling from house to house on the reserve in 1907 with M. R. Harrington collecting for museums in New York City.[2] Gibson discharged his commission so well that few old Delaware or Iroquois specimens escaped them. He remembered Frachtenberg, who came for Tutelo and learned Mohawk in a few weeks, and Edward Sapir, from Ottawa, who retained the Gibson family—Chief John and his sons, Hardy and Simeon—as collecting agents for the Victoria Memorial Museum, and as impresarios for F. W. Waugh, A. A. Goldenweiser, and Sir Francis Knowles. Simeon doubled at carrying the camera tripod for Waugh and operating the gramophone for Goldenweiser. It amused him to relate how, as youths in their twenties, he and his brother Hardy broke in anthropologists to field work. The first time Waugh attempted to take a plaster cast, Simeon was the guinea pig, but Waugh forgot to grease his face or provide straws to his nostrils, and Simeon well-nigh suffocated before the frantic Waugh succeeded in freeing him from the plaster mask by breaking the cast with a hammer. He got five dollars for submitting a second time. Next to Sapir, who paid hurried visits, Gibson esteemed Goldenweiser the smartest white man who studied among his people. "There was a man!" he would say, and launch into his favorite Goldenweiser tale—how the Columbia Professor later confessed to having carried a revolver as protection from the wild Iroquois the first time he ventured over the river to call at Gibson's, or perhaps how Goldenweiser bought a canoe to paddle on the Grand River at sunset, or how Goldenweiser had a dream of being chased by a pig and Chief Gibson advised joining the Onondaga Medicine Men's Society for which Goldenweiser "put up a feast" at the longhouse every time he came out there. After Chief Gibson died in 1912, Goldenweiser brought his wife and stopped with Simeon, who was then married. The Gibsons served corn soup and their Russian guests made tea in a samovar which impressed the Indians enormously. I mention these incidents because they made earlier Iroquois studies live for me years later when I acquired Waugh's notes through Professor Sapir, and at Goldenweiser's suggestion I sought out the Gibson brothers to interpret the notes and texts which Goldenweiser had then entrusted to me, and the more when, after 1939, Hewitt's mantle fell upon me at the Bureau.

Simeon remembered the circumstances under which texts were

taken, who gave certain genealogies, and informants like old Oneida Chief John Danforth who, after his own dialect, habitually transposed his interrogator's name to "Goldenwissla." He could read Hewitt's phonetic transcriptions and actualize my bad Seneca into several dialects. He used to ask, "In what language do you want this?"

His mother, Mary Skye, was a Cayuga matron and guardian of the title of her brother, Chief Abram Charles, Hewitt's second informant. With maternal descent, Simeon was therefore a Cayuga, although "Onondaga on the list." Chief John, his father, was head chief of the Seneca tribe and knew that dialect from his mother, who was full Seneca, but his father was Onondaga and that was the language of their longhouse and neighborhood.

"It is a funny thing—I learned two languages at home. My mother was Cayuga. I always talked Cayuga to her and to Uncle Abram. Mother spoke Cayuga to father and he replied in Onondaga. My father always spoke Onondaga and I always replied in Onondaga to him, even if my mother was present, for she knew both dialects. Father's mother was Seneca and I learned Seneca talking with her, for she never gave up her language. Father also spoke Seneca and Cayuga, but he preferred Onondaga, the language of his father and of our longhouse. And then when I went to day school I picked up Mohawk and Tuscarora from the children, and some English."

At the same time, the modesty of the man was disarming. In World War I he had enlisted in the Indian Battalion of the Hamilton and Dufferin Rifles and served overseas as a machine gunner during sixteen months, largely in front lines at Passchendaele, Vimy Ridge, Arras, etc., and he was gassed during the last great offensive. Yet he seldom spoke of the war or of his role in it, but he loved to describe Oxford, Cambridge, Aldershot and the British Museum—places that he visited on furlough.[3] In 1939 when Royalty paused at Brantford, he loaned his military decorations to a veteran comrade and stayed home to hoe his corn. Wholly devoid of political ambition among his own people, he managed to avoid successfully all important roles in the longhouse ceremonies. Not that he wasn't qualified; his youth was literally passed in council in the longhouse. As guide for his unseeing father, he had accompanied him to innumerable councils over muddy roads in all kinds of weather to sit long hours while the chiefs deliberated, sometimes for several days, on matters affecting the nation; he had attended Condolence and Installation ceremonies walking with the Eulogy singers on the road to the longhouse of the mourning phratry of tribes; and he had made yearly visits to other Iroquois reserves in New York State when Chief Gibson, as prophet of the Handsome Lake doctrine, delivered the good message of adherence to the old way. Thus he knew the old time Senecas at Coldspring, Cattaraugus and Tonawanda, and the Handsome Lake Religion was his second nature. Yet Simeon never became a longhouse preacher or a chief.

He used to tell me, "When the day came that my mother told me that she had decided to put me in the Council for the Cayuga nation, I didn't say anything. I knew what it was to be a chief—an upright man. It means long hours of sitting, it means traveling in all kinds of weather and getting home late. I resolved that I had had enough of that. Let them make my brother chief, I thought. When the day came for the Ceremony of Condolence and the raising up of a new chief, I hid in the bush. When they set out for Cayuga longhouse, I was not to be found. I wanted to be free. So they installed my brother. He is a good chief."

Such passion for anonymity is atypical even of the Iroquois, who often feel it necessary to pass themselves off as chiefs when away from the reservation among the white people.

Simeon Gibson leaves no list of publications. His pride was in knowing the archaic language of the Iroquois League, and I believe that he derived deep satisfaction in interpreting for me the texts of laws and rituals that his father and uncle had given to Hewitt and Goldenweiser. In 1939 we reviewed Waugh's notes on medicines and related activities and took paradigms in several dialects. The next year he demonstrated his grasp of native religion by outlining and detailing the entire ceremonial cycle of Onondaga longhouse, including many of the prayers and announcements. The gas attack that left him the victim of asthma, spoiling his voice for singing and speaking, had not impaired his memory. He urged me to get on with the translation of texts: "There are only myself and my brother who can explain the meanings of the old words. You can read them, but when we are gone the meanings will be lost."

In the winter of 1941 we made recordings of a large number of songs from the Iroquois longhouse and of the rites of the Medicine Societies. It was Simeon's ambition to arrange for me a complete documentary film with recordings of the fast failing Condolence Ceremony for making League Chiefs, but conditions have conspired to postpone the project, and it may never be possible of fulfillment since the Life Chiefs of the old Council that went underground in 1924 are rapidly falling by the trail.

Plans were made to bring Simeon Gibson to Washington in 1941 for purposes of translating the Deganawi:dah legend, but his barn blew down and he could not leave home. There were two versions of this Legend of the founding of the Iroquois Confederacy—both in Onondaga by Chief Gibson. Hewitt recorded it first in 1899 on 189 typescript pages; Goldenweiser had it again thirteen years later, this version comprising 525 pages. Translation of the Hewitt version was completed in 1941 at Brantford, but Goldenweiser's manuscript hung over two more years until this past September–October, when the translation of the final 100 pages was completed at Ohsweken, leaving the great bulk covered by the Hewitt version untouched and concentrating on that section which comprises a complete record of proceedings of the Condolence and Installation Council, or the ceremony for raising up new candidates to chiefship in the League.

Whatever may be remarked of Simeon Gibson's ambition, industry, or intelligence among his farming neighbors, it can be said that he seemingly derived as much satisfaction from completing such intellectual pursuits as does the ethnologist. He passed up reenlistment in the armed forces because he wanted to continue the work on which we had embarked, and it is with no little regret that the ethnologist, in paying this brief tribute to the passing of his informant, confesses that he has spent far too much time in the office, engrossed in the seemingly inevitable busywork of bureaucracy, and all too little time with his informant in the field.

Mr. Gibson is survived by an elder sister, Jemima Gibson; a brother, Chief John Hardy Gibson; several grown daughters by his late first wife; his present wife; and three small children. His keen wit and sober nature will be missed by all his neighbors, both the Indians and the white people over the river whom he helped at harvesting. The Six Nations Reserve will not seem the same again without Simeon trudging along the road, pushing with one of his innumerable sticks which he uncannily produced from beside the store at Ohsweken, from a fence corner, or from beside the road where he had cast it for a passing ride. Weather prognostication was one of his principal pastimes, and it amused him greatly when he looked at the heavens, felt the wind, and his signs failed to come true. Perhaps it is the irony of fate that he forecast an open winter this year because there were so few hickory nuts.

Notes

1. See A. A. Goldenweiser, *The Death of Chief John A. Gibson* (*American Anthropologist*, 14, 1912), pp. 692–694.

2. M. R. Harrington, *Some Unusual Iroquois Specimens* (*American Anthropologist*, 11, 1909), pp. 85–91.

3. See Fenton, *Songs from the Iroquois Longhouse* (1942), p. 27.

Twí-yendagon' (Woodeater)
Takes the Heavenly Path

On the Death of Henry Redeye (1864?–1946),
Speaker of the Coldspring Seneca Longhouse

Henry Redeye, who gave many a funeral address over the coffin of a fellow tribesman, has himself gone on the Heavenly Path. I shall not see him again in the Coldspring Longhouse of the Seneca Nation, his eyes tight shut, his hands grasping the wampum strings which are the *light* of the council fire. I shall not hear him recite again the message of the prophet, Handsome Lake. He was buried in the moon of blossoms in the little cemetery just west of Quaker Bridge NY where he had lived.

When I first heard of Henry Redeye in June of 1933, I was living among the Senecas at Coldspring beside the Allegheny River. A white missionary recommended Henry as possibly suiting my interests as an anthropologist by listing him among those who caused most consternation in the work of the Christian uplift. The missionary's boast of his progress with the *pagan Indians*, as he called them, was that they now let him speak first at their funerals before Henry rose to deliver his address and tell the people not to believe what the white preacher had said.

During the summer I came to know *old Henry* or *djíwa'*, as the Indians fondly called him. In August he was making elm bark bowls to exhibit at the New York State Fair, and he showed me an elm bark cradle, of a type mentioned by J. F. Lafitau in his *Moeurs des sauvages amériquains* (Paris, 1724, 2 Vols.). From a discussion of handicrafts and their uses in the old culture, our conversation drifted to herbal medicines, the content of the ceremonies, and the ritualistic forms of address. Unlike others of the Senecas who were unsure of themselves about such matters, Henry Redeye had full confidence in his knowledge and he was always willing to impart accurately just what the old people told him. He invited me to come stay at his house during the Midwinter Festival of 1934, and I returned the next summer to live in the Redeye household.

With the old man as informant, his son clarifying what the old man had said while biting his pipestem, and his son's wife interpreting, we—Henry, Sherman, Clara and I—worked at ethnology at the dinner table, around the stove while wiping dishes, on summer evenings propped up in chairs facing the Quaker Bridge–Coldspring road. Sometimes to my regret but to his own interest, the old man would tire of my questions and retire to hoe his garden, or he would vanish into the bush to return with some medicinal plant for the herbarium. Often there were visitors, his or mine. Sometimes the Coldspring Singers Society came to dance, or just to sing; and when these activities flagged we *put up* the False Faces or held a feast for some other medicine society. And then there were the public affairs at the Longhouse which the *family* attended. There we listened to Henry, now formally designated Twí-yendagon', the principal speaker for the officers, and sometimes, as my ability to take Seneca texts phonetically increased, he would dictate *for the book* what he told the people.

In late July of the second summer Henry agreed one evening to dictate the long address which he was accustomed to deliver at the funerals of the Longhouse people. Four days passed in writing down and checking the text, which ran to 60-odd pages. Curiously enough, death struck the community twice within the next week, providing the opportunity to verify information with performance.

So it happened that I went with Henry to Quaker Bridge to hear him preach over Chesley Snow. There had been two nights of wake and playing the moccasin game, and the day of the funeral had dawned clear. We had been home to sleep, and it was before noon that we returned. Chesley's was a welfare funeral. The Salamanca undertaker would get a mere $65.00 and would have to supply a coffin, although the Senecas would have preferred burying Chesley in a pine box of their own making. The Christian missionary, who was also welfare officer, would receive $10.00 from the state. These two had come down together in the undertaker's utility truck (it would not pay to bring out a hearse), and they were in the house when we arrived.

Both the mourning family of Chesley's mother, who spoke no English, and the master of ceremonies representing the opposite four clans, who were conducting the funeral, let the missionary speak first. After all he was the welfare officer and they were all on relief.

The Longhouse men stood around the woodpile outside as the missionary began. I wondered as he went on whether Chesley might find space in the *"house of many mansions"* which the mourners, such of them as understood English, could hear being promised for their clansman. They all listened politely. The conductor thanked the white speaker and came to the door to summon Henry Redeye inside. There he made his formal address.

As Henry and I walked home from the cemetery, he said, *"Chesley was there among his relatives. He know what I say this morning. I told them it was no good for the missionary to talk because it is hard language to understand. Some do not know what he said. I told them today that somebody should choose one preacher. It is no use to have two preachers. Poor Chesley will not know where to go. He will be all mixed up. There are two roads. The missionary directs one, I another. He can't go on both. Chesley stays on the middle and he does not know where he goes. . . . I did the best I could."*

As we approached Henry's house near a tall pine, he told me how he would like to have his own funeral.

"They used to get a horse to take the body to the Longhouse at Coldspring, if a man had gone there during his life. I want to be buried in a plain board coffin. Just the body uses it. The soul has gone out of it. He sees the body lay down. He don't know what is the trouble.

"*The Indian poormaster, appointed by the people, has no money to pay, but men at Coldspring can make a board coffin.*

"*This is how it should be with us Indians.*"

I wondered whether *djíwa'* got his wish or whether they buried him in a cloth-covered coffin such as he abhorred. According to the local press, he died in the Salamanca City Hospital and his body was taken for the funeral to his home in Quaker Bridge, and thence for further ritual to the Coldspring Council House. Considering these circumstances it is creditable to his own people that *djíwa*'s wish was carried out. When his body was brought home from the hospital, they dressed him in Indian costume and buried him in a pine box that his neighbors made for him.

Henry grew up under the tutelage of his foster mother's brother, Oscar Crow, from whom he learned the message of the prophet, Handsome Lake, and how to speak it in the Longhouse. Much participation as well as hard listening to older speakers at the ceremonies etched in his mind the content of the whole Coldspring ceremonial cycle. While walking in the woods and when felling timber he used to practice the learning of the Longhouse. Old men must have liked him in his youth because they told him many things to remember.

At times Henry had been a seasonal farmhand, a railroad worker, a pretty fair carpenter. He had felled timber in the woods and, during the last lumber boom along the Allegheny, he had ridden the rafts downriver into Pittsburgh. He had owned teams and cattle, and he had built the house where he lived.

Broken knuckles in his later years attested to his many summers of playing baseball without a glove. The Coldspring people, like all Senecas, are ardent fans. I have seen the old man stop a hard-hit liner with one bare hand. He loved Lacrosse and had played it well in his youth. He never told me of his prowess as a runner, but it is said at Quaker Bridge that he and *Deerfoot* had gone across the ocean as youths to defeat the best runners on the Continent. With failing health, he gave up his games, and he sold his carpenter's tools to buy groceries for his last days.

As a ritual speaker and preacher of the Handsome Lake revelation, there was demand for his services at home and abroad on such occasions as the Green Corn and Midwinter Festivals and at the annual revivals of the Longhouse People which they call *Six Nations*. It was usually Henry whom the people of other Longhouses—Newtown at Cattaraugus, Tonawanda, Onondaga (Syracuse); Lower Cayuga, Onondaga, Sour Springs, Seneca at Six Nations on Grand River; and Munceytown (London, Ontario)—summoned in the fall with notched message sticks and a short string of white invitation wampum to preach at their meetings.

"We like to hear that old man from Allegheny speak Seneca," I was told last autumn in Ohsweken. And I believe that what he said was most like the words of the ritual spoken at Burnthouse (Cornplanter PA) a century and a half ago.

Henry Redeye and I never got around to making a transcript of the *Gaiwiiyo'* (Good Message of the prophet, Handsome Lake). It was 1941 before I could take dictation in Seneca phonetics swiftly enough to record what he said when speaking in normal preaching style. The next year the war called me to other tasks. However, with the new recording machines that wartime activities have put within reach of the ethnological field worker, I had planned to go to Quaker Bridge this season to let *djiwa'* dictate as he was wont to preach.

It is easy to say that Henry Redeye was the last holder of the rituals, the last preacher of Handsome Lake's message, but it would not be true. Will the officials of Coldspring Longhouse find another to replace him? It is possible, for in the two decades of his preaching others heard him. His own son lived at home during this time and learned many things of the old man. And there were other younger men among those who sat by the door apparently inattentive, but listening. They seldom spoke for they were not appointed by the officers to do so. Possibly some of them know how. I know of one or two who had studied under Hiram Jacobs and old man Abrams who were *djiwa*'s predecessors at Coldspring. These younger men were waiting for the day when the Chiefs would turn to them. Surely the officers will find someone to elevate to the bench that now stands empty.

"*Now he on whom our minds depend has fallen, even as a tall pine is uprooted by the high winds. Now the place is empty where he used to sit on whom the people looked in confidence. And so he has taken with him 'our' words.*"

John Reed Swanton, 1873-1958

Swanton was no minor figure in anthropology. In addition to making substantial contributions to the ethnographic literature of the Northwest Coast tribes, for which alone he would be famous, after 1905 he erected "... his largest monument: the Southeast ... to such a degree that it remains undisputedly his and that mention of the area automatically brings to all of us the association of his name" (see bibliographic note; Kroeber 1940:2). At the time of his retirement he had published over 200 articles and a score of monographs on the Indians of North America. The most famous of his historical and regional summaries are: *Indian Tribes of the Lower Mississippi Valley and Adjacent Coast of the Gulf of Mexico* (Bulletin 43, 1911); several studies on the Creek Indians and their neighbors; and *Final Report of the United States DeSoto Expedition Commission* (1939), now a collector's item. He put a capstone to his monument with *Indians of the Southeastern United States* (Bulletin 137, 1946), and added a finial to the capstone with *The Indian Tribes of North America* (Bulletin 145, 1952). Although he did not found the present movement known as ethnohistory, he was its greatest exemplar. During the 44 years of his professional career, Swanton was associated with the Bureau of American Ethnology, Smithsonian Institution, where he was a research associate until the time of his death.

Born February 19, 1873, Swanton grew up in Gardiner, Maine, with the poet Edwin Arlington Robinson. He attended Harvard and graduated with the class of 1896, taking the master's degree the following year. Subsequently he was a student of Boas at Columbia for two years until completing the requirements for the doctorate at Harvard in 1900; he was one of the first anthropologists to receive the degree. After fieldwork on the Northwest Coast, he went immediately to the Bureau of American Ethnology. Though not a joiner, Swanton was professionally associated with the usual anthropological associations; he served as editor of the American Anthropologist and as president of AAA, and vice-president of AFS; he was a Fellow of the AAAS and of the Linguistic Society of America; and he was elected to the National Academy of Sciences.

Kroeber has ably evaluated the work of Swanton in the volume that honored Swanton's 40th anniversary with the Smithsonian, so the task of writing his obituary is immensely simplified. We need only summarize his principal accomplishments, for those who may not have access to Kroeber's appraisal, indulge in some personal reminiscence, and bring his bibliography up to date.

Swanton's accomplishments touch five major areas of anthropology: ethnography, method, linguistics, ethnological theory, and folklore.

1. In ethnography he discovered, identified, traced the movements, and wrote the histories of ethnic entities—a kind of taxonomy that represented real drudgery, but which will not have to be done over again; it is fundamental to later work.

2. In methodology he developed and refined the methods used in ethnohistory, which have affected archeology and ethnography alike.

3. In linguistics, besides compiling standard lexicons for Dakota, Haida, Tlingit, Muskhogean, and Tunica, he contributed to classification and to understanding of kinship systems.

4. There is no Swantonian system nor a long methodological treatise, but he contributed repeatedly to cultural theory. *The*

Social Organization of American Tribes (1905) first disproved evolutionary contentions about these phenomena, and opened the way for later historical work.

5. He contributed major collections of folk tales recorded in original texts from two cultural provinces.

In 1933, I had gone to Philadelphia to see Professor Speck before commencing fieldwork with the Iroquois. If possible, I was to go on to Washington to see Swanton. On climbing the stairs of College Hall, I encountered an elf of a man seated on one of the deep window ledges outside Speck's office. I told him that I was hoping to meet Dr. Speck and he replied that so was he. After extolling Speck's virtues as a field ethnologist—that no one had quite the same approach or the same success in the field with native Indians—my informant allowed that he also was an ethnologist and that his name was Swanton.

Our next meeting was after I joined the staff of the Bureau of American Ethnology in February 1939, when Swanton and the late David I. Bushnell called and welcomed me to the tradition of historical ethnology. On occasion Swanton would drop in on colleagues to hand them an inscribed copy of something that he had written. Swanton was not exactly garrulous, but he was helpful and courteous to a younger colleague beginning his research career and in need of help. He would put aside whatever he was doing and listen to queries and explain at some length what he thought would be a reasonable approach to the problem. It was out of such conferences that I decided to write an exploratory paper to begin for the Northeast the type of systematic approach that Swanton had accomplished for the Southeast.

Preparing *Essays in Historical Anthropology of North America* to celebrate Swanton's 40th year with the Smithsonian Institution was a rewarding experience, and I am confident that the other contributors treasure as I do the letter of acknowledgment from Swanton after he had received the volume and read the papers. Though he was much gratified at the kind of recognition tendered him by his anthropological associates at the Smithsonian that year, the presentation ceremony which occurred just before the staff's annual exodus to summer fieldwork was a somewhat drab and desultory occasion. Swanton, though he insisted it was all a complete surprise, delivered himself of one of the most fitting speeches of the kind ever heard. He was pleased, of course, but accepted the honor with his usual modesty.

Swanton's modesty was proverbial among his friends and colleagues. The most recent *Who's Who* sketch does not even list the honors he received—the second Loubat prize in history 1913 or the Viking Medal of the American Anthropological Association in 1948. He insisted that he should retire on June 30, 1944, and make way for younger men, but was persuaded to stay on during the war years. The two contemporaries, Swanton and Secretary Abbot, occupied adjacent offices on the second floor of the old Smithsonian building, and the line of visitors waiting to see Swanton often exceeded in length that waiting outside the door of the Secretary's office. His Harvard classmates recall how difficult it was to get him to come back to reunions, but the Class of 1896, 25th Anniversary Report carries his autobiography. He had no wild oats to confess, but he had published more than anyone else, including Thorndike, the psychologist.

Swanton considered his greatest success was marrying Alice Barnard of Washington DC in 1903. They spent their honeymoon at Sitka and Wrangell in the Alaskan panhandle while Swanton was engaged in ethnological work among the Tlingit Indians. They had three children—two sons and a daughter—to whom he was a most conscientious father. This was the reason he did nothing heroic during World War I "like enlisting as a private." Swanton's life was touched by tragedy and he was ill himself much of the time, but it scarcely affected his work. He had a bright and cheerful side and could quote Gilbert and Sullivan endlessly, both notes and lyrics.

Swanton was a conscientious but not a militant liberal: "In particular I am free to say that I cordially loathe from the ground up the entire competitive system, a system which rewards desert about as intelligently as a Ouija board. However, I have not tried to reform anything except to make the most unpromising material over into a half-way decent father for three of the rising generation of famous men and women. . . ." In his later years he retired to live with his daughter and one of his sons in Newton, Massachusetts, where he became a most indulgent grandparent to five grandchildren, and where he passed away on May 2, 1958, in his 85th year.

In explaining ethnology or anthropology to his classmates he wrote: "Ethnology is but one aspect [and] is a comparatively young science. It might be described as a backward extension of history, a history relying for its evidence upon something older than written documents or monumental inscriptions, or from another point of view it might be called the last chapter of paleontology. It conducts its researches by means of an intensive study of the physical characteristics, languages, material culture, art products, social and political institutions, ceremonies, and beliefs of the various tribal and national aggregates of mankind, but particularly the more primitive peoples, and also by an examination of the remains left by the forefathers of these peoples or by races which have entirely vanished. While it has its natural place as a complement of biology, paleontology, and the great group of historical and social sciences, anthropologists believe it has a leading part to play in the international and interclass rapprochements which are pressing fast upon us" (Harvard College, Class of 1896, 25th Annual Report, 1921:568). It was his idea that the "Bureau" should become an American Bureau of Ethnology, with a world-wide focus.

After retirement Swanton went on publishing in archeology, linguistics, history, ethnology, the beginnings of civilization, the state of the world, and his own personal interest in spiritualism. His *Source Material on the History and Ethnology of the Caddo Indians* (1942), written in 1939, combines the best of his historical, ethnological, and archeological research on an area.

He undertook two papers for the Smithsonian War Committee. The first was concerned with the "Evolution of Nations" (1942) and traced the development of states from bands to tribes to nations; it discussed some of the factors such as race, geography, and language that operated in their growth, and added some observations on structural and functional deficiencies and on freedom. In the second he asked: "Are Wars Inevitable?" (1943). The idea that war was not an original human institution—that as an abnormal extension of the state it had roots in primitive society, and was not the only way of settling differences—came as somewhat of a shock to certain staff officers of the day. Swanton was attracted to Andean civilization and wrote *A Note on the Quipu* (1943). Though this topic lay outside his usual range, it was an extension of method of using historical sources to solve an intriguing problem of how society kept its historical records and manipulated ideas.

Swanton was seldom roused to monumental ire and he engaged in few controversies. He did reply to J. B. Griffin's question about the proof of the identity and situation of certain Siouan tribes in the Ohio Valley (1943). *The Wineland Voyages* (1947) had long fascinated him. Speaking of the vast literature on the Viking voyages to America, he wrote: ". . . the data are just strong enough to tempt one to theorize and just weak enough to open the door for an immense amount of speculation, especially if one has an undisciplined imagination and a plentiful supply of local pride or wishful thinking. . . . It is one of those investigations which enable men who pride themselves on their acumen to prove it by leaving the problems ostentatiously alone or by registering skepticism, the cheapest way there is to acquire a reputation for scientific ability" (1947:4). In 1952 he took up one more cudgel to answer comments on his DeSoto Commission "Final Report" (1939, 1952). It had been a difficult assignment because officially he had to make absolute determinations for placing markers. When archeologists failed to find the sites identified from documentary sources, they criticized the whole structure of Swanton's report. He answered: "It was an illusion to suppose that there must invariably be an identifiable town site at every point where explorers report towns. Indian populations . . . were not so tied down to locations or so deeply engaged in manufacturing potsherds for archeologists to exhume" (1952).

Swanton had early been touched by spiritualism and avidly followed the experiments on extra sensory perception, having himself been a student of James at Harvard. But knowing the skepticism, if not outright antagonism, in the scientific community toward an orthodox member engaging in such a pursuit, Swanton thought it appropriate to sever his connections with the more austere scientific bodies to pursue this inquiry. His views were summarized in a series of communications which he shared with his friends during 1950 and brought out privately under the title *Superstition—But Whose?*

Bibliography

[An evaluation of Swanton's work was made by A. L. Kroeber in *Essays in historical anthropology of North America* published in honor of John R. Swanton in celebration of his fortieth year with the Smithsonian Institution (Smithsonian Misc. Colls., vol. 100, Washington, 1940). A full bibliography of Swanton's writings to 1939 appears here, prepared by Francis S. Nichols (except for numerous articles on religious subjects). We are therefore listing only his subsequent publications, again excepting his non-anthropological writings.]

1940   Linguistic material from the tribes of southern Texas and northeastern Mexico. Smithsonian Institution, Bur. Amer. Ethnology, Bull. 127.

The first description of an Indian tribe in the territory of the present United States. (Studies for William A. Read: 326–338.) Louisiana State University Press.

1942   Source material on the history and ethnology of the Caddo Indians. Smithsonian Institution, Bur. Amer. Ethnology, Bull. 132.

The evolution of nations. Smithsonian Institution. War Background Studies, no. 2.

Obituary of David I. Bushnell. American Anthropologist 44:104–110.

1943   Siouan tribes and the Ohio valley. American Anthropologist 45:49–66.

Are wars inevitable? Smithsonian Institution. War Background Studies, no. 12.

Annotations on Indians, pp. 131, 132, 179, 194, 209; notes by, 193. *In* Travels in Georgia and Florida, 1773–74; a report to Dr. John Fothergill (by William Bartram) Francis Harper ed. Transactions of American Philosophical Society, vol. 33, part 2.

The Quipu in Peruvian civilization. Smithsonian Institution, Bur. Amer. Ethnology, Bull. 133, Anthrop. Papers no. 26.

1944 Arikara pottery making. American Antiquity 10:100–101.

Data and comments supplementing Buckingham Smith's notes. *In* Memoir of Do. d'Escalante Fontenada respecting Florida written in Spain, about the year 1575; translated from the Spanish with notes by Buckingham Smith, Washington, 1854, David O. True, ed. Univ. of Miami and the Hist. Assn. of So. Fla.

1946 The Indians of the southeastern United States. Smithsonian Institution, Bur. Amer. Ethnology.

1947 The wineland voyages. Smithsonian Misc. Coll., vol. 107, no. 12.

1948 The primary centers of civilization. Smithsonian Institution. Annual report, 1947.

1952 The Indian tribes of North America. Bur. Amer. Ethnology, Bull. 145.

Hernando DeSoto's route through Arkansas. American Antiquity 18:156–162.
n.d.Superstition—but whose? [ca. 1953]

Howard Sky, 1900-1971

*Cayuga Faith-Keeper, Gentleman,
and Interpreter of Iroquois Culture*

Scholars who attended the International Congress of Anthropo-logical and Ethnological Sciences held in Philadelphia in 1956 will recall as perhaps its most memorable feature the appearance and participation of a delegation from the Six Nations Reserve in Canada who came at the invitation of the organizing committee to honor the memory of Professor Frank G. Speck. It was Professor Melville Herskovits' idea that we should have them; I was delegated to carry the invitation, and Alfred Kidder, II, the treasurer, held that whatever the cost, it would be that much less of an occasion without them, for our foreign guests would surely want to see some Red Indians. I got in touch with Howard Sky whom I knew to be thoroughly reliable, confident that he would produce one or two elder sachems and ritualists, bring along several clan mothers, and round up the best singers and dancers, including some children. Mr. Sky had been putting on demonstrations of the traditional culture of his people throughout Canada, and he had arranged to take his troupe abroad. Once during the summer before the Congress, perhaps because I was apprehensive over the quality of the performance for the sum appropriated, I went up to Six Nations Reserve, which lies along the right bank of the Grand River below Brantford, Ontario, to see Mr. Sky and hear his plans. He received me graciously in his home at Silversmith's Corners, near the Onondaga Longhouse; he inquired about the health of my family, and he asked for details about the nature of the meeting and the character of the audience. Then he told me whom he planned to include and something of their specialties. I explained that this would be a sophisticated audience, perhaps I remarked that we expected a sterling performance, and I asked whether they would rehearse. He replied, "Indians never rehearse. On the way down I shall think over in my mind what we shall do, and when the time comes they will perform. Don't worry, they are the best singers and dancers. And they will come dressed for the ceremony." That they did and more.

Of the many pleasant recollections of that intercultural encounter, I like Ted Kidder's story of introducing Howard at his bank. Howard was wearing a bear claw necklace over a buckskin shirt and the proper Iroquois gastóweh (headdress) with twirling feather. "This is Mr. Sky. He wants to cash a check." While Howard proceeded to endorse it, the obviously startled bank clerk stared at the necklace without flinching, and neither party gave any sign to the other that the transaction was extraordinary. It was probably the only time in the long history of Indian and White relations in Philadelphia that an Iroquois in native costume and a local banker had such a confrontation.

Philadelphians recalled years later when planning the celebration of Dr. Froelich G. Rainey's twentieth anniversary as Director of the University Museum that our Iroquois guests had then adopted him since he was both President of the Congress and their host. The planners of the fete asked me to get the same Indians to renew his honor.

Again I went back to Mr. Sky who found several survivors of the first party, and there were others who were eager not to miss a Philadelphia happening which had become legendary on the reserve. Although I was now an honorary Consulting Fellow of the University Museum, I had yet to attend a formal dinner meeting of its patrons. When the day arrived, it was gratifying to see colleagues and their wives in formal dress mingling with "Main Line" society who were more awed by the costumed Iroquois guests than the "People of the Longhouse" were impressed by them. When a society reporter inquired how they knew my daughter so well, Councillor George Buck commented, "Long ago we took her as a little girl, we adopted her, and we raised her up as one of us."

After dinner Mr. Sky presented Dr. Rainey with a condolence cane which carries the roster of Iroquois chiefs in pegs and pictographs (Fenton 1950). And he himself climaxed a superb program by his troupe in a solo performance of the Discovery Dance, which demands great agility in a man of his years.

As I write these words in tribute to my friend where I am snow-bound at home, I know that the appointed speaker will presently stand and intone the "bare words" of condolence to the mourning relatives and to the Six Nations people. For surely they are depressed in their minds at the loss of their great one. For certain a tree has fallen, uprooted by the storm, and a great hole looms in the earth. Every bench must be taken on both sides of the Onondaga Longhouse where Teyohtsʔíkréhkonh, "Cloudy on both sides," was Keeper of the Faith, moiety leader and treasurer these past thirty years. Though a Cayuga through his mother, and son of a Cayuga chief, he understood and spoke Onondaga fluently, although he preferred Cayuga, since both languages prevail in that longhouse. A master of the ceremonies, he knew the main speeches and songs of the Longhouse way; but neither orator nor singer, he was rather conductor and prompter of those appointed to these roles. He was, moreover, the trusted keeper of the sacred Kano: da bundle, the tribal medicine, sometimes referred to as the Little Water Medicine, or simply as the "Great good medicine." No one else more enjoyed the confidence of the Longhouse people, the respect of the Christians at the "Upper End," as well as their White neighbors over the river. This was a good man. He had the capability of uniting the bitter factions on the reserve, but he was too wise to attempt it, although he maintained relations with all of them.

Ethnologists who were privileged to work with Howard Sky admired the quality of his mind. He was equally interested in us and was obviously challenged by our discipline. He shared some of our intellectual curiosity and spent hours and days on his own trying to satisfy our questions and exploring problems that arose from our sessions. Although I had known Howard for a number of years, we commenced working regularly after the death of Simeon Gibson (Fenton 1944), when as a relative (a patrilateral cross-cousin), he volunteered to assist me in deciphering the now famous Cranbrook condolence cane (Fenton 1950), to help me with Hewitt's texts, and to guide me through the rehearsals for the great ceremony for mourning and installing chiefs (Fenton 1946).

Ever courteous, friendly, and modest, Mr. Sky maintained a professional attitude toward our work. Although in the 1940s I regularly attended the public ceremonies at Onondaga Longhouse, where he was an officer, he never let our work relationship intrude upon his responsibilities to his people. At public ceremonies he treated me like any other visitor, greeting me by my Indian name, and perhaps assigning me some chore about the cookhouse. In our work sessions he spoke candidly of public and restricted rites in which he participated at which my presence might have become an issue, and he went out of his way to satisfy my questions about their history, content, purpose, and meaning (Fenton and Kurath 1951). Clearly he sensed the intellectual challenge posed by ethnology and he enjoyed it.

While ethnologists speak commonly of good informants and interpreters—and surely Howard Sky fulfilled the ideal—at Six Nations the visiting anthropologists are graded and ranked. Howard remembered Goldenweiser working with his father's generation, and "J. N. B. Hewitt once came to our house—he spoke pretty good Onondaga"; he knew and admired F. G. Speck; but of the living Iroquoianists he put Floyd Lounsbury at the head of the list. Lounsbury and Mr. Sky worked on Cayuga one season, when they commenced the translation of the Onondaga text of the Deganawi:dah legend that Goldenweiser had taken from Chief John A. Gibson in 1912, which I had partly translated and then put aside. Howard regarded

Lounsbury's knowledge of Iroquoian as something of a marvel, and he invariably inquired about him.

During the seventeen years when administrative duties claimed my attention and prevented my going to the field for more than a few days at a time, I saw Howard infrequently. At each meeting we promised to go on when we could. When in February, 1969, we resumed a series of intensive sessions spread over two years, Howard looked at me and said, "How old a man are you?" (I was then just 60.) "I am 69," he added. "If we are to finish this Deganawi:dah business, we had better get on with it, for no one else ever will." That prophecy unhappily stands.

Howard died March 3, 1971. At the close of the previous year he went into hospital to relieve some difficulty that his own considerable knowledge of "Indian medicine" would not alleviate. (We had discussed a field study of Iroquois herbals with the intent of ascertaining their pharmaceutical properties.) His difficulty lay beyond the reach of Western medicine. During a remission we resumed in June of 1970, when I went off for the summer to transcribe the results of our most productive session, with only sixty-five pages of the long "Goldy" manuscript remaining untranslated. Over the summer Howard contracted a respiratory infection that was rampant on the reserve; it put him back in hospital and left him with little reserve to fight his primary enemy. He never lost interest in our work and reaffirmed his determination to recover his strength, when we talked periodically by telephone. By Christmas it was already too late, although he lived to see the new moon of midwinter when I presume ceremonies were done for his recovery. The word of his passing reached me in the night, and then a card confirmed the sad news with this laconic message: "Howard left us all this morning. 3/3/71."

One wonders how the reserve will fare without him. People looked to him with confidence, they entrusted money to him, and they depended on him to organize various enterprises. For years his Jeep was a familiar sight, slogging its way through muddy side roads in spring, or furnishing the power for wood-cutting bees in the fall. At home he made lacrosse sticks, and betimes he was the center of a cottage industry to fill outside orders. He popularized the favorite Iroquois winter game of snowsnake among Canadians. Howard took a broad view of Indian questions, perhaps because he lived so long among the Whites whom he understood, and although his loyalty and sympathy lay with the old chiefs of the Confederacy and he adhered to the Longhouse way, he was a realist and he considered it poor policy to exclude White people from the longhouse ceremonies.

Little is known of his youth. He spent much time listening to the old people who recognized his keen mind. "When I was small I could name all fifty of the chiefs," he once told me, and he undoubtedly would have been named to one of these offices had he remained on the reserve. But he also enjoyed the companionship of his own generation. He attended Indian district school for the minimal number of years, barely learning to read and write, although he picked up other Iroquoian dialects from schoolmates for whom English was then a second language. "As lads we ran the six miles to Caledonia to play pool, we stayed until the pool hall closed at ten, and then we ran all the way home. We had no cars or bikes." Small wonder that Six Nations produced such rugged lacrosse players.

Howard was good with animals, and he soon went to work for the Alan McBay family whose century farm lies north of the Grand River and west of Caledonia. One Sunday in June, 1969, he took me there to call—a day that he said was on him—so that I might meet his particular farmer friends whom he hoped would confirm the location of the early nineteenth century Onondaga longhouse north of the river. Our conversation in the McBay kitchen that Sunday morning supported Howard's memory that the site was on the Adam Allan farm where Howard had turned up broken crockery and dishes one spring when plowing. Although the talk reminded me of my own rural background in western New York, I soon realized that Howard was employing my techniques of interview to confirm his own recollections. He elicited more information about the intercultural relations of the Six Nations people and Brant county farmers during the past half-century than I had learned in previous years of fieldwork. Our hosts produced axe and hammer handles of ash and hickory that had been brought over the river by Indian craftsmen and laid away to season years ago. The story of the Indians moving their longhouse is still recalled by pioneer families in Onondaga township. Pressure of White settlement, particularly of squatters on Indian land, influenced the Indians to sell and remove south of the river. The Indians dismantled the building, marked the logs, and floated them down the creek; having rafted them across the Grand River, they snaked them up the bank to the present site on MacKenzie creek where the building was re-erected. Afterward one White observer paced off the distance: "It was the same distance to the creek at the old site as it is now south of the river." Why had he done that? "Because White men are just curious, I guess."

Howard left the reserve in 1918 to work as a stockman on an Ohio farm. He was away twelve years, returning in 1930. He developed a considerable affection for his adopted family, one of whom tutored him in English and arithmetic, and he kept up with them for years. When I first knew him he was steadily employed in an asphalt mill near Hamilton, coating gas and water mains, which somewhat limited his availability. He told me that even during the great depression when no work was to be found, how he organized cooperative buying of flour and other staples at wholesale prices for his people.

Howard was twice married, and a son by his first wife survives him. I remember his mother in the 1940s as a grand old Cayuga lady with classic Iroquois features. His sister was then married to Dr. Silversmith at the Corners. He is survived by his second wife Mabel who is much beloved in the community.

He leaves no publications—only the works of ethnologists whom he assisted. When the Deganawi:dah epic is ready for the press, he will share joint authorship. In looking over old vouchers, I note that he formerly used the Scottish spelling "Skye," but of late years he signed simply "Sky," perhaps on the correct assumption that his name had an Iroquoian origin.

For his Indian name and for the account of the obsequies which I could not attend we are indebted to Michael K. Foster, Mr. Sky's last co-worker in American ethnology.

References Cited

Fenton, William N.

1944 Simeon Gibson: Iroquois Informant, 1889–1943. American Anthropologist 46:231–234.

1946 An Iroquois Condolence Council for Installing Cayuga Chiefs in 1945. Journal of the Washington Academy of Sciences 36:110–127.

1950 The Roll Call of the Iroquois Chiefs: A Study of a Mnemonic Cane from the Six Nations Reserve. Smithsonian Miscellaneous Collections 111(15): 1–73.

Fenton, William N., and Gertrude Kurath

1951 The Feast of the Dead, or Ghost Dance, at Six Nations Reserve, Canada. Symposium on Local Diversity in Iroquois Culture, No. 7. Smithsonian Institution, Bureau of American Ethnology, Bulletin 149:139–165.

Goldenweiser, A. A.

1912 The Death of Chief John A. Gibson. American Anthropologist 14:692–694.

Conference on Iroquois Research

Conference on Iroquois Research

The second Conference on Iroquois Research, which met for the first time last year, assembled a good attendance of anthropologists from the northeastern states and Canada at the Allegany State Park, Red House NY, October 4–6, 1946. As chairman of the Allegany State Park Commission, Mr. Charles E. Congdon of Salamanca again made available to the Conference the Administration Building on Red House Lake, which is situated in a wilderness area, flanked by the Allegany Reservation of the Seneca Nation. Merle H. Deardorff of Warren, Pennsylvania, was co-host.

Sessions were devoted to a report and discussion of field studies in Iroquois ethnology (with Fenton presiding), to remarks on history and the Iroquois (by Arthur C. Parker and Paul A. W. Wallace), and to a lively discussion of the Owasco culture and its relation to Iroquois origins (by Ritchie and others).

The will to do something about problems of Iroquois research was manifest in increased attendance, in an attitude of genuine interest that marked the discussions, and in reports of research accomplished since the first conference: by Speck, Dodge, Witthoft, and Fenton in Ethnology; by Voegelin and associates at the summer Linguistics Institute on the Seneca language; by Parker on history; and by Kidd, Schaeffer, Ritchie, and McIlwraith in archaeology. It is hoped that new projects and an opportunity for collaborative research will appeal to the scholars who were welcomed to the conference this year.

Those present included: Disher, Cleveland; Hout, Columbia; Carl Guthe, Albany; Stout, Syracuse; Parker and Ritchie, Rochester; Plassman and Hirscher, St. Bonaventure; G. Brown, Emerson, Kidd and McIlwraith, Toronto; Hatt, Cranbrook; Griffin, Jones and Witthoft, Michigan; MacNeish and Ted Guthe, Chicago; Schaeffer, Harrisburg; de Laguna, Bryn Mawr; Wallace, Annville; Carpenter, Speck and Stearns, Pennsylvania; Johnson, Andover; Dodge, Salem; Hadlock, Bar Harbor; Setzler and Fenton, Smithsonian Institution.

The Conference has so far avoided formal organization, and it has no officers; it exists to promote Iroquois studies and as a vehicle for discussion and informal exchange of information.

Fourth Conference on Iroquois Research

For the fourth time since 1945, anthropologists of the northeastern states and Canada met at Red House, New York, October 8–10, 1948, to hear reports of progress and to discuss next steps in Iroquois studies. The conference owes its attractive place of meeting, the Administration Building of Red House Lake, to the continued interest of the Hon. Charles E. Congdon, chairman of the Allegany State Park Commission, who with M. H. Deardorff of Warren, Pennsylvania, issued the invitations and acted as host. W. N. Fenton continued as general chairman of the conference.

The conference opened Friday night with an informal address by C. E. Congdon on "The Allegany Country and its Settlement," which he concluded by reiterating a hope that the Allegany State Park might again become a center of studies. An impromptu contest in singing Indian folk songs from l'Ancienne Lorette was set off by Marius Barbeau and F. G. Speck. And the spirit of whimsy carried over to the report of the Committee on Museum Studies in which Ernest Dodge assessed collections awaiting the student of Iroquois material culture and disclosed certain archival sources previously overlooked by ethno-historians. Discussion pointed to the obvious need of putting a student on the trail of this material, testing his findings in the field, and producing a series of topical reports.

The outstanding accomplishment in Iroquoian studies during 1948, however, was in the field of linguistics as manifest in the presentation

Saturday morning of "Comparative Iroquoian" by Floyd Lounsbury. Barbeau led the discussion and appraised the sources for the study of Huron-Wyandot.

A seminar led by James Griffin paraded substantial achievement in archaeology on sites scattered from Maine to Georgian Bay and from Bay of Quinte south to the Maryland border. Of less interest to archaeologists, perhaps, than Byers' report on his excavations in Maine and those by which Ritchie extended his New York pre-histogram to Ontario, but of greater interest to ethnologists, were the reports by Ritchie on large Seneca cemeteries from which Schoff and Wray have taken several hundred human skeletons, Kidd's report on excavating a historic Huron ossuary, and Emerson's account of the excavation of a Huron longhouse. Carpenter and Witthoft gave parallel reports on New Jersey and Pennsylvania.

The above discussion left but an hour for the seminar on "Locality and Kin in Iroquois Culture," which was originally scheduled to set the theme for the conference. Fenton developed the theme of local differences, drawing materials from community studies at Coldspring, Tonawanda and Six Nations, and then Anthony Wallace reporting on new field work at Tuscarora and Augustus F. Brown on Onondaga, New York, brought new points of view to the field, stressing personality and culture more than structure of society. For the first time it appears likely that the Iroquois like the Navaho are becoming a social science laboratory.

The Seneca Indians of Coldspring Longhouse have virtually included the conference in their yearly round of activities. Led by Albert Jones, a larger number in costume and more besides turned out with enthusiasm for the annual Indian party in honor of F. G. Speck. They afforded abundant materials for illustrating G. Kurath's discussion of "Structural Types of Seneca Dances." They proceeded to manage their part in traditional manner, insisting on their own sequence of numbers and choosing their own speakers and interpreter. To our amazement the Johnny Johns performed the dance of the False-faces, and the Hawk Clan gave a name to Dr. George Snyderman.

Discussion turned Sunday morning to the need of a check list of manuscript materials relating to the Iroquois; second, to the applications of research and its techniques to general education; and third to the need of enlisting a physical anthropologist to work up the expanding series of crania from the area.

Those present included: Barbeau, Leechman, National Museum of Canada; M. Barnett, Carstairs, Holmberg, Leighton, M. E. Opler, Sasaki, Cornell University; Mrs. M. Blaker, Fenton, Smithsonian Institution; Brown, Miss M. Lamberson, Snyderman, Speck, Van Stone, Anthony Wallace, Miss Jane Willets, University of Pennsylvania; Byers, Andover; Carpenter, Emerson, Kidd, McIlwraith, Toronto; Congdon, Walter Edson, Allegany State Park Commission; Count, Hamilton College; de Laguna, Mrs. C. Dryden, Miss Alta Mae Harris, Bryn Mawr; Dodge, Hadlock, Peabody Museum, Salem; Griffin, A. K. Guthe, Jones, G. Kurath, Lee, Spaulding, University of Michigan; C. E. Guthe, New York State Museum; Kent, Webb, Witthoft, R. P. Wright, Pennsylvania Historical Commission; Knoll, Ritchie, Rochester; Lounsbury, Yale; Lucy, R. Wright, Society for Pennsylvania Archaeology; Miss P. Pollenz, Brooklyn; Paul Wallace, Annville; Peter K. Smith, Six Nations Reserve.

Seventh Conference on
Iroquois Research

The value of an informal gathering for reporting research accomplished, for stimulating new research, and for integrating methods of related disciplines, was again demonstrated October 5–6–7, when students of the Iroquois met for the seventh year at Red House, New York, to discuss the theme of stability and change in Iroquois culture history. The annual Iroquois Conference, which owes its inspiration to the late F. G. Speck and looks to W. N. Fenton to arrange the program, comprises mainly anthropologists, but specifically ethnologists, archaeologists, linguists, historians, a psychiatric case worker, museum directors, lawyers, a superintendent of Indian affairs—who are either professional or amateur students of some aspect of Iroquois culture. From the principal universities, museums, and research institutions in Canada and the northeastern states, students of Iroquoiana come to Red House Lake for the weekend, without consideration of status. They join no society, pay no dues, and they have happily resisted organization. The place of meeting has contributed enormously to the success of these meetings, and Charles E. Congdon, chairman of the Allegany State Park Commission, issues the invitations and annually proclaims the weather and welcomes the Conference to the Park. People come to see the wild life and the autumn foliage, and enjoy the hospitality of M. H. Deardorff of Warren, Pennsylvania.

In previous years we tried sectional discussions of research areas, substantive reports of field work, summaries of abstruse topics such as linguistics, a rigorous symposium on a theme, meeting separately and in plenary session, but this year the conference returned to the plan of general sessions interlarded with section meetings, so that everyone could hear the main papers and yet share his problem with a more intimate group having similar interests. Rapporteurs summarized research trends in a final general session. The success of the recent conference depended on the high level of general papers, the plan of conducting the meetings, the quality of personnel in attendance, and tightening up the program.

The conference moved forward on a central theme, which Fenton set in a paper entitled "Stability and Change in Iroquois Culture History" on Friday night. Discussion sought possible indices of stability in linguistics, archaeology, ethnology, and history. Apparently historic contacts have produced rapid change, diversity, and early conservatism in different areas of Iroquoia, the eastern groups remaining most conservative in archaeology and language from early times. The western groups show early change and later conservatism. The theme carried over into the presentation, Saturday morning, of "Iroquois kinship" by Harry Basehart (Goucher), which proved the display piece of the meeting, and was followed by spirited discussion led by F. Lounsbury (Yale). Basehart finds in changing kinship evidence of both historic contact and internal evolution.

While the ethnologists retired to explore possible methods for three related projects in personality and culture by A. F. C. Wallace (Pennsylvania), M. Randle (Brantford), and M. Teicher (Toronto), the archaeologists and historians heard Charles Wray (of Rochester) describe the excavation of historic Seneca cemeteries. If it is true, as J. Witthoft (Pennsylvania Historical Commission) claims, that the Iroquois conferences have changed the face of archaeology in Pennsylvania, New York, and Ontario, we at least note with pleasure application of the direct historic approach to Huron and Iroquois town sites and the beginnings of sociological interpretation of settlement patterns, in which the findings of ethnology are employed to explain what the ground yields. The work of Ritchie (New York State Museum) and his associates in New York is being paralleled by the University of Toronto group for whom Norman Emerson spoke on "Historical Archaeology in Ontario," describing the splendid cooperative endeavor of the staff of the Royal Ontario Museum of Archaeology with amateur scholars of whom Frank Ridley (of Islington), discoverer of the Lalonde pottery complex, which may be ancestral to both Huron and Onondaga ware, was present to display a magnificent collection of pottery vessels. K. E. Kidd, co-discoverer with Ridley, of the Ossossané ossuary, described by Pere Brébeuf in the *Relations*, shared some observations on ossuaries in general; Kidd is currently studying trade goods as Guggenheim Fellow from Canada.

The Saturday night Indian party, a tradition at the conference, witnessed the Red House premiere of *The Longhouse People*, a documentary film in color, directed by Alan Worgon and produced by the National Film Board of Canada with Iroquois actors from the Six Nations Reserve. The picture appeals to persons familiar with the culture who recognize the people of Six Nations Reserve as represented by Deskaheh (Chief Alex General, Cayuga), George Buck (who sang for the first Fenton album), and Howard Skye. The piece features several conspicuous incidents in Iroquois ceremonialism, including War Dance for rain, the False-faces, and the Hymn to the Dead Chief and the Charge to the New Chief from the Condolence Council. Use of the French flute introduces a malapropism for the reedy note of the native flageolette, but the theme is in keeping with the picture, although its use in the mourning scene is puzzling. The best comment came from Senecas present, who, in characteristic local pride, avowed they could themselves make as good a movie at Allegany.

Using two Seneca informants, Joe E. Pierce, a student of C. F. Voegelin, demonstrated the Indiana method of recording and testing intelligibility of Indian languages, which involves two magnetic recorders, and offers possibilities for translating long ethnological texts. The recorded document is dubbed onto the second machine, stopping at junctures to record parallel strips of English translation. The test can be repeated on several subjects in the same and in distant communities. Lounsbury, addressing the Senecas present in Oneida, showed how similar results can be achieved without the apparatus, if the linguist knows one other related language.

A substantial number of persons remained for the Sunday morning session to hear the rapporteurs summarize progress in ethnology and in archaeology. Martha Randle pointed up the relation of several research projects in ethnology to the theme of the conference. A drift away from studies in ceremonialism and more conservative topics may be noted; Basehart's kinship study links Morgan with the present; and three current projects approach personality and culture. Investigating ambitions of children at Six Nations Reserve, Randle finds no significant differences in aims of children from Longhouse and more acculturated families. Wallace's projected study of the life and times of Handsome Lake, the prophet, may entail devising new TAT's to employ situations arising in Longhouse life, possibly patterned after native Indian drawings. Teicher's study at Deseronto represents pioneer work in the most acculturated Iroquois community.

Besides the trends already noted in archaeology, Witthoft, seconded by historians and archaeologists present, suggested featuring ethno-history at the next conference, an area in which archaeologists want help. What are the critical means of deciding where a town mentioned in the records is located?

The chairman then turned to Lt. Col. E. P. Randle requesting a private estimate of the crucial administrative problem in the affairs of the Six Nations to the solution of which a team of anthropologists and others might make a significant contribution. Representative government, though nearly thirty years old at Six Nations Reserve, has failed to gain the support of more than a minority of the population, and the hereditary council of chiefs, which went underground in protest against the Indian Act of 1924, remains the governing body of the Longhouse people seconded by a faction of Christians called the Mohawk Workers who otherwise withdraw from active participation in the life of the community. The people of Six Nations unite on one issue only—the integrity of their "Nation" and the preservation of their lands. In common they fear enfranchisement. What is the real basis of factionalism? How is factionalism related to the process of acculturation? What can be done toward producing unity in such a situation? What lessons does the history of the last generation at Six Nations Reserve hold for the administration of native peoples, and more important, what lessons does it hold for predicting the outcome of contracts between the great powers and peoples of so-called underprivileged areas? Here is an example of what administrators may expect wherever native cultures are suppressed in the name of progress. Here is a laboratory for training students in the behavioral sciences.

The Iroquois Conference will continue on its present informal basis so long as present personnel desire to meet and share interests. It was decided, however, to go ahead with an *ad hoc* committee to explore ways and means of forming an Institute for Iroquois Research to get support for larger cooperative projects, to administer fellowships for the development of social scientists in the field of its interests, and to center its resources and activities in one of the institutions already identified with Iroquois research.

Editor's Note: This long report, aside from its intrinsic interest for many readers, exemplifies quite well the operation (and achievement) of the *informal working conference*. Archaeology particularly seems to flourish in such sessions. For whatever value it may have in encouraging other state or regional groups to gather and discuss mutual problems, this statement has been printed unabridged.

Iroquois Research

The usefulness of the informal research conference for exploring some central theme, for identifying new research problems, and for reporting research accomplished was again achieved 14–16 Oct. 1955 when students of the Iroquois Indians of New York and Ontario met for the ninth time in 10 years at Red House NY to discuss the theme, "Exploring ways of achieving cooperation in anthropological studies in the Northeast." This theme provided a vehicle for discussing state and local relationships in archeology, professional and amateur responsibilities in archeology and ethnology, the roles of local and regional museums, and relationships between universities as training centers and the opportunities provided by the conference for field work.

The conference was limited to 35 invited participants who had recently contributed to the advancement of Iroquoian research, of whom 28 attended. The Red House conferences are traditionally family affairs; until the rains of this year, the glorious autumn weather has made these week-ends a pleasant outing. For the continued use of the administration building and quarters of the Allegany State Park, the conference is indebted to Charles E. Congdon, chairman of the Allegany State Park Commission, and to M. H. Deardorff of Warren, Pennsylvania, who was host at the "doings" of the Very Little Water Society.

The annual Iroquois Conference owes its inspiration to the late

F. G. Speck and has from the beginning been organized and chaired by W. N. Fenton, who this year was assisted in planning by W. A. Ritchie and C. E. Gillette. The conference has no formal organization and no regular members. The attendance comprises mainly anthropologists, many of whom are part-time workers in archeology, ethnology, language, and history—the only prerequisite is an active and contributing interest in some phase of Iroquoian studies.

The agenda included the following discussions: State and Local Relations led by John Witthoft (Pennsylvania Museum Commission); Professional and Amateur Relations led by William A. Ritchie (New York State Museum and Science Service); Museum and University Relations, Irving Rouse (Yale University); Ethnologist and Indian, Anthony F. C. Wallace (University of Pennsylvania); and the Structure of Support, W. N. Fenton. The discussions lasted throughout Saturday and were actively engaged in by everyone present. Those who did not have a chance to say all that occurred to them in the meeting carried on in small groups far into the night. On Sunday morning, we heard from the "new voices" in Iroquoian research, who were introduced by Wallace. These included Jacob Gruber (Temple University) on a study of artistic styles in Iroquois masks; Cara B. Richards (Cornell University) on a study of women's roles at Onondaga; David Landy (Harvard University) on child-rearing practices of the Tuscarora; and Annemarie Shimony (Yale University) on the longhouse communities of Six Nations Reserve, Ontario.

The chairman summarized the high points of the conference as follows:

1) The need had been identified for an archeological extension service from the New York State Museum and Science Service to local societies, schools, and collectors of New York antiquities.

2) The present type of conference on the theme of improving state and local relationships in antiquities of New York should

be repeated at the local level; such additional conferences are contemplated.

3) Sentiment favored education and diffusion of professional scientific knowledge to the use of legal sanctions to prevent vandalism of sites; it was held that an antiquities act would be unworkable.

4) Universities such as Yale and Toronto should encourage research by state and local museums but must evaluate these programs in the light of national responsibilities. It is recognized that Iroquoian studies in archeology, ethnology, and linguistics have provided part-time research opportunities for the faculties and field training for graduate students.

5) It was evident that in arriving at an over-all program for the conference, one must know the number of students available in the universities of the area and what parts of the program each university would assume. There is a need to identify a few solid projects in language, social relations and political organization, personality studies, archeology, and linguistics to show how the main concept of conservatism can be studied in relation to change, using the Iroquois field as a laboratory.

6) From the "new voices" came the suggestion of a clearing house of research in progress and research in the recent past so that young scholars might approach the field in an intelligent manner.

The discussions and recommendations on Saturday and Sunday followed the presentation of a paper appropriate to the theme for the conference that was delivered this year by Thomas Grassmann of the Mohawk-Caughnawaga Museum at Fonda NY on "The excavation of historic Caughnawaga." Grassmann's talk was illustrated by slides; it highlighted, very appropriately, excellent cooperation between professional and amateur scholars in a local setting.

Of the conference last fall, two things can be said: it identified a new field of research in the area of Indian education that is in the trend of the times, when education and anthropology are finding common research interests. In the selection of the theme and in the candor with which it was discussed, the conference touched one of the significant problem areas in the organization of scholarship—namely, how to foster good communications among national, state, and local levels of the community of science without control flowing from the top, and how to provide the amateur, part-time scholar with a sense of full participation.

History and Purposes of the Conference on Iroquois Research

On the 20th anniversary of the Conference on Iroquois Research, which has met more or less regularly in October since 1945, it may be helpful to those who have come to it lately to summarize its history and point out its purpose. Two of the founders, Merle H. Deardorff and the writer, attended the vigesimal celebration in Glens Falls, while a third, Charles E. Congdon, stayed at home "on the back of the bed," as the old Iroquois say. In the beginning, we three had formed a Turtle's War Party and went on a raid to Hamilton College to read the Kirkland Papers, and to the Mohawk Valley to visit Father Thomas Grassmann at historic Caughnawaga, and somewhere on the path the idea occurred to us to have a party honoring Carl E. Guthe, the then new Director of the New York State Museum, and to hold it at the Allegany State Park Administration Building in Red House. Frank G. Speck, who was then alive and very active in ethnological work among the Six Nations, and I had been discussing the need to bring students of the Iroquois together; they represented the entire spectrum of anthropological and historical studies after World War II and would help us to see where we stood and what could be done. The first conference was such a success intellectually and socially that we kept on meeting yearly. A wide range of persons attended: scholars, students, and amateurs. At times the meetings grew too large and included fringe people. The history of these early conferences is in print, and most recently I summarized it, as of 1958, in the foreword to the *Symposium on Cherokee and Iroquois Culture* (Fenton and Gulick 1961: 3–8). Since then it has met more or less irregularly.

There have been but four full-scale conferences since 1959. That was the last time we met at Red House. Edmund Wilson attended, Merle Deardorff gave a memorable sketch of the Kinzua Dam controversy, and Annemarie Shimony read on Iroquois conservatism. After that there was a desire expressed to meet elsewhere. The Senecas at Allegany were in deep trouble with Congress over the Kinzua Dam and we Iroquoianists had not been particularly effective in helping them. Consequently, it seemed inappropriate to discuss cultural problems in their midst.

The next year I was on leave writing, and Floyd Lounsbury acted as host to a small 1-day working session of ethnologists and linguists at Yale. As I recall, Chafe, Shimony, Sturtevant, Tooker, White, Rouse, Mintz, and the writer attended.

For a number of years we were urged to come to Canada, and in response to an invitation from the President of McMaster University, Iroquoianists met at Hamilton under the most favorable auspices in 1961. Frank Vallee was our host. The occasion was the anniversary of Pauline Johnson, the Mohawk poetess. In 1962, because of the rising interest in ethnohistory and the contributions of Iroquoianists to its development, one session of the American Indian Ethnohistoric Conference which met in Albany was denominated the "Fifteenth Conference on Iroquois Research" and was devoted to hearing new voices in Iroquois studies: Blau, Funk, Gauss, and Diamond. Chief Corbett Sundown came down from Tonawanda and blessed the mask collection in the New York State Museum, burning tobacco and imploring the masks not to be unhappy and injure the curators. There was a field trip to an Iroquois site in the Mohawk valley and to Johnson Hall, followed by a dinner with an address by Milton Hamilton (1963), editor of the *Sir William Johnson Papers*.

There were no formal conferences during the next two years. In the fateful November of 1963, several Iroquoianists lunched together in San Francisco during the American Anthropological Association convention, and the year after we met for dinner in Detroit. Efforts to hold a full-scale conference at Lake George in 1964 had found a majority of Iroquoianists bound to other commitments. Elisabeth Tooker had undertaken the correspondence and continued as Program Chairman for the Glens Falls meeting, with the writer making local arrangements. We were supported by two volunteers from the Anthropology Club at Vassar, Constance Turnbull, and Lauree McMahon, who assisted with registration.

The range and diversity of the papers read at Glens Falls is surprising when one considers the irregularity of meetings and the absence from the program of some headliners of recent years. Several comments are in order. First, there is a genuine community of interest among Iroquoianists and they seem to regenerate themselves or produce fertile offspring with amazing vigor. Second, the Iroquois Conference has no formal organization and no regular members. The mailing list comprises active scholars, amateur or professional, who are interested in the Iroquois, who have published, or are engaged in research. Students are encouraged. Not a penny of foundation support has been solicited or paid for travel to these meetings. People come on their own, or they are sent by their institutions. Part of this interest arises from a real hunger for small academic meetings where everyone listens to all the papers, even those outside his specialty, where one can really talk with colleagues without keeping one eye on the academic slave market, and where one can hear the new voices. In contrast with the huge and bewildering conclaves of learned societies today, the Iroquois Conferences are definitely low key. Consequently, people feel relaxed because their reputations are not at stake. Informality extends to the program. We have a tradition of informal communication, or "un-papers," which allows the beginner to formulate some idea and the oldster to retread his science. Some of these sessions have produced interesting research leads to important discoveries. There was MacNeish's (1952) report on Iroquois pottery at Red House. Wallace came first, as Speck's student, and gave some of his earliest papers (Wallace 1958) on prophet movements. Under Lounsbury's aegis, Chafe (1960–61 and 1963) described the Seneca language. We could go on.

Our most famous tradition is the "Very Little Water Society" meeting, presided over by Merle Deardorff. An obvious parody on the Little Water Medicine Society of the Senecas, it fits the anthropological culture nicely, and it has a unique flare that belongs only to these meetings and to its birthplace at Red House.

The present offerings are made to the spirits of the humanities and the social sciences in the trust that they will be acceptable and helpful to all who read them.

References and Bibliography

Chafe, W. L.
1960–61 Seneca Morphology. J. of Am. Ling. 26: 11–22, 123–130, 224–233, 283–289 and 27: 42–45, 114–118, 223–225, 320–328.
1963 Handbook of the Seneca Language. N.Y.S. Mus. and Sci. Serv. Bull. 388.

Fenton, W. N. and Gulick, John (*eds.*)
1961 Symposium on Cherokee and Iroquois Culture. Bur. of Am. Ethnol. Bull. 180.

Hamilton, M. W.
1963 Sir William Johnson: Interpreter of the Iroquois. Ethnohist. 10: 270–286.

MacNeish, R. S.
1952 Iroquois Pottery Types: A Technique for the Study of Iroquois Prehistory. Nat. Mus. of Can. Bull. 124.

Wallace, A. F. C.
1958 The Dekanawideh Myth Analysed as the Record of a Revitalization Movement. Ethnohist. 5: 118–130.

Iroquois Research
Conference after 25 Years

The 1969 Conference on Iroquois Research met at the Institute for Man and Science, Rensselaerville, New York, October 17–19. Some 50 persons attended. These conferences, which have no formal structure, continue under the informal leadership of William N. Fenton (SUNY Albany) by co-opting the students of the various aspects of Iroquois culture, including linguistics, ethnology, history and prehistory. The content of the program varies from year to year according to work under way. Recently there has been unprecedented activity in linguistics.

The meeting opened with an informal report by Garrett Cook on a Classification of Iroquois Material Culture which he had devised during an internship at the New York State Museum under the sponsorship of the Committee on Anthropological Research in Museums of the American Anthropological Association. These internships are awarded to selected undergraduates to afford them a museum experience in the hope that they will be attracted to graduate work which will involve museum collections as research materials.

Symposiums, rather than individual papers, followed by informal discussion are the rule at these conferences. A single paper serves to start discussion. William C. Sturtevant (Smithsonian) presented an analysis of Pan-Iroquois Ritual Pattern which introduced a symposium on ceremonialism shared with Elisabeth Tooker (Temple). A short paper on the Corporate Structure of Delaware Ceremonials by Ives Goddard (Smithsonian) afforded a comparative view.

A session on Iroquois linguistics chaired by Floyd Lounsbury (Yale) featured a presentation by Wallace L. Chafe (Calif. Berkeley) on Semantic and Objective Distinctions in the Surface Structure of Iroquois Languages. A group of younger linguists, undertaking their first fieldwork in Iroquoian languages, participated in the discussion.

Fieldwork among the Iroquois has been going on for more than a century since Lewis Henry Morgan began it in 1846. A paper by Sally Weaver (U of Waterloo, Canada) set the tone for a symposium on Problems of Entry and Re-entry to Fieldwork in which Fenton, Don Cassie, Superintendent of the Six Nations Indian Reserve, Brantford and others participated.

The Iroquois have produced their own scholars. Ernest Benedict of St. Regis Reservation, Cornwall Island, Quebec, presented his concept of the North American Indian Traveling College with a film.

Robert Funk (NYS Museum) organized a symposium on the Strategy of Current Researches in Iroquois Archeology. Marian White (SUNY Buffalo) presented hypotheses for ascertaining patterns of warfare from archeological evidence, and James Wright (Natl Mus of Canada) reviewed evidence for comparable interpretations of related events in the prehistory of Ontario and Quebec. Archeological collections from the Iroquois contain some 5000 pottery pipes which have resisted description. Cynthia Weber (Harvard) indicated how she proposes to analyze their attributes and work out their distribution in time and space. The archeology of the Mohawk Valley offers a unique example of the continuity of ethnographic information into the protohistoric past. Donald Lenig, an amateur who has distinguished himself by publications of professional grade, outlined the strategy for synthesizing the ethnohistory and the archeology of the region.

The Iroquois Conference plans to meet jointly with the Algonquinists at Trent, Peterborough, Ontario in 1970.

Index

Page numbers in italic indicate illustrations.
WNF = William N. Fenton

acculturation: as a folklore topic, 7–10
acculturation studies, 56
Adams, John, 203
Adams Express Company, 236
Adon:weh (personal chant), 255
adoption: cases opposed by the Senecas, 260–62; as clan function, 264n1; formal speech of, 257; the Iroquois and, 245; and naming the adoptee, 256; of Olive Fenton and her children by the Senecas, 262–63; pledges of friendship following, 257–58; of WNF by the Senecas, 245, 250, 251, 255–58
Albany NY, 139–40
Allan, Adam, 340
American Academy of Arts and Sciences, 203
American Anthropological Association, 149, 177
American Anthropologist, 182
American Association for the Advancement of Science, 126
American Council of Learned Societies, 129, 130
American Documentation Institute, 13, 45
American Indian Ethnohistoric Conference, 360
American Museum of Natural History, 236
annuities, 71
anthropology: academic councils and, 129; and alienation of Six Nations Reserve, 169; A. L. Kroeber's description of, 126–27, 129; applied, 148–49; Claude Lévi-Strauss on, 131–32; communities and, 138–43; concerns of, 126; culture and, 132–33; defined, 128; field work and, 146; historical knowledge of, 41–43; museums and, 128, 149, 180–83; participation in government, 130–31; participation in World War II, 129–30; recommendations for the study and advancement of, 52; social sciences and, 125,

127, 128–29; at State University of New York at Albany, 144–50
Apologies to the Iroquois (Wilson), xvii, 214, 216, 218
archaeology, 145
Arden, Harvey, 225
"Are Wars Inevitable?" (Swanton), 332
Armstrong, John, 100, 247
Armstrong, Sarah, 163–64
atomic bomb, 131
Avery, Jimerson, 254
Awenha:ih (Ripe blossom), 106
Awenhaniyonda (Hanging Flower), 112
axes, 86, 90n22
Ayer Collection, 45

Bailey, Nick, 213, 214, 219
Ballston Spa NY, 73
Barbeau, C. Marius, 4, 15, 119n4, 347
Barber Black, 204
Barnard, Alice, 330
Basehart, Harry, 351
Bear Dance, 157–58
Beauchamp, William M., 235
Beaver clan, 262–63
Beaver Wars, 310, 311
beggars, 124, 160
beliefs, 3–4
Benedict, Ernest, 364
Benedict, Ruth, 134
Benedict model, 134–36
Bennett, Hanover, 165
Big Tree, Treaty of, 71
Billy, Elsina, 259
Birket-Smith, Kaj, 187
Black, Eddie, 167
Blackfoot Indians, 60–61
bluebirds, 116
Boas, Franz, 40; culture area concept and, 183;

In The Iroquoians and Their World

Nation Iroquoise: A Seventeenth-Century Ethnography of the Iroquois
By José António Brandão

Your Fyre Shall Burn No More: Iroquois Policy toward New France and Its Native Allies to 1701
By José António Brandão

Gideon's People, Volumes 1 and 2: Being a Chronicle of an American Indian Community in Colonial Connecticut and the Moravian Missionaries Who Served There
Translated and edited by Corinna Dally-Starna and William A. Starna

Iroquois Journey: An Anthropologist Remembers
By William N. Fenton
Edited and introduced by Jack Campisi and William A. Starna

William Fenton: Selected Writings
By William N. Fenton
Edited and introduced by William A. Starna and Jack Campisi

Oneida Lives: Long-Lost Voices of the Wisconsin Oneidas
Edited by Herbert S. Lewis
With the assistance of L. Gordon McLester III

The Texture of Contact: European and Indian Settler Communities on the Frontiers of Iroquoia, 1667–1783
By David L. Preston

Kahnawà:ke: Factionalism, Traditionalism, and Nationalism in a Mohawk Community
By Gerald R. Reid

A Description of New Netherland
By Adriaen van der Donck
Edited by Charles T. Gehring and William A. Starna

To order or obtain more information on these or other University of Nebraska Press titles, visit www.nebraskapress.unl.edu.

www.ingramcontent.com/pod-product-compliance
Lightning Source LLC
Chambersburg PA
CBHW021807270326
41932CB00007B/85